An Intro

Language

Learning About Language
  General Editors
  Geoffrey Leech & Mick Short, Lancaster University

*Already published:*

Analysing Sentences 2nd edition
  Noel Burton-Roberts

Patterns of Spoken English
  Gerald Knowles

Words and Their Meaning
  Howard Jackson

An Introduction to Phonology
  Francis Katamba

Grammar and Meaning
  Howard Jackson

An Introduction to Sociolinguistics
  Janet Holmes

Realms of Meaning: An Introduction to Semantics
  Th. R. Hofmann

An Introduction to Psycholinguistics
  Danny D. Steinberg

An Introduction to Spoken Interaction
  Anna-Brita Stenström

Watching English Change
  Laurie Bauer

Meaning in Interaction: An Introduction to Pragmatics
  Jenny Thomas

An Introduction to Cognitive Linguistics
  Friedrich Ungerer and Hans-Jörg Schmid

Exploring the Language of Poems, Plays and Prose
  Mick Short

Contemporary Linguistics: An Introduction
  William O'Grady, Michael Dobrovolsky and Francis Katamba

An Introduction to Natural Language Processing Through Prolog
  Clive Matthews

# An Introduction to Child Language Development

Susan H. Foster-Cohen

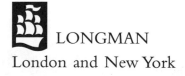

LONGMAN
London and New York

Pearson Education Limited
Edinburgh Gate,
Harlow,
Essex CM20 2JE,
United Kingdom
and Associated Companies throughout the world.

*Visit us on the World Wide Web at:*
www.pearsoned.co.uk

© Addison Wesley Longman Limited 1999

First published 1999

ISBN-10: 0-582-08729-5
ISBN-13: 978-0-582-08729-3

Visit Addison Wesley Longman on the world wide web at
http://www.awl-he.com

**British Library Cataloguing-in-Publication Data**

A catalogue record for this book is available from the British Library.

**Library of Congress Cataloging-in-Publication Data**

A catalogue record for this book is available from the Library of
Congress.

10 9 8 7 6
09 08 07 06

Set in 11.5/12 pt Mono Bembo by 35
Printed in Malaysia, LSP

For Avi, Naomi and David

# Contents

# Preface: How to use this book

Like any respectable field of enquiry, child language research is by no means monolithic in its methodologies, its basic tenets of belief, the way it sets about interpreting data, or the conclusions it draws. In particular, there are real and serious differences of opinion between, on the one hand, those who view children as extracting regularities from the language they hear with the aid of innate propensities that are not specific to language learning, and, on the other hand, those who think there is a serious role to be played by genetically encoded linguistic information, currently known as 'Universal Grammar'.

Trained in the first tradition as a student, but seduced by the elegance and intellectual attractiveness of the latter, I have for many years thought that the chasm between these approaches is both unfortunate and ultimately unproductive. Over the years, therefore, I have tried to see how the best of both approaches could be made to work together to enrich our understanding in ways that are not possible given any one approach alone. The result is the book you are now holding. It is time introductory textbooks on language acquisition routinely made the ideas of Universal Grammar (UG) and its role in language development available to students not yet ready to read the complex details of the most advanced analyses. At the same time, many of the explanations for language development that have been developed from any of the non-UG perspectives continue to provide insight and inspiration. You will find, therefore, that I weave insights from the theory of UG and the parametric approach to language development throughout this text without apology. As far as I am concerned, it is now part of the general knowledge that ought to be possessed by even the most novice of language development students. However, because of this focus within a fairly short book, you will find that sociolinguistic approaches to language acquisition are less well represented than in other introductory books. The book is more psycholinguistic than sociolinguistic, although references are provided to allow students to expand their knowledge into sociolinguistic topics. Of particular interest is *An Introduction to Sociolinguistics* (1992) by Janet Holmes in the same series as this book.

It is difficult in an introductory text to provide definitions for all the new terminology that must inevitably be learned. In those cases where a term is opaque to you, and you have no one around to help you out, I recommend other volumes in the Learning About Language series. Of particular value will be *Contemporary Linguistics: An Introduction* (1997) by William O'Grady, Michael Dobrovolsky and Francis Katamba, *Meaning in Interaction: An Introduction to Pragmatics* (1995) by Jenny Thomas, *An Introduction to Phonology* (1998) by Francis Katamba and *Analysing Sentences* (second edition, 1997) by Noel Burton-Roberts.

The style of this book is intended to be direct and accessible. I have referenced the literature relatively little, particularly in the early part of the book (you will find a steady increase in the density of references as the book progresses), and have presented prevailing ideas in as comprehensible a form as I can manage, providing pointers to further reading where appropriate, particularly at the end of chapters. Each chapter contains a number of in-text exercises, suggested solutions to which are to be found at the end of the relevant chapter. At the end of each chapter, there are also questions for discussion, some suggested activities, and suggestions for further reading. The questions for discussion and the activities come with solutions where appropriate. Since many of the discussions and activities are open-ended, however, my comments are not intended to be exhaustive, only suggestive. Finally, since many of the suggested activities involve collecting and analysing data, Appendix 1 provides some tools for doing that.

I hope that I have been provocative in my presentation and that students and teachers alike will disagree with me. If you engage with this text enough to disagree and to go out and search for evidence to back your position, then I will have succeeded in my primary task: to make you *think* about the issues involved in understanding children's language acquisition. If you have reactions to this text (positive or negative) that you are willing to share with me, I hope you will write to me:

Department of English
The British Institute in Paris
9–11 rue de Constantine
75340 Paris cedex 07
France
fosterco@ext.jussieu.fr

# Acknowledgements

This book has been really fun to write, and has been enlivened throughout by titbits of data from my children, Abraham (Avi) and Naomi, whose language development I did not study systematically, but whose utterances feature throughout this book. My husband, David, has, as always, been a pillar of support and encouragement, particularly appreciated during a period of our lives when he has had to put his own career on hold in order to allow us to move to France for mine. My thanks also go to the British Institute in Paris, which has given me a new home, and to Christophe Campos, who has allowed me the time to continue my writing.

My greatest thanks for this book go to all the people (teachers, colleagues, friends) whose works I have read, to those I have met, talked with, and thought with about language development, including Mike Breen, Robert Hoogenraad, Elaine Andersen, Elinor Ochs, Nina Hyams, Sharon Klein, Bonnie Schwartz, Carol Moder, Cheryl Scott, Matt Rispoli, Marie Helt and many others. Over the years, I have tried to come to terms with the various influences from the wide variety of formal and informal training I have received, and have pieced together a rather eclectic view of language development, which incorporates approaches that are frequently pitted against each other in the primary literature. While those who know the field will see the seams, I hope that for those who do not, the overall effect is coherent. May I also express my sincere thanks to two special women: Elizabeth Mann, my patient and long-suffering editor at Longman, and Julia Harding, the copy editor assigned to me. The former encouraged me to keep going when the project seemed never-ending, and the latter is not only meticulously careful, but also knows linguistics well enough to ask all the right questions. She helped me avoid several embarrassments; the remaining ones are entirely my own fault!

Finally, I would like to send belated condolences to the parents of the little boy called Ross whom you will meet in these pages. I learned only recently that Ross died while still a child. To me he will always be the perky little guy with the winning smile who talked so energetically about getting up in the middle of the night and running around in the dark.

Paris, March 1998.

The publishers are grateful to Prentice Hall Inc for permission to reproduce extracts from *CHILDREN'S LANGUAGE AND LEARNING*, 1st edition (1980) by J. W. Lindfors, pp 114/5 & 307/8.

## CHAPTER 1

# What do children bring to the language acquisition task?

## Chapter summary

In this chapter, the issue of whether children bring innate knowledge of linguistic principles to the language acquisition task is raised in broad, mostly philosophical, terms. The issue of how one can know what children know (innate or not) is discussed. Two approaches to language acquisition research are identified – the 'observational' and the 'logical' – and examples of each are given

## Introduction

Perhaps the most hotly debated topic in child language research today concerns how children's mental and physical capabilities help them learn languages, and what they know in those months and years before their talk is recognisable. There are those who believe that children 'know' a great deal about language – much more than might at first appear from what they say (or are able to say). There are others, however, who believe that children know very little about language, and must work it all out from hearing (or seeing, in the case of sign languages) the language of others and from their own attempts to use language.

The reason why we can't decide what infants know or don't know is that we cannot observe knowledge directly. We can't get inside children's heads, but have to use more or less subtle methods of observation and experimentation that we hope will give us the clues we need. However, children's behaviour, even in response to the most controlled experiment, is often ambiguous and could be interpreted in more than one way. And they certainly can't sit down and tell us any of what they know, until they are at least three or so. In fact, even then, they can only tell us what is available to conscious reflection. Most of what anyone, child or adult, 'knows' about language is not directly accessible, and must be probed in ways only slightly more direct than with small children. (A detailed discussion of how children learn to talk about language is contained in Chapter 8.) How can we know what children know about language?

## A challenge to ingenuity

Trying to determine what someone knows when they are unable to tell you takes plenty of ingenuity.

### Thought experiment 1

How might you figure out what each person in the following four situations knows without using language?

1   Imagine that someone you know is secretly in love with you.
2   Imagine that someone you know has been awarded a prize which they must go to receive from a distinguished dignitary tomorrow.
3   Imagine that someone you know won a prize yesterday.
4   Imagine that someone you know knows the 126 times table.

In the first case, unless the love is to remain unrequited, eventually the person will show by some look, touch, or conventional action (such as sending flowers) that they love you. In the second case, patience is called for. You will discover they have been awarded a prize if you wait around long enough to see them get dressed up and go to meet the dignitary, who then gives them the prize. You will know that the person already knew they had won a prize from the fact that they dressed up specially to meet the dignitary, although perhaps meeting the dignitary was known, but receiving the prize was a surprise. If the latter is the case, then you would expect some betrayal of surprise when the prize is given; perhaps a gasp of 'Ooh' accompanied by raised eyebrows.

In the third case, you have a greater problem. Something has happened in the past. You might be able to figure out that the prize had been awarded by the presence of the prize on a shelf, or perhaps by the respectful way others treat your friend. But you have missed the opportunity to observe the event directly. In the fourth case, you have an almost insurmountable problem. It is conceivable that a situation may arise that calls for the instant multiplication of 126 by some number, and that your friend provides the number either by saying it, or, if language is not to be used at all, by counting the product of the multiplication in matchsticks or some such.

Each of these situations mirrors part of the problem of determining what young children know about language (or about anything else, for that matter). Some things they are able to 'betray' directly by their actions. Children betray directly that they are hungry, dirty or tired, for example, by crying (although it remains to be seen whether these are distinguishable from each other on the basis of the cry alone). Children can also betray an understanding of language by doing what is asked of them, by looking at objects named by someone else, or picking them up, for example. These indicators are, however, pretty minimal given the complexity of language, and it is often not clear with very small children that they have responded to the language rather than to gestures or other clues to what a speaker meant. We can also observe children's beginning attempts at speech; but that too is limited by the fact that they may 'know' far more than they can say. In fact, language comprehension studies with small children indicate that children do indeed understand a great deal more than they can say, and thus observations of child speech (language production) may be woefully inadequate as a way of determining what they know about language. However, we must do the best we can with what we've got. As the thought experiment is intended to suggest, just because we cannot observe something someone knows even indirectly, does not mean that that person doesn't know it. You may know (consciously) many things you have never told a soul; an infant may know (unconsciously) many things it *cannot* tell a soul. And if we are interested in that knowledge, we will just have to get more ingenious at deducing it by indirect methods.

In some cases, we can figure out what infants know by waiting around for them to produce utterances, either as initiating contributions to conversations or as responses to other people's utterances, that can plausibly be said to indicate knowledge of specific kinds. For example, when children say things like 'no water' when they are offered a cupful, we may presume they know what words are (unconsciously, of course), that words can be combined, that words carry meaning, that words in combination carry a meaning that is in some way a combination of the meanings of the individual words (i.e. that 'no' and 'water' each carry a meaning singly and in combination), that directing words to other human beings is a sensible thing to do, and that it is likely to have some effect. We might also presume that some of this knowledge may have been learned through experience with language; other linguistic knowledge may be innate (built in as part of the genetic code of human beings). Knowing that communicating with others is a sensible thing to do, for example, is a particularly likely candidate for innate knowledge. Knowing that words are the building blocks of communication may also be a candidate for innate knowledge. Knowing that 'no' means 'no' and 'water' means 'water' is a highly *unlikely* candidate for innate knowledge. Children learn what the individual words of specific languages mean by observing those around them, otherwise we would have to assume that all children are born knowing the meanings and forms of all the words in all the world's languages – a patently absurd conclusion (although they do seem to be born with some preconceptions about words – that they can refer to objects and activities, for example). Thus it seems clear that some parts of language are candidates for innate knowledge, and some must certainly be learned from input (the language children hear around them). The trick to language acquisition study is trying to figure out which type of knowledge belongs to which category.

## Two different approaches

Researchers differ on the extent to which they are willing to credit children with innate knowledge of language. The differences result in (or are indicative of) two rather different approaches to language acquisition in general. Let's look briefly at these two approaches.

## The observational approach

If one presumes young children know nothing innately, then one could decide to credit them with specific knowledge of language only when there is some substantial direct evidence for doing so. For example, let's say you've been observing young children aged about two, and you've noticed that they keep producing utterances without subjects. That means that instead of saying, 'I/me want cookie', they routinely say, 'want cookie'. Instead of saying 'Mummy do it', they say 'do it'. What I am calling the 'observational approach' would lead you to say that these children do not know what subjects are or how to use them. (As we will see in the section below, the 'logical' approach leads to a very different conclusion.) The observational approach is a very sensible approach to take. It prevents one from making wild claims about what children know in the absence of fairly direct evidence. It leads to the assumption that if children produce utterances with certain features (say, having subjects, or showing subject–verb agreement marking, as in 'He wants cookie' (rather than 'He want cookie')), then they must have learned those features from listening to the language that is spoken to them or around them, analysing it in some way (and there's the rub, but more of that anon), and then reproducing it in their own speech.

However, there are those for whom the account of language acquisition I've just summarised just doesn't work. Their observations lead them to conclude that children know much more than they could have figured out from observing the language of others. These researchers bring a particular kind of logical deduction argument to their analysis of what they see. They pursue what I will call here a 'logical approach'. However, please note that by calling this second approach 'logical', I am not at all implying that the observational approach is somehow illogical. The term 'logical' in this context simply means that making a logical deduction is at the heart of the second approach.

## The logical approach

In the 'logical approach', children are hypothesised to *know innately whatever they could not have learned from observing and analysing the language they hear.* Researchers in this second camp believe that there *must* be a great deal that children know about language from birth because they produce and understand utterances with features they could not possibly have deduced from the input. Examples of this claim get a bit complicated because they depend on a pretty sophisticated understanding of the structure of adult language, but let me try a fairly simple example.

Look at the four sentences below:

(1)   *Who do you think that knows Mary?
(2)   Who do you think knows Mary?
(3)   Who do you think that Mary knows?
(4)   Who do you think Mary knows?

Sentence (1) has a star by it because it is generally judged by speakers of English to be ungrammatical, i.e. could not have been produced by the speaker's linguistic system functioning normally. Please note, however, that many of the utterances that are judged ungrammatical by prescriptive grammarians such as school teachers and other guardians of 'proper' English (such as 'I ain't got none') are not regarded as ungrammatical by linguists (just socially 'non-standard'). Linguists, therefore, are interested in the difference between grammatical and ungrammatical utterances viewed descriptively in terms of what people actually say (rather than prescriptively, in terms of what they ought to say), and a '*' by a sentence or utterance is the conventional way linguists denote descriptive ungrammaticality.

Returning to the sentences above, while the first is impossible, the other three are perfectly grammatical. In other words, in sentences where the structure leads to the interpretation that *someone knows Mary*, the 'that' cannot appear before 'knows'. In sentences where the structure means that *Mary knows someone*, the 'that' can appear. In structural terms, we can say that if the missing 'someone' in these sentences is the subject of the embedded clause, the 'that' may not appear. If the missing 'someone' is the object of the embedded clause, the 'that' is free to appear or not, as the speaker chooses. Below are the same four sentences with the missing someone represented by an [e] (= empty). I have also indicated the boundaries of the embedded clauses with square brackets:

(1')   *Who do you think that [e knows Mary]?
(2')   Who do you think [e knows Mary]?
(3')   Who do you think that [Mary knows e]?
(4')   Who do you think [Mary knows e]?

OK, so what does all this have to do with children's language development? Well, presumably, children's language development eventually results in adult language knowledge of these (and myriad other) facts. And notice that this knowledge is unconscious even in adults, unless they have had it pointed out to them, or have engaged in direct linguistic analysis themselves. (Did you know this about your language before I told you?)

Thus, somehow, children know or come to know that sentences such as (1) are not part of the English language. However, apparently no one teaches them that fact. They do not, for example, hear people saying such sentences, and then correcting themselves to produce the legitimate one (2). Or, at least, if people do that, we haven't observed it yet. It certainly would not seem to be a major part of language experience for the young child. It is more likely, say those in the 'logical approach' camp, that this knowledge is somehow innately specified in a very general (and abstract) form. It is *general* in that the feature being exemplified here doesn't apply only to simple English sentences such as those shown in the examples, but, properly described, is a very general feature of human languages. It is *abstract* because in order to show up in all the world's languages, it cannot be represented in the child's mind initially in terms of involving the word 'that' because that is a word of English only, so the rule itself must be more abstract, i.e. not specific to English.

So, the 'logical approach' argument is as follows:

1    Here is an odd and rather difficult to describe feature of the
     English language.
2    We have no evidence that it is taught to children; and we have
     no evidence that the particular pattern of appearances and non-
     appearances of 'that' in such sentences is deduced from
     observation.
3    If adults know it (unconsciously), and children don't learn it,
     then it must have been known innately.
4    Obviously, children are not going to know innately that these
     particular English sentences pattern this way, so there must be
     an innate formulation of this pattern that can apply to all
     languages. That this might be the correct view is bolstered by
     the fact that many other languages, perhaps all, reflect the same
     type of patterning, thus lending credence to the view that this
     is innately known knowledge.

Clearly this is a rather more complicated approach than the observational one, but it leads to some very interesting claims. The argument I've just summarised, for example, can lead to the prediction that children learning English will never naturally produce sentences such as those in (1). This can be tested, perhaps by trying to get children to repeat sentences such as these, and seeing how resistant they are to saying such things.

Logical arguments about language acquisition also clearly depend on some crucial assumptions about what can and cannot be learned from experience, and it is actually very hard to say what children do *not* learn from experience, since no one has been able to follow even a single child around long enough to be able to document *everything* the child hears and every attempted utterance he or she produces. The absence of this kind of complete record is one of the reasons the debates between the 'observational' and the 'logical' approaches remain so active and energetic. Those in the 'logical' camp think it is a waste of time to go looking for such an extensive record because all the input (i.e. language exposure) in the world won't be enough to 'teach' language. Those in the 'observational' camp are persuaded that since so much *has* been discovered about children's language experience, the 'logical' group are slamming the doors shut on explanations without having given more sophisticated observational and experimental techniques time to contribute to the debate. They accuse the 'logical' folks of sitting idly cogitating in their armchairs, while *they* are doing the work of running around the world collecting data in time-consuming and even dangerous situations. Meanwhile, the 'logical' folks think the 'observationalists' are wasting time and money chasing around after something they will never find. Of course, if observationalists didn't go on getting grants to run around the world collecting data from children learning Samoan, or Sesotho, or whatever, the 'logical' folks wouldn't be able to test their hypotheses, nor would they have challenging language acquisition data to keep the fires of cogitation going. No wonder child language research can be so contentious. Anyway, let's put the politics on one side for a moment.

To return to the 'logical approach': in this approach children are assumed to know many things about language before they even begin to speak or to understand much of the language around them. They will begin by using the innate principles they possess to make sense of the language they hear, and to produce the things they want to say. A consequence of this way of thinking is that even the most simple utterance is seen as the result of a quite complex system of knowledge of language, a system of a far greater complexity than might be apparent from the simple utterances produced at first. Proposing such complexity for very simple utterances is anathema to the 'observational approach' and is one of the very basic issues on which the approaches disagree, and will be addressed more directly in the next section.

## Competence versus performance

That the system of knowledge underlying language production might be rather different from – in fact, much more complicated than – what children actually say is captured in the contrast between 'competence' and 'performance,' a distinction Noam Chomsky introduced to modern linguistic discussion (although he was building on ideas from linguists of an earlier age, such as Ferdinand de Saussure at the end of the nineteenth century). Let's do a thought experiment that might help you see the distinction between competence and performance.

### Thought experiment 2

Have you been in a situation the same as, or similar to, the following?

1    You have taken two years of college French. You are walking down the road one day and you are accosted by a woman who asks you a question in French. You get the gist of what she is asking, although you don't catch every word. When you go to reply, you cannot remember the proper way to conjugate the verbs, your prepositions are all wrong, and you hear yourself doing far worse than you (and your French teacher) would have liked. After the Frenchwoman has gone, you go over the exchange in your mind and are able to figure out what you should have said, much to your chagrin.

2    You have a bad cold and you've lost your voice. You are unable even to say 'good morning' to your office/room mate.

3    While you are talking on the telephone, an old friend with whom you had a terrible fight three years ago, and whom you haven't seen since, walks into your office. You try to continue your conversation on the phone, but you find yourself hesitating and faltering, until you finally have to end the phone conversation and attend to the new arrival in your office.

4    You have rehearsed a speech in a Shakespeare play. On the opening night, what you always feared would happen happens. You 'go blank'. You cannot, for the life of you, remember the next line. As soon as you walk off the stage, the whole speech comes flooding back to you.

Situations like those above are fairly typical. There is a wide range of ways in which, as adults, we don't say what we mean or what we are able to say. Something gets in the way; whether it is memory, nerves, interference from other emotions, sickness, etc. When such situations arise, we don't assume that the person has somehow forgotten the language (except perhaps in the second-language (French) example). Rather, we assume that something has gone wrong with the 'performance' of the language.

Competence is the knowledge the person (whether adult or child) possesses of the language; it is the mental representation that the speaker of a language, no matter how old, has of that language. So, that competence may not be fully 'competent' in the usual sense of that word. A child is not fully competent in the way we might claim an adult is, for example. But the child none the less has a competence *in* that language. When we actually speak, it is argued that we engage that knowledge, that competence, along with the actual mechanisms that allow us to speak. If those mechanisms are faulty for some reason (because we have lost our voice, or are frightened or embarrassed, or even suffering from certain kinds of brain damage), the 'performance' may not reflect the competence.

What's the relevance of this for child language study? Well, if adults do not reveal all they know in what they say, then why should we expect children to? And if children don't reflect all they know in what they say either, then we are back to the possibility that children may know a great deal more about language than they let on.

## Some recurring questions

In the chapters that follow, the ideas presented in this preliminary discussion will reappear. Watch for them, and keep asking yourself:

1   What knowledge of language might underlie children's actual utterances?
2   Where might that knowledge have come from? Could it have been learned from experience? Could it be innate knowledge possessed from birth?
3   How do children use the information they possess about language, whether innately provided or learned from experience, to become proficient speakers of one or more languages?

These are three crucial questions in language acquisition research. Though there are plenty of observations of children using language at all stages of development, these questions are extremely hard to answer. The problems of observation I have outlined in this chapter make interpreting the data (i.e. the observations of children using language) extremely problematic. However, that is the enterprise of studying child language acquisition, and that is what this book will explore.

Before I close this section, let me say a last word about the polarising and often acrimonious debate between the two different approaches to language acquisition research outlined here. I deliberately emphasised the differences between approaches in order to make it clear how things can degenerate (and, I am afraid, often have degenerated). However, there are clear signs that things are getting better. The 'logical' approach, which for much of its early history, and for very good intellectual reasons, focused only on a few languages in forming its hypotheses, has now begun to branch out into the study of a wide range of languages, and the effect is interesting. Many of the original hypotheses are being changed or abandoned, while many of the most robust observations noticed by the 'observationalists' are being reinforced and then reinterpreted in different theoretical terms. The overall effect, to my way of thinking, is a truly useful rapprochement which can drive the field in really productive ways in the twenty-first century.

## Some premises

Finally, let me (re)state six of my firmly held premises about language and language development so that as you read on you will have no illusions about the filters (and blinkers) through which I view language acquisition.

1    I am persuaded that some aspects of the linguistic system are innate and specific to language. Like Noam Chomsky, who has been the impetus for much of this research, I think there is reasonable evidence that certain parts of syntax (the way sentences are structured out of words), morphology (the way words are structured out of smaller units known as morphemes), phonology (the way morphemes are structured out of sound units) and semantics (the meanings that words and sentences encode) are so 'weird' that only accidents of genetics could account for them.

2    I am persuaded that some aspects of the linguistic system are innate but *not* specific to language. For example, I think that the basic way in which people make communicative sense of the language they hear (pragmatics) has much in common with

the way they make interpretative sense of pictures they see, or non-linguistic sounds they hear. Taking (1) and (2) together, I endorse Chomsky's distinction between the computational (1) and interpretative (2) aspects of language, and think that maintaining that distinction is useful in trying to understand children's language.

3   I am persuaded that there are some aspects of language that are not innate at all, but are learned from the environment in which children grow up. Most notably, this includes the words that make up the vocabulary of the languages children are learning, along with various pragmatic conventions for being socially acceptable when using language.

4   I think language is modular. In addition to the boundary between the computational and the interpretative alluded to above, I think there are a number of internal divisions, certainly within the computational, and maybe within the interpretative. Work on the sub-modules of the computational part of language is considerably ahead of research on the sub-modules of the interpretative part. In fact, some (e.g. the philosopher Jerry Fodor) think there are no sub-modules in the interpretative portion, rather there is only an undifferentiated central processor.

5   I am persuaded that there is a distinction between linguistic knowledge and linguistic processes. That is, I think there is a three-way distinction between *production* of language, its *comprehension* (production and comprehension making up performance) and its mental *representation* (competence). Correspondingly, I think it is important when studying children's language to consider equally, 'what they say', 'what they understand' and 'what they 'know' about language – whether or not they can articulate that knowledge.

6   Finally, I think that both children and adults, but particularly young children, can communicate without using the computational part of their system at all. Particularly at the pre-linguistic stage (but at any time when the linguistic system gets bypassed: by fear, for example), communication can be achieved through gesture and action.

Early gestures and actions are certainly the means by which children first start to communicate. And even if the system of gestures and actions is distinct from the linguistic system, a well-rounded view of children's emerging communicative competence should start with these first attempts. The next chapter, accordingly, considers how children are able to communicate before they have language.

## Questions for discussion

Here are a few questions you might like to discuss as a class or in small groups. They are all designed to put your current knowledge and expectations out on the table, so that you can use them as a basis for exploration as you work through the book. I am a great believer in being honest with oneself as a way of recognising more easily where knowledge gaps are, as well as where personal expectations and prejudices might either help or hinder comprehension.

1    What are your own prejudices about language development? Coming into this class, or opening this book, how do you think languages are learned? Is your first reaction to the possibility of innate language knowledge one of scepticism, or are you willing to consider the idea seriously?
2    Why are you taking this class or reading this book? Are you interested mostly in how children learn language? Are you more interested in helping children who have problems of one kind or another with language? Are you interested in knowing how young children learn language so that when you work with school-aged children, you will have a better appreciation for the amount of learning that has gone on already?
3    What do you hope to take away with you from this class? A better ability to work with children? A better understanding of the *process* of language acquisition? A better understanding of the philosophical issues surrounding language acquisition? A better understanding of the kinds of theories linguists and others working in the field have proposed? What?
4    You might like to place the answers to these and any related questions you or your teacher propose in a time capsule to be opened at the end of the course (or at least at the end of the portion of your course for which you are using this book). This will enable you to see what has changed and what has stayed the same in your thinking about children's language acquisition between the beginning and the end of the course.

## An activity

If you do not have children of your own, or do not have contact with small children on a regular basis, you might want to find a few tame ones that you can visit fairly regularly as you work with this book. Children constantly amaze and delight linguistically, and sometimes it is simply worth being around when they do so. It can often set you thinking about an issue in child language acquisition that simply had not occurred to you before. Here's an example. When my son was four, he said, 'Mom, did you know that "pizza" has "pee" in its name?' His analysis of 'pizza' was, of course, wrong (no matter how amusing), but it told me a lot about how he was dividing words up. Along with other questions, such as 'Mom, what does "-er" mean?' (in 'checkers') and 'Mom, what does "siz" mean?' (in 'scissors'), it told me that he was dividing words not really into morphemes (pieces of words that carry the pieces of meaning), but into syllables which might or might not coincide with the morphemes: they do in the case of '-er' in 'checkers', but not in the case of the 'pee' in 'pizza', and not straightforwardly in the case of the 'siz' in 'scissors' (although he is not to know that). My son's questions got me thinking. And the innocent questions of children can get you thinking too. Try it!

## Further reading

Baron (1992) takes an 'observational approach' to children's language. Although, as I have said, I do not agree with those who see no role for innate knowledge of language, you will find Baron's book to be full of useful (and fun) information on the things children say. Her book is intended for people with little or no familiarity with linguistics and for parents who may be interested (or worried about) the progress their own children are making with language. Baron makes many good points about the variability in the pace of development between children (a topic which I will talk about in Chapter 6), so you might like to read this book in preparation for that discussion.

If you feel you are ready to jump into a general discussion of the relationship between innate and learned linguistic knowledge, I recommend Pinker (1994). Much of it deals with the same issues we have been looking at in this first chapter. The approach Pinker takes is substantially the same as the one I take in this book.

Another book, and one that is substantially shorter and very accessible, is Jackendoff (1994). Jackendoff discusses many of the issues raised in this chapter, and also plunges into reflections on other areas of human functioning that seem amenable to explanations involving innate knowledge, particularly vision, music appreciation and social organisation. For those who would

like to see linguistics meet up with the humanities more successfully, this is a particularly valuable book.

A book which galvanised my own thinking and approach
to language acquisition some years ago is Atkinson (1982). In
this book, Atkinson presents many of the same arguments I
have presented in this chapter, while being more critical of
the 'observational' folks than I have been. I owe much to his
discussion in my own presentation, and recommend his book
highly.

## CHAPTER 2

# How do children communicate before they can use language?

## Chapter summary

This chapter is about how babies and very young children can convey meanings when they are just entering the social world of human communication. Using both vocal and non-vocal signals (gestures) in context, they convey quite complex messages. They are also beginning to make sense of the speech sounds they hear from others, and the chapter will explore what babies can perceive of the language around them. Finally, the question of how the pre-linguistic system might be related to later linguistic development is addressed.

## Clues for understanding

Let's begin with what may appear to be a digression. When you are talking to your friends, you probably are not very aware of the effort you make to understand them. But make the understanding process more difficult, and immediately you will find that you make very heavy use of contextual cues to determine what they mean.

### Thought experiment 1

Your friend has just been to the dentist and cannot talk clearly. She is trying to tell you that at the dentist's she was subjected to several injections of anaesthetic because the first two or three attempts to numb her tooth appeared not to work, so the dentist added more anaesthetic. Unfortunately, all of the shots eventually became effective, leading your friend to bite her tongue very badly because she couldn't feel anything.

1    Can you imagine your friend trying to tell this story without using her hands?

2    If this were not your friend telling you the story, but some
     stranger sitting next to you on the bus whom you could not
     understand clearly enough to comprehend that he or she had
     been to the dentist, would you be inclined to move to another
     seat?
3    If your friend were trying to tell you this story over the
     telephone, how much more difficult would it be to understand?

This simple example should be enough to show you that
when there is a problem understanding the words that are said,
whether because of temporary (or permanent) speech difficulties
on the part of the speaker, or because of a lack of ability to
understand the words on the part of the hearer, other indicators of meaning assume a very great importance.

Children in their first year or so are often in a situation akin
to the poor dental patient above. They may want, often desper-
ately, to communicate something, but often cannot. However,
that does not deter them from making the effort as they follow
what seems to be an inborn desire to communicate. Neither
does it mean that we cannot understand the messages children
try to send until they are using adult words. We use their
actions, their gestures, the tone of their voices and our knowledge of their immediate or more distant pasts to interpret – or
at least make a good guess at – their meanings, just as we do
with the dental patient.

As children gradually add words and phrases to their communicative repertoire, the problem of insufficient information
diminishes; but for much of the first two to three years of a
child's life, conversations are crucially dependent upon those
'peripheral' things which in adult conversations usually only
provide added context: facial expressions, hand gestures, objects
and people in the vicinity.

## Facial expressions

Among the first interpretable facial expressions are smiles and
the puckerings of hunger or hurt. Researchers (and parents)
differ on when they believe smiles first appear. Both the professional and the popular literature has suggested, on occasion,
that what looks like a smile may be indigestion. However,
smiles that involve the whole face, particularly the eyes, are
hard to interpret as indigestion, and this kind of smile appears
within the first few weeks. Some believe true smiling has

emerged by the third week of life, when fleeting upturns of eyes and mouth have been observed in response to people's voices, and, a few weeks later, in response to people's faces. Other researchers believe that true smiling emerges around the third month.

Whatever the actual chronology for smile development may be, there is no doubt that the earliest smiles are produced with no understanding of their precise social and emotional effect on those around them. Early smiling is in response to something someone else does at this first stage: a noise someone makes, a toy someone presents, etc. It only gradually becomes something the child can *use* to effect certain responses in others and to affect their behaviour.

Watson (1973) has argued that infants delight in what he calls the 'Contingency Game' in which something the infant does calls forth a predictable reaction in other people. So children gradually realise they can get other people to smile and interact with them if they smile first. One of the highlights of my day when my son was a baby was the smile he gave me when I picked him up from day care, but I couldn't say exactly when he shifted from smiling at me because I smiled at him, to smiling spontaneously at me. It was somewhere between his fourth and sixth months. It is probably important to survival that it *doesn't* exactly matter to a parent whether the smile is initially truly welcoming or not. That it occurs at all is one of the things that keeps an infant cared for by the human 'pack'. But parents certainly are delighted when they feel recognised and appreciated by a child who offers them a genuine smile of greeting. The interpretation that this cements the parent–child relationship is bolstered by the fact that though blind children produce the first stage of smiling, in reaction to others, they do not usually move into this second stage of using the smile to initiate interaction. This often puts a strain on the parent–child relationship, and parents have to be taught to look for other signs of greeting from their children, learning to expect these other behaviours rather than the (genetically) expected smile.

Expressions of apparently quite astonishing sophistication play across the faces of young babies – disdain, contempt, bemusement – but we would not want to suggest they are motivated by the adult feelings these descriptions suggest. Young children simply exercise the facial musculature to produce these, often comical, results. Some of the funniest can be elicited by exposing an infant to new food sensations. I remember when my son first tasted a piece of lemon. He looked as if someone had suggested he should work on a slug farm when he grew up. (That did not, incidentally, prevent him from returning the lemon to his mouth repeatedly for the next several minutes! Or from later smearing it over his face and into his eyes. Ouch!)

Colwyn Trevarthen has studied infant expressions for many years, and has shown that a wide range of expressions appear, and (at least in Western middle–class families) are mimicked by parents, long before their conventional meanings can be understood by the infants. In one of his papers (Trevarthen 1979), there are some sample photographs of these expressions which you might find both amusing and instructive. A class activity in connection with this study is suggested at the end of this chapter.

## Cries, coos and grunts

Although cries are similar to speech in that they involve the same kind of quick intake of breath followed by an extended noise on the out breath, they do not start out having the communicative value of genuine communication. Like smiles, cries are at first simple responses, be they to the discomfort of wet clothing, or an empty tummy, or the disappearance of a loved person. However, they quickly become ways of eliciting particular behaviours from others (manipulating others, some would say).

Most parents of newborns are familiar with situations where they are trying to determine whether their child is hurt, uncomfortable, or just trying to avoid settling down and going to sleep. Some parents, on the other hand, are very sure that they can distinguish various different cries (frustration, pain, anger, etc.) early in their child's life. It is not clear, however, whether they really can, or whether they are depending on other, contextual, information for their interpretations. For example, a child who hasn't eaten for several hours is likely to be hungry. One who hasn't been changed for a while is likely to be wet. One of the problems for those of us who are working parents, is that we need that crucial conversation with the baby-sitter before we take our children home (how long did he sleep?, when did he wake up?, what has he eaten today?, how long ago was he changed?), in order to avoid having to run through the gamut of possibilities and being more likely to 'get it wrong' later in the evening.

While the first couple of months are characterised by the production of cries and involuntary grunts and sighs, the second to fourth months see the beginning of voluntarily produced comfort sounds or coos, usually in response to another person. These sounds are not yet quite like speech sounds, although they do sound a bit like sounds called 'velar fricatives' (the sound at the end of the German 'Bach' or at the beginning of the Hebrew 'Chanukah'). After this stage, from the age of about four months, and on up to about seven months, comes a stage of vocal play. During vocal play, the child plays with pitch and loudness, resulting in squeals, yells and growls, and with various parts of the vocal tract, producing characteristic 'raspberries', murmurs and snorts (Vihman 1996).

Throughout these early stages of vocalisation, children show quite a lot of responsiveness to other people. They prefer to vocalise when the other person is not, rather than at the same time (i.e. they engage in rudimentary turn-taking), to imitate sounds produced by others, and generally behave more and more as if they are in a genuine conversation. When babbling emerges, the child's vocalisations become more obviously speech-like, and the range of sounds produced is strikingly greater. Before moving on to a consideration of babbling, however, let's look at how babies perceive the sounds they hear around them. After all, it is these which they have to decipher in order to make sense of human speech.

## Infant speech perception

Speech sounds are complicated things requiring the producer to coordinate the production of a stream of (usually) outgoing air from the lungs, the modification of that airstream to a greater or lesser extent by tongue, teeth, lips, etc., and the presence or absence of voice produced in the vocal cords down in the throat. For the listener, the task is to extract the crucial information and ignore the rest. Thus, variations owing to such things as personal voice quality (male versus female voices, a smoker's gravelly voice versus a child's clear voice, etc.), accent, and high pitch owing to excitement, must be tuned out in order to get the basic meaning out of what has been said (although such variations do of course have a role to play in further interpreting the speaker or the speaker's message). The question to ask about children is, when can they tell one speech sound from another?

It turns out that children are able shortly after birth (perhaps innately) to make various distinctions for which evolution seems to have predisposed them. The most studied is the ability to tell whether a sound is voiced or voiceless (/d/ versus /t/ in English, for example; see Appendix 2 for explanations of the symbols used in this chapter). You perceive a sound as a /d/ rather than a /t/ because in the /d/ the speaker's vocal cords start vibrating around the beginning of the sound for the /d/, but for the /t/ (if you just say it by itself) they don't vibrate at all. Actually, it's quite hard to produce just a /t/, and if you try, you will almost certainly actually say /tə/. In other words, you will put a vowel after the consonant, and since vowels (in English at least) are always voiced (always involve the vocal cords vibrating), you will probably feel there is some voice in the /t/ too. Actually, there is, because when you put a voiceless consonant next to a (voiced) vowel, the voicing for the vowel actually starts before the consonant has finished. So in /da/ versus /ta/, it is actually a question not of whether one consonant has voice and one does not, but of where in the syllable the voicing starts, early (for /da/) or later (for /ta/).

Well, babies seem innately capable of distinguishing those voice onset times. They can tell the difference between /da/ and /ta/ just like adults can. And just like adults, when the voice onset time is varied little by little from left to right (early to late) through the syllable, there is a point when it is perceived as /da/ and then there is a point when it is perceived as /ta/, and the shift is sudden; there is a sharp change from one category of sound to the other, and both babies and adults perceive it.

## Exercise 1

Not only do babies have the kind of categorial perception just described, but so do chinchillas and macaque monkeys. What problem does this fact pose for saying that human babies are uniquely predisposed to acquire spoken languages? What alternative reaction to these facts might you have? (See the end of this chapter for a possible response.)

Now, there are a number of other contrasts, like the voicing contrast we have just seen, which appear to be naturally perceived by infants. Not surprisingly, these are contrasts which show up frequently in the world's languages. After all, if humans are predisposed (by the nature of their auditory mechanisms,

and/or the nature of their brains) to pick up on certain kinds
of sounds, it is not surprising that languages make use of them.
What is interesting is that infants do not need to be growing
up in a linguistic community which actually has all those sounds
in order to perceive them. For example, infants can easily perceive the difference between /a/ and /ɔ/ even if, as in French,
their language does not contain that distinction. Interestingly,
however, their skills of discrimination start to disappear at about
eight months when the relationship between sound and meaning in their particular language begins to assume greater importance for them. And even before that age, their discrimination
is not as good when the contrast being tested is embedded in
a language-like context. For example /ba/ versus /du/ is easy
enough when isolated like that, but when embedded in /kotiba/
versus /kotidu/, it is much harder. The problem is unlikely to
be the overall processing of a string of sounds, since at this age
(around six months) children are producing multi-syllabled strings
like this themselves (see the next section). Rather, the problem
is focusing on a sub-part of a string and ignoring change in the
rest, since in the example above, the part attached to the /ba/
and /du/ also contains change from one syllable to the next:
/ko/ versus /ti/ (Goodsitt *et al.* 1984).

## Babbling

Babbling is the stringing together of consonants and vowels,
at first in simple repeated sequences (known as canonical babbling) and later in more varied sequences of sound (known as
variegated babbling). Many of the consonants in babbling are
ones that occur in the language the child is being exposed
to, but, particularly early on, there are often ones that belong
to others of the world's languages, or perhaps to none. The
sequences are often quite long, and may defy exact repetition
on the part of an adult. (I tried to imitate some of my children's
babbles once, and found it really difficult.) It's not surprising
that any child can learn to pronounce any of the world's
languages perfectly with that kind of flexibility.

   Babble must be conceptually distinguished from words, even
if it is actually difficult in practice, to be sure one can tell
which is which. Babbling is assumed to be contentless sound
play or sound practice, whereas words have specific meanings
and are usually produced to communicate. As we shall see,
early words need not bear much resemblance to adult words,

but at least for the child, they must have a degree of stability of form, and they must be used to communicate a fairly stable concept (even though those concepts change over the course of development, often quite radically).

The relationship between babbling and speech has been fairly hotly debated over the years. If there is a consensus emerging, it is that, though children often produce sounds that are not a part of the language they are learning, there is a systematic relationship between the types of sounds and sound sequences that appear in babble and those that characterise the earliest words. For example, babbling tends to involve what are called 'open' syllables. These are ones which start with a consonant and are followed by a vowel, but without a second consonant to close off the syllable at the end. A typical sequence of canonical babble, for example, might consist of a sequence of /ba/ syllables one after the other. Early words, too, typically consist of open syllables. Thus, 'dog' is often rendered as /do/ and 'duck' as /dʌ/. In both cases, note the absence of a final consonant, even though one occurs in the adult word. Another similarity between canonical babbling and early words is that both involve the repetition of identical syllables, what is known as reduplication. A typical example would be the rendering of 'water' as /wawa/, of 'bottle' as /baba/, and so on. Babble also seems to contain many of the same sounds across the world's languages, and Roman Jakobson (1968) suggested that some speech sounds are just easier than others and tend not only to occur in the vocalisations of young infants, but also to be more common among the world's languages.

As the child matures, the mouth cavity changes to be more adult, the child gains increasing control over the speech muscles (tongue, lips, palate) and more of the babble contains a wide range of sounds rather than being just simple repeated sequences of the same consonant–vowel pair. This marks the emergence of variegated babble. There are also some changes which make the babble sound more like the language the child is exposed to, most noticeably in the intonation (the inflections, or tune, of the voice) with which the babbling is pronounced. It becomes very like that of the language the child is exposed to. In fact, parents of children at this stage sometimes feel their children are carrying on long and involved (if incomprehensible) conversations. Certain consonants, particularly those made with the lips (labials), also start to sound more specifically like the language the child is exposed to. Labials are probably mastered early because these are easily 'visible' ones, and the child can imitate the face movement as well as the sound. Most other babbled sounds, however, seem to be independent of any particular language, and there are a number of studies which show native speakers of different languages being unable to tell whether children's babble comes from their own or some other language group (Vihman 1996). In fact, some argue that even early speech is not reliably assigned to the correct language.

## The transition to language

At the beginning of the true word stage, grunting often reappears, both as an indication of the effort children are putting into making the vocal musculature do their bidding, and, apparently, as communication. At this stage, children will often produce strings of sounds that include both babbling and words, and some of those words are not recognisably adult, but ones the child has largely invented.

### Exercise 2

Table 2.1 shows some data from Vihman (1996) on the relationship of words and babble in three children (Alice, Aurie and Rick) aged between 11 and 16 months. Just the figures for babble and word production are shown, the rest of the vocalisations being grunts of various kinds. Look at the figures in the table and try to answer the questions.

1    What is the general pattern of the relationship between babbling and words as shown by these figures?
2    What strikes you about the children's development when you compare them with each other?
3    The author of this study identifies for each child the point at which real use of words as a means of referring to things appears. Can you decide where that point is for each child on the basis of these figures?

(See the end of this chapter for a solution.)

Combining 'words', which have a stable meaning, and strings of babble, which do not, is a pretty intelligent solution to the problem of having only a few words at one's disposal. You may remember I said that children get the language's intonation down pretty early. Well, eventually that intonation will

Table 2.1    Proportions of babbling to words in three children aged 11 to 16 months

| Age in months | Babble (%) | Words (%) |
|---|---|---|
| Alice | | |
| 11 | 73 | 18 |
| 12 | 61 | 8 |
| 13 | 67 | 12 |
| 14 | 42 | 49 |
| 15 | 28 | 52 |
| 16 | 17 | 51 |
| Aurie | | |
| 11 | 92 | 0 |
| 12 | 85 | 0 |
| 13 | 69 | 4 |
| 14 | 73 | 10 |
| 15 | 35 | 12 |
| 16 | 52 | 24 |
| Rick | | |
| 11 | 80 | 3 |
| 12 | 87 | 0 |
| 13 | 67 | 12 |
| 14 | 75 | 0 |
| 15 | 59 | 19 |
| 16 | 30 | 36 |

*Source:* Vihman 1996: 132

carry/be carried by all the words in the child's utterances; but until he or she has enough words to do that, the babbling stays in the system to fill out the intonation contour. And since intonation carries so much communicative meaning – desire, anger, distress, frustration, questioning, demand, surprise – the child is able to communicate much more efficiently than the size of his or her real vocabulary might lead one to expect.

Some children also appear to use 'filler syllables' to fill in gaps in the utterance. Bernhardt and Johnson (1996) have discussed a pair of language-disordered children who made extensive use of nasal syllables as fillers, but such syllables are to be found in many normal children's repertoire at a certain stage as well. One child studied by Lois Bloom used /ə/ for this purpose. She said, '/ə/ write', '/ə/ pen' and '/ə/ bag'. Since in the adult language the /ə/ is in the position of either the first person pronoun 'I' or the indefinite article 'a', Bloom argues that at this time in the child's development it corresponds to neither. It is simply a 'sound' (a babble, if you like) that extends the intonation contour of the utterance, but does not truly enter into the structure of the utterance. (See page 71 for discussion of a similar example in my own data.)

So babble and words appear to co-occur in the transition to speech, and as children enter the first word stage, their meanings can be deduced from the words they can say, the expressions on their faces, and the expression in their voices.

## First words

As we saw above, first words emerge before the end of the babble period, and are often idiosyncratic to the child. The very first attempts, which are not really true words at all, are often sequences of sound which children decide to use for various communicative purposes. These are often called 'proto-words'. For example, one child used [diː] as a general marker meaning 'That's interesting!' and another used [diduba] apparently to mean 'Stop that barking' (Stoel-Gammon and Cooper 1984). Michael Halliday (1975), studying his son Nigel, concluded that /ə/ said on a mid-low to low falling tone meant 'Yes, we're together', whereas the same vowel said on a mid to low falling tone meant 'Look, that's interesting'. A study of a child learning French found that low-pitched utterances were either attempts to label things or (on a mid pitch) to give or show things to someone, and high-pitched utterances were demands, with repeated demands the highest of all (Marcos 1987).

Other precursors to words can be traced to attempts at adult words, although it is not always obvious at first that they are attempts to imitate. Carter (1979) suggested that a single syllable beginning with [d], and with some kind of a vowel after it, eventually sorted itself out in an English-speaking child's repertoire to a whole range of adult words ('this', 'that', 'there', 'those', etc.). As true first words appear, however, it is usually more straightforward to see how children get their versions from what they hear, and there will be more in the next chapter on the systematic variation between adult words and child words.

As the true word stage takes off, the range of speech sounds under the child's control gradually expands to encompass the adult system. With physical control over voicing, for example, children's systems can contrast /p/ with /b/, /t/ with /d/ and /k/ with /g/. With control over the lips and the soft palate, there is control over /p/ and /b/ versus /k/ and /g/. However, there is a difference between being physically able to produce the different sounds and understanding that the adult language is organised along these lines. As we shall see in the next chapter, children's understanding of the linguistic system (their mental representations of the sounds of words) first go through a period of treating the whole word or syllable as a unit, and only later treating each sound (each segment) as a unit.

## Gestures

The evolution of speech sounds is quite gradual. Meanwhile, gestures are still doing much of the work of communication. Let's go back to the beginning and see how this part of the pre-linguistic system emerges. The most studied early gestures are hand gestures. Pointing and reaching are the first to be used; and, at first, it appears that children do not understand the function of these movements. They don't realise that these hand movements have a meaning that can be interpreted by others as 'I want that' (reaching) or 'Look at that' (pointing). Children reach in order to grasp; and they explore with the finger tip, at first on the object, later at distance, as they pay attention to the object and its features. Then, somewhere in the last quarter of the first year or the first quarter of the second, a major change occurs in children's understanding of the social world they have been born into. They begin to realise that they can get other people to fetch things for them if they reach for or point at them, and that people will comment on objects they point to. At that point, a leap forward in the ability to communicate happens because real meanings come to be carried by the gestures themselves.

Recognising that this leap has occurred is not always easy because the hand movements continue to be used in the same contexts. A crucial indicator that the change has taken place, however, is reflected in the use of the eyes. Children who don't realise that they can get adults to do their bidding, i.e. who don't realise that gestures communicate, will simply gaze at the object reached for or pointed at. Children who realise that these gestures communicate will glance to check that the person they are with has seen the gesture and is either complying with the request or responding to the point. Children who realise that gestures communicate will also tend to continue pointing or reaching until a response is forthcoming, and may also show distress at an object or a person until there is a response. Moreover, they may reach for or point to things that are clearly out of reach, once they realise that someone with greater power can respond to the request.

As these behaviours emerge, children move from communicating *unintentionally* to communicating *intentionally*. (The notion of intention is by no means as simple as I am letting you believe here, and has been the focus of much philosophical and psychological speculation. See, for example, the respective work of psychologist John Shotter and philosopher John Searle.) At this stage, children move from a state in which they can concentrate only on an object or only on a person to a stage where they can share interest in an object *with* a person.

The repertoire of gestures expands quickly, and, by the end of the second year, children can typically reach, wave bye-bye, push objects away as an expression of rejection, request to be picked up by raising their arms, point at objects and at people, show or offer objects to people (and relinquish them) and shake their heads in a conventional negative gesture. But what exactly is the status of these gestures in the big picture of language development?

## Language and gesture

Young learners of both spoken and sign languages usually use gestures in advance of words. So, from a communicative point of view, the non-verbal system both precedes the verbal system and shoulders the burdens of getting the messages across until the verbal system is sufficiently developed to take over the task. At that point, the non-verbal system assumes the role of a largely optional accompaniment to language. But does the fact that gestures precede language mean that gestures are necessary precursors, required for the development of language?

It turns out that gestures are almost certainly not a requirement for language development, and there are two important sources of evidence for this. One is from children who, for reasons of disease (e.g. cerebral palsy), are unable to use their musculature either for gesture or for talking. As the wonderful autobiography of Christopher Nolan (Nolan 1987) shows, their language acquisition continues unabated. When Nolan was given a toe-operated typewriter, he poured out a detailed account of his experiences in language sophisticated enough to win him literary prizes.

The other source of evidence about the role of gesture comes from studies of children learning sign languages. Here, where the connection between gesture and language would seem to be so obvious, we would expect a clear and steady path from gesture to (sign) language. In fact, no such thing occurs. As Laura Pettito has shown in a series of studies (Pettito 1988), pre-linguistic gestures occur in deaf learners of sign language just as they do in hearing learners of spoken languages, and are no more connected to the emergence of the linguistic system than gestures are connected to words. The clearest example of this comes from her work on the emergence of the pronouns 'I' and 'you'. In American Sign Language, as in gesture, 'I' is expressed by pointing to the self, and 'you' by pointing to the listener. But after an initial phase of using these gestures as gestures, they drop out of the deaf child's repertoire, re-entering as bona fide signs, and, when they do, the children make mistakes of pointing to themselves (i.e. using the sign for 'I') when they clearly intend 'you', and using the sign for 'you' when they mean 'I'. Even more interestingly, hearing children learning spoken languages make exactly the same kinds of mistakes, substituting the spoken 'I' and 'me' for each other. So, we have clear evidence that the gesture system and the language system are quite separate from each other. One does not lead into the other, even though, from a practical point of view, the non-verbal system does the work of communication until the linguistic system (spoken or sign) is ready to take over.

This 'dissociation' between non-verbal and linguistic systems serves to emphasise a very important point: that the non-verbal system must not be considered a 'language' if that term is to have any technical status in our discussion. It does not constitute a language because, as we will see in the following chapters, language involves greater structural complexity, greater displacement from the here and now, and greater arbitrariness in the relationship between the meaning and the message than the pre-linguistic system (or the systems non-human species can use).

However, though it is not language, the pre-linguistic communication system is an important part of communicative development. It provides a means for children to communicate before they are able to use language, and lets them enter the social and physical worlds of which they are a part. Moreover, their simple communications get other people to respond, to show them what communication is about, to provide for their needs, and to expose them to lots of language.

## Discussion of in-text exercises

Exercise 1

Obviously, if other species have categorial perception, it cannot be special to the human speech capacity. However, the fact that it appears in other species is good evidence that it is innate in humans rather than learned. And, given that it is innate, it is clearly put to good and immediate use by the language learner. Presumably, humans (or pre-human ancestors) and other species have found evolutionary advantage in having hearing attuned to these subtleties, although only humans now use this ability to acquire speech. We must not forget, however, that the existence of sign languages shows that the ability to hear is not a prerequisite for *language*, only for speech.

Exercise 2

Question 1: Clearly, babble is used a great deal more than words at this stage, although for Alice, by 14 months there is an even balance between the two, with babble dropping off dramatically after that time. The other two children do not show such a clear substitution of one system for the other, but none the less the use of babble does decrease fairly steadily across the age period.

Question 2: A comparison across the children shows some differences. Alice is using words, although not referentially, from the beginning of the period studied, whereas neither of the other two are (there being just a few tokens for Rick and none for Aurie). The big surge in word use – for Alice at 14 months, for Aurie at 14 months and for Rick at either 13 or 15 months – shows a similarity among the children, but the percentage of word use among the children is different, at least when Alice is compared with the other two.

Question 3: Referential word use is identified for each child at the point of the surge in word use. For Alice, this is at 14 months, for Aurie at 14 months, and for Rick at 15 months. (Although at 13 months Rick had 12% word use, at 14 months it dropped back to zero again, suggesting an aberration at 13

months. After 15 months, on the other hand, the trend continues upwards.)

## Questions for discussion

1    The obvious naturalness of human interaction for humans
often leads students and others to speculate on the origins of
communication in our species. A related question concerns
the extent to which animal communication systems are like
language or can be seen as precursors to language. What do
you think? Read Chapter 11 of Steven Pinker (1994) to give
you some ideas.

2    Despite the evidence from paralysis and from sign language,
there are still researchers who argue for a continuity between
gesture and language. What evidence would they bring to bear?
How might you adjudicate between a researcher who claims
pre-linguistic communication is a necessary precursor for
language and one who sees the two systems as separate? What
kinds of experiments and observations would you want each
one to carry out? What kinds of results might be expected?
How would you (and they) interpret various possible results?
(Some suggestions are given at the end of the chapter.)

## Some activities

1    If you have a camera and access to a baby under a year old, try
taking a roll of film one afternoon and see how many of the
facial expressions to be found in Trevarthen (1979) you can
capture. You will find that you get some pretty interesting
expressions by capturing a moment when the face is *changing*
from one expression to another (e.g. on the way from a smile
to a cry). You should also find that even a very young baby is
quite an accomplished mimic. Try making faces at the baby, and
see what happens. If you want a silly but fun follow-up activity,
try to find 'captions' for each expression.

2    Experiment with what it takes to get a baby to smile. Compare
your efforts with how the baby's parents can get him or her to
smile. Can the baby you are observing laugh? If so, what makes
him or her laugh? Note: Babies laugh some time later than they
are able to smile. In some cultures (e.g. Navajo), the first laugh
is an important event celebrated with a special ceremony. Why
might this event be so culturally significant?

3    Experiment with the kinds of sounds infants appear to be
interested in. With a baby old enough to support and, at least
partially, turn its head, try producing sounds of various kinds
just behind the baby's head – a rattle, a bell, a familiar human

voice, an unfamiliar human voice, etc. (be creative). Which sounds do they prefer? How easily do they get bored with repeated sounds? Are there any sounds that get them really excited?

4    If you have access to a child between the ages of five or six months and a year, set a tape recorder near his or her cot or pram when the child is getting ready to go to sleep and when he or she wakes up. Try to tape a short segment of babbling once a week for three months. Then try to transcribe what you hear. (See Appendix 1 for discussion of transcription, and Appendix 2 for the phonetic symbols you will need.)

5    Try to decide whether the infant you are observing is able to coordinate attention to an object with attention to you. Begin by observing the child's behaviour with objects, and particularly when the child is hungry, how 'requests' for food are accomplished. If you are able, observe two children (one under nine months old and one at least 15 months old) and see if you can detect the difference. You should expect the younger infant not to be able to coordinate object and person attention, and the older to be able to do so. By the way, the technical terms often used to describe the first stage is 'primary intersubjectivity' and the second (more social) stage 'secondary intersubjectivity' (Trevarthen and Hubley 1978). Other authors who have discussed the emergence of intention and the ability to communicate are Patricia Greenfield (1980) and Jerome Bruner (1974).

## Solutions to and comments on discussion questions and activities

Discussion question 2

Those who see the pre-linguistic and linguistic systems as continuous must show that there are data that support the continuity and have an explanation for the change. Carter's (1979) study of the development of 'this', 'there', 'that', etc., mentioned in the chapter, is a good example of data suggesting continuity. In such cases, the explanation for the evolution might be either that children notice the general 'th'-initialness of a range of 'pointing' words in the adult language or that the adult language has developed a range of words that begin with 'th' because of children's propensity to produce them in 'pointing' contexts. Carter suggests children may be pointing with the tongue and thus producing the interdental /ð/ and /θ/ sounds. This latter explanation is only plausible for languages such as English which have the interdental sound on such words. It is hard to see how a similar explanation could be worked out for 'celui-ci' and 'celui-là' in French, for example. So, your continuity adherents would need to show:

1    that there is a range of cases such as that described by Carter, and not just restricted to English;
2    that there are plausible gestural or other explanations for the development.

Another source of evidence would be cases where, for one reason or another, a child cannot produce the pre-linguistic system, perhaps because of paralysis or cultural behaviours that prevent the kind of behaviours described in this chapter. An example might be the extensive use of binding or a cradle-board. Some Native American societies bind children with their arms at their sides and place them on a curved board from which they can easily (and very calmly, I might add) watch what goes on, but without moving their arms and legs, and (I have observed) without the incessant chatter of Anglo babies, at least while the child is in the board. The issue is, whether no, or less, use of the pre-linguistic system has any effect on the development of language. A large-scale study might be needed to explore the cultural patterns approach, but any pre linguistically silent cerebral palsied child who develops language normally (even though speech is difficult or impossible) is a case against the continuity argument (see Nolan 1987) unless it can be shown that, despite appearances, pre-linguistic communicative behaviours are actually being produced. So, your continuity adherent would also need to show:

3    that disruption of the pre-linguistic system leads to disruption of the linguistic system.

Your discontinuity adherent, on the other hand, would need to show:

1    that paths of development such as the Carter case are rare, and that the Carter case is a lucky accident of English, in which natural sounds produced by babies happen to connect with a set of words in the adult language;
2    that there are either no plausible accounts, or, if there are plausible accounts, they cannot be made to work generally for children in a variety of situations;
3    that disruption of the pre-linguistic system does not lead to a failure to learn the adult language.

Can it be done?

## Further reading

Although it is now a rather old volume, Bullowa (1979) contains many useful articles that still warrant careful study. Particularly useful are the many photographs of babies making the kinds of facial expressions described in this chapter. Another volume of similar vintage, but also still very useful, is Schaffer (1977). A more recent volume is Nadel and Camaioni (1993). Locke (1993) develops a view of language acquisition that sets greater store by the pre-linguistic behaviours of young children as part of the development of language proper than I am willing to entertain, but it is an interesting account, and reviews in detail the literature on pre-linguistic behaviours of the kind I have mentioned here.

A comprehensive summary of research on phonological development is given by Vihman (1996). Finally, an extremely accessible book about working with blind children and helping them and their parents compensate for the non-verbal cues that are missing is Fraiberg (1977).

## CHAPTER 3

# When does language development start?

## Chapter summary

This chapter is concerned with children's early verbal communications. Specifically, it tries to answer the question: How should we analyse children's one- and two-word utterances? Beginning with the development of the sounds of first words, and progressing through the levels of language, it tries to demonstrate that there are multiple levels of linguistic analysis in even the simplest utterances, and that what may differentiate early utterances from more mature language is the behaviour of certain special *grammatical* features of the system: features that are arbitrary from a communicative perspective, but which are what make human language 'language'. The overall conclusion is that even though early utterances are clearly limited, they are none the less the product of a rich linguistic system.

## What's in a word?

In the previous chapter, we saw that children begin very early to imitate adult words. These imitations are often surprisingly accurate, and imaginative adults can make some sense of most of them. You might think that children simply progress in a linear fashion to perfect adult renditions, but actually they often appear to get worse for a while, making mistakes they were not making before. However, rather than being a regression, it is actually indicative of an advance, because there is a major reorganisation taking place towards the adult system. It is similar to what happens when children begin to read with a global method, recognising whole words from memory, and then move to a phonic approach, and start making mistakes on words that were previously perfectly memorised. In both developments, there is a reorganisation from large units (whole words) to small (individual sounds/letters).

Even before the reorganisation of word pronunciations, some aspects of the adult system are well in place. Specifically, those aspects of phonology which apply to large units, and which naturally emerge first. Intonation, the up and down tune of an utterance which tells the listener, among other things, that it is a question, a statement, or a command, for example, emerges even during the babbling stage because it affects whole words or strings of words. Word stress, too, is learned early, and seems to be picked up with each word as it is learned. As the segmental system emerges (i.e. as words become constructed out of individual speech sounds (phonemes) rather than being imitated whole), the segments of an attempted word are often quite different from the adult model, but the stress and intonation are usually recognisably adult.

The sounds of children's words do eventually come to match those of adult models, and the sounds of familiar words are more likely to be mastered early, but many words are systematically and interestingly different. Before we go on, see if you can do the following exercise.

**Exercise 1**

Table 3.1 shows three sets of words from children between the ages of one year and six months (1;6) and two years and six months (2;6)

Table 3.1   Phonological processes in early words

|       | Adult form | Child form | Source |
|-------|-----------|-----------|--------|
| Set 1 | see       | /tiː/     | Smith 1973 |
|       | shoe      | /zu/      | Velten 1943 |
|       | leg       | /jek/     | Ingram 1986 |
| Set 2 | duck      | /gʌk/     | Ingram 1986 |
|       | tickle    | /gigu/    | Smith 1973 |
|       | bacon     | /buːdu/   | Velten 1943 |
| Set 3 | train     | /ten/     | Ingram 1986 |
|       | potato    | /dedo/    | Ingram 1986 |
|       | bib       | /bi/      | Ingram 1986 |

*Source:* Smith 1973, Velten 1943, Ingram 1986 (as presented by Goodluck 1991: 25)

with their adult equivalents. Within each set, the same phonological process is involved. Can you see what is happening in each set? The data are taken from Goodluck (1991), who herself took them from the authors indicated.
Now read on.

David Ingram (1986), from whom much of this data is taken, categorised children's modifications of adult words into the three groups you see here. The first represents processes of *substitution* (where one sound is substituted for another) the second *assimilation* (where a sound changes to become more like the one next to it) and the third *reduction* (where a sound is deleted), although in many cases more than one process is going on in the same word. Let's look at the data in detail. In Set 1, an /s/ becomes a /t/, a /ʃ/ becomes a /z/ and an /l/ becomes a /j/. (Use the table in Appendix 2 to remind yourself how these symbols sound, and for basic information about speech sound articulation that will allow you to make sense of the following discussion if you have never met this sort of analysis before.) When the /s/ becomes a /t/, a fricative consonant is substituted for a stop consonant. When /ʃ/ becomes /z/, the place of articulation moves forward from being on the palate to being on the alveolar ridge behind the teeth. And when /l/ becomes /y/, the glide /y/ is substituted for a liquid consonant (/l/).

In Set 2, sounds become more like each other. So, when 'duck' becomes /gʌk/, the child anticipates the velar /k/ at the end of the word, and substitutes the velar equivalent of /d/, namely /g/, for the /d/. When 'tickle' becomes /gigu/, both the /t/ and the velar /k/ become voiced like the vowel that separates them, and the /t/ moves to be velar like the /k/, the same process as we saw in the previous example. And when 'bacon' becomes /buːdu/, not only do the consonants become more similar to each other, but the vowels change to become the same.

Finally, in Set 3, we see things missing from the adult versions. The consonant cluster /tr/ is simplified to /t/, the three syllables of 'potato' are reduced to two, and the final consonant on 'bib' is simply absent. (As I said before, there are often multiple processes going on in the same word, so /dedo/ also shows assimilation of the /t/ to /d/, for example.)

Why do children make these changes? Is it because they cannot say certain sounds? Is it because they cannot hear the

adult sounds accurately? These are good questions that still
have not been satisfactorily answered, but we have some clues
for some children. For example, children often recognise that
their own pronunciations do not match those of the adult, and
get quite annoyed if an adult tries to pronounce the words the
same way. A child who says 'fis' for 'fish' may say, 'No! not
"fis", "fis"!' when an adult tries to use the child form. Cases
such as these provide clear evidence that it is not always a
question of perception. Neither is it simply a question of production difficulties. Neil Smith's son Amahl (Smith 1973) pronounced 'puddle' as 'puggle'. Ah! you might say, he can't say
/d/ in the middle of a word. But at the same time period he
pronounced 'puzzle' as 'puddle'. So, clearly, it was a question
of having systematic correspondences between adult and child
sounds, rather than a simple question of getting the muscles to
cooperate.

Some children do, however, have problems perceiving some
speech sounds. Getting the distinctions between /θ/ and /f/,
and between /r/ and /w/, for example, is difficult for many
children until as late as three years old, sometimes beyond.
What is odd, is that these same differences can be perceived by
infants in the pre-linguistic stage when treated purely as sounds,
unrelated to language. So, the capacities of the ear and the
capacities of the language learning brain are not always in step
with each other. Another effect of this mismatch is that children may be able to perceive and produce certain sounds in
words with which they are very familiar, but not be able to
produce these very same sounds in words that are less familiar.
A child who can say his brother's name 'Matthew' may not be
able to say /θ/ in any other word.

While the substitutions of the type seen in Set 1 in Exercise
1, as well as the 'puzzle'/'puggle'/'puddle' type, can be described as the result of changes of segment from adult to child
word, other processes, such as simplifying consonant clusters
('train' /ten/) or deleting final consonants ('bib' /bi/), seem to
be the result of children having fixed notions of what a word
can be like. For example, many of the distortions of adult
words result in simple consonant–vowel (CV) or CVCV structures for words. Others, such as the assimilation processes, lead
to word structures where all the consonants are in harmony
with each other (all the same or similar). A child learning
Catalan had the following pronunciations (from Lléo (1990)
cited in Vihman (1996: 226)):

| | |
|---|---|
| 'arecada' (= earring) | /kaʀaʀa/ |
| 'bicicleta' (= bicycle) | /bleblɛka/ |
| 'sabates' (= shoes) | /papatɔs/ |
| 'toronja' (= orange) | /ʒɔʒɔnta/ |

You should be able to see how regular the pattern of each word is, and how they all seem to conform to a CVCV pattern, with repetition of the vowel, and in many cases repetition of the consonant, i.e. reduplication of the kind seen in babbling. This kind of forcing of adult words into a predetermined phonological template typical of babbling is quite common among children, although some do it more extensively, and more strictly, than others.

Let's look now at how early words are used to convey meaning.

## Meaning through word and context

A child who says /wandæt/ (= 'want that') while reaching for a plate of biscuits on the table has mastered the phonology of English sufficiently that the utterance is recognisable, and the component words can be understood by the person listening. That person can then make other assumptions about the utterance. In particular, what exactly each word means, and what they mean in combination. They will undoubtedly assume that the word 'want' expresses desire for (in this case) an object, and the word 'that' picks out a particular object. From a syntactic point of view, the fact that the two words occur in the order they do, allows us to interpret their meaning in combination as that someone wants something specific. Finally, the hearer can interpret the whole utterance as having a particular pragmatic or communicative meaning: it is clearly either a request for action on the part of someone else who is expected to give a biscuit to the speaker, or the child is simply stating that he or she wants a biscuit without any expectation of getting one. (There may be other possible interpretations, but request and expression of desire are the most likely here.)

Notice that in the utterance of 'want that', the communication of meaning succeeds through a combination of the words themselves and the context in which they are uttered. The hearer must fill in various gaps in the expression to retrieve something along the lines of '[This child who is speaking now] wants [right now] [a particular thing which can be interpreted as] that [biscuit which is on the plate, or one of the biscuits on the plate]'. Moreover, we assume this child wants the hearer to understand that a request is being made, and expects the hearer to comply with the request and be the supplier of a biscuit. As such, the child is assuming that the hearer can reach the biscuits, is capable of supplying one, will see the supplying of one as reasonable, etc. More may, of course, be at stake. Perhaps the child was earlier refused a biscuit until she finished her spinach, in which case other assumptions must be supplied by the hearer. Maybe the child knows perfectly well she is not allowed a biscuit, but is trying to get one nonetheless. Clearly the possibilities are endless.

Now, why should I spin this example out to such a (possibly ridiculous) extent? In order to make the following points. First, that much of the success of an utterance such as this depends upon the hearer doing the work. And second, to suggest that such work is normal in all utterance interpretation, no matter who the speaker is. An adult who said 'I want that' would similarly have to have his or her utterance interpreted by a cooperating hearer. It is just that, in general, children give fewer linguistic cues to work with, so the hearer has more work to do.

## Exercise 2

Below are some utterances from a child in the one- and two-word stage. Look at the examples and try to decide what each one might mean. You should have more than one conclusion for each. Then look at the contexts provided below and decide whether, with this additional information, you can narrow down your original hypotheses, or even change them altogether.

1   'Go'
2   'Up'
3   'Waddat?'
4   'No more'

Contexts: (1) said while buttoning up the child's coat; (2) said while the child watches a parent mount the stairs, the child remaining at the bottom prevented from going up by a child-proof gate; (3) said while pointing to a new toy which has just been brought by an aunt; (4) said while pushing away some dessert and reaching towards the mashed potato, a large bowl of which she has already eaten. (Comments on this exercise are offered at the end of this chapter.)

## A word about (over-)interpretation

Parents are often guilty of crediting their child with more
language than he or she actually has. Even half-way plausible
interpretations of children's utterances are eagerly seized upon
by parents as correct, even if they represent knowledge far
in advance of what might otherwise seem reasonable for the
child to be communicating. My husband was leaving the room
one day when our son was almost a year old, and Avi said,
/badada/, and both of us heard it as 'Bye Daddy' (even though
we always call my husband 'Papa'). We were clearly over-
interpreting what our child was saying. But that's OK. In fact,
it's more than OK for *parents* to over-interpret their children's
utterances because it exposes the child to important experiences of being understood a certain way, and exposes him or
her to specific, contextually relevant, language. When Avi said
(we thought), 'Bye Daddy', we responded by saying, 'Yes,
Papa's going out. Wave bye-bye' or some such. We produced,
in other words, language relevant to the situation, containing
key words such as 'out', 'Papa', 'bye-bye', etc. and reflected
them back to our child. I doubt he learned any of them in that
instant (although one never knows: see Chapter 5) but repeated over-interpretations by parents may be quite helpful to
the language learning child. (Since cultures vary in the extent
to which they (over-)interpret children's utterances, we must
recognise the variability of the relationship between child utterance and adult interpretation. Moreover, although the crucial
experiment cannot be done for ethical reasons, it may well be
that the way parents of children incapable of recognisable
speech (cerebral palsied children, for example) treat them 'as if'
they were a conversational partner, is at least part of the reason
such children learn language.

What is good for parents to do, however, is not good for
*researchers* to do. Researchers struggle to interpret only to the
extent that there is fairly strong logical or observational evid
ence (see Chapter 1) for the interpretation. As a researcher, I
stepped back from the 'Bye Daddy' episode after it had happened, and thought, 'Hmm, Avi is several months away from
the two-word stage, so if he really said "Bye Daddy", he must
have been using it as a single word. Then, again, he hasn't
heard the word "Daddy" much if at all applied to his father.
On the other hand, his baby-sitter refers (in the third person)

to his father as "Daddy", so maybe the "Daddy" was genuine, though I'm unconvinced because the use of "Papa" so clearly overwhelms the frequency of use of "Daddy", and Avi is not yet old enough (I think) to be seriously affected by the peer pressure towards the more common "Daddy" . . . For the "bye" or "bye-bye" part, I thought, well, /baba/ is the way Avi has been saying "bye-bye" when he clearly means it, waving his hand as someone departs (or appears, or just simply looks interesting to him), so maybe that interpretation is legitimate. But even here there's a wrinkle: my husband said "Bye-bye" to both Avi and me, just before Avi said /badada/, so maybe it was a simple imitation. Besides, /badada/ contains only one syllable that could be assigned to the two-syllables of "bye-bye", so it would have to be seen as a blend in any case . . .' You see the problems, I hope.

The efforts by researchers not to overdo their interpretations in the manner of parents has led many, particularly those within the 'observational' tradition discussed in Chapter 1, to be sceptical that the children mean as much as they are credited with meaning. However, while caution is always a valuable scientific state of mind, we always, whether talking to children or adults, interpret more than is strictly contained in the utterance itself. We need to be careful, therefore, not to diminish children's abilities by applying stricter standards of interpretation to them than we would to each other!

## Early vocabulary

In the early stages, children use words (in combination with gestures and other pre-linguistic communications) mostly for things in their immediate environment ('drink', 'bottle', 'hat'). They also describe actions or states ('down', 'allgone'); and they produce words that facilitate social interaction ('hi', 'bye'). By the end of his first year, my son had the little vocabulary shown in Table 3.2 (always presuming I'm not overdoing my interpretation of his utterances!).

All these words were produced during the month he turned a year old, but it was the beginning of an explosion of vocabulary that has continued unabated ever since. At one year and three months (1;3), I estimated his vocabulary as (at least) 72 words (see Activity 1 at the end of this chapter).

I represent the vowels in the words in Table 3.2 with some trepidation because first of all they were not stable, and second

Table 3.2   Avi's vocabulary at one year old

| /baba/ | 'bottle' or 'bye-bye' | /papa/ | 'Papa' |
|---|---|---|---|
| /ha/ | 'hat' | /mama/ | 'Mama' |
| /haːiː/ | 'Hi!' | /duːduː/ | 'doodoo' (faeces) |
| /ba/ | 'ball' | /dædʰiː/ | 'Odette' (Portuguese) |
| /bebi/ | 'baby' | /tʃiː/ | 'cheese' |
| /dɔ/ | 'dog' | /pɪpɪˀ/ | 'pipik' (tummy button) |
| /gʌ/ | 'duck' | /ʃø/ | 'shoe' |
| /kʌgʌ/ | 'kitty' | /buː/ | 'book' |
| /kʰiː/ | 'key(s)' | /bɪbø/ | 'Big Bird' |

they often did not truly match any of the adult vowels in the phonemic system of representation shown in Appendix 2. Thus the vowel in 'ball' would sometimes come out clearly as represented here (i.e. the vowel in 'father') and sometimes be closer to /æ/ (the vowel in 'bat'). I am sure it didn't help him that he was growing up in a Western American English community with a mother who speaks the (remnants of) a southern English dialect replete with exceedingly unstable vowels herself. However, don't expect *any* child's early pronunciations to be very stable, and if you decide to try to record and transcribe a young child's utterances you will have to decide whether you want to focus on pronunciation – in which case you will need to use a much narrower, phonetic, transcription than I have used here – or whether you want to focus on the semantics (meanings) of the early vocabulary, in which case a broader (less precise) transcription of the kind I have used here should be sufficient.

From this list of Avi's first words, it is clear that his meanings are both *referential*, that is they refer to specific objects he can see, feel and (usually) put in his mouth, and *social* (or affective), such as 'hi' and 'bye'. That 'hi' is a social word is very clear in Avi's case since he would vary its pronunciation depending on the extent to which he wanted to use it as an invitation to cuddle up with his 'blankie' and the word's recipient, or was simply happy to see the addressee but was more interested in getting on with his own activities afterwards (see the discussion of intonation and proto-words in the previous chapter). At the end of the day, I often received a delighted /haːiː/ with long drawn out vowels (represented by putting a colon after the vowel). At other times I might be greeted (or re-greeted, if I had just returned from another room) with a much more peremptory /hai/.

So, we have seen so far in this chapter that words can convey meaning by being recognisably similar to those of the adult language, and by being interpreted graciously by co-operative others in context. At this point we have to ask whether a word to a child has the same status as a word to an adult. To an adult a word is a multi-faceted thing. It has phonological form, it has semantic meaning, and it has syntactic positions in an utterance that it may go in. We have seen that the first two of these are fairly straightforwardly credited to the child. It is in the final aspect that deep disagreements among child language researchers emerge. There is a strong tradition (in the observational approach) of analysing early utterances only in semantic terms, and not crediting children with a full linguistic system. The work of the late Harvard psychologist Roger Brown (Brown 1973) exemplifies this tradition, and in the next section I will outline how he analysed early utterances semantically, and then indicate why I think he was wrong not to credit children with a syntactic system. Although Brown's analysis was done twenty-five years ago, the principles it embodies are still very much current in child language research. A detailed analysis of Brown's work allows us to see why a semantic account only takes us so far, and why there are arguments for a richer account.

## Semantic descriptions of early utterances

Roger Brown claimed that there are a small group of ten 'major meanings' which can be used to characterise utterances at the two-word stage, and at the one-word stage, if we use the context to supply missing elements. Here are Brown's 'major meanings':

1 *Nomination* is the naming category. Brown applied it to an utterance when its function was to remark on the simple existence of an object or to demonstrate that the speaker knew the name of the object. Brown's examples included 'This doll' said by a child in response to an adult asking 'What's this?', and saying 'Here baby' when asked 'Where's the baby?'

2 *Recurrence* Utterances such as 'More noise', said when the child began turning a toy wheel in order to make noise, and 'Nother raisin', said when the child extended a hand towards the mother

who held some raisins, were both categorised as meanings that express recurrence. This meaning might be described as including expressions of desire that something happen again, or comments that there are more of something, or that something is happening again.

3   *Non-existence* Brown put in this category cases such as the child who looked at an empty plate and said 'Allgone egg'. Another example was a child who said 'No more noise' when stopping a toy wheel that the child had been using to make noise.

4   *Agent–action* In this and all the remaining categories, the meaning, or perhaps we should say the 'semantic function', of each of the words in the two-word utterance were labelled. Thus both 'Mommy write' and 'Daddy go' were examples of the agent–action meaning type. The first word of each pair is the agent (the 'doer' of the action), and the second describes the action they were doing, or were about to do, or had done. The notion of agent has to be fairly freely interpreted, since presumably expressions such as 'Cookie fall' would be considered as belonging to this category, even though the 'cookie' is not an agent in the sense of an entity that can deliberately do something.

5   *Action–object* 'Throw ball' and 'Eat raisin' were examples of this category. They each involved the expression of an action someone was performing (or had performed or would perform, depending on the context) and the object on which that action was performed. The notion of 'action' must be broadly interpreted if this classification system is not to fail to categorise many utterances with a similar structure. 'Want cookie' and 'Hate that', for example, would have to fit in this category, even though 'wanting' and 'hating' are states of mind rather than actions.

6   *Agent–object* When a child's mother was busy making bread, the child said 'Mommy bread', and when the child's mother was putting a book away on a shelf, the child said 'Mommy book'. These were classified by Brown as instances of agent–object, since the 'doer' of the action was specified as well as the object that was acted upon.

7   *Action–location* When an adult asked, 'Where did Janet go?', and the child answered, 'Go movie', this was classified as action–location. Similarly, if the child was asked, 'Where did you put your socks?', and the child answered, 'Put there', this was also categorised as action–location.

8   *Agent–location* The child's doll was 'eating' at the table, and the child said 'Baby table'. The adult asked the child, 'Where's Mommy?', and the child replied, 'Mommy kitchen'. In both cases, the first word labelled the person involved and the second indicated the place. The notion of agent must be interpreted

loosely here, too, since, in the second example, it is hard to describe 'Mommy' as an agent (a doer) by simply being in a particular place. Similarly, utterances such as 'Cookie there' would have to be included in this category, when 'cookie' does not even have the option of being a true agent.

9   *Possessor–possessed* A child pointed to the father's chair and said, 'Daddy chair'. A child's mother was taking a new dress out of its box, and the child said 'Mommy dress'. These were both examples of the possessor–possessed relationship. They were no different from the way they would be expressed in adult English, except the '-'s' is missing.

10   *Object–attribute* This expressed a relationship between an object and something that could be said about it. The form of the utterance may have been equivalent to either an adult predicate structure, as in 'Microphone hot', equivalent to 'The microphone is hot', or to an adjectival structure as in 'Animal book' said about a book about animals.

These are the ten categories Brown used to classify the bulk of the two-word utterances in the data from the three children he studied intensively in the 1960s. While these categories have been used extensively by researchers over the years, and have advanced the field considerably, there are some problems that lead me to advocate a rather different view of classifying children's language.

## Arguments for a richer account of early utterances

First, a reminder. Adult utterances are analysable in terms of several subsystems: *pragmatically* in terms of how and what they communicate in context; *semantically* in terms of word and sentence meanings; *syntactically* in terms of how words can be recognised as nouns and verbs (etc.) and can be combined as subjects and objects (etc.); *morphologically* in terms of how words are made up of pieces (roots, prefixes, suffixes, etc.); and *phonologically* in terms of the sounds that make them up. (See further reading suggestions at the end of this chapter for more on these levels of language.)

Take the following sentences:

(1)   Max threw the biscuits on the floor.
(2)   The biscuits fell on the floor.
(3)   Did the biscuits fall on the floor?

From a *pragmatic* point of view, sentences (1) and (2) are likely to be used as statements of information, whereas sentence (3) probably demands a 'yes' or 'no' answer. It could also be used, however, to confirm a state of affairs. Imagine a situation in which a small child has thrown the biscuits on the floor, and the adult says, 'Oh dear! Did the biscuits fall on the floor?' Since the adult knows the answer, it would be better to say that the pragmatics of this utterance, in this context, is as a description of what has happened, possibly with the aim of saying 'accidents happen'. If she had said, 'Did you throw the biscuits on the floor?', it could have been more of an accusation than an observation. It is also pragmatics which dictates the choice of 'the' in front of 'biscuits' since the speaker assumes the hearer is already familiar with the biscuits.

From a *semantic* point of view, sentence (1) contains an agent, Max, who did an action, throwing the biscuits on the floor. The floor is the location to which the biscuits went, as a result of Max's action. In sentence (2), we find reference to an action and a location, but not to an agent. Because there is no agent, the action itself becomes a rather different thing. It no longer carries the meaning of a deliberate action, but rather assumes the sense of something which simply happened, an event.

From a *syntactic* point of view, the utterances can be described as all having subjects: in (1), it is 'Max', and in (2) and (3), it is 'the biscuits'. There are verbs in all three sentences: 'threw' and 'fell/(did) fall'. There are prepositional phrases: 'on the floor', and so on. We can also describe sentences (1) and (2) as declarative sentences (statements) and sentence (3) as an interrogative sentence (question). From a *morphological* viewpoint, we can describe the noun 'biscuits' as being made up of two morphemes, a 'free'-standing lexical item 'biscuit' and a 'bound' morpheme '-s' which marks the plural. We can also draw attention to the irregular past tense 'threw'. Finally, from a *phonological* point of view, we could discuss the kinds of syllable structures, stress patterns, consonant clusters, etc. that these sentences would reveal if they were spoken by a real speaker rather than just appearing on the pages of this book in regular English spelling.

It is very clear that for analysing adult sentences we need to make reference to all these subsystems, and that all subsystems operate simultaneously all the time. Now, let's get back to child language. Many researchers believe that it is going too far to credit the young child at the one- and two-word stage with (implicit/unconscious) 'knowledge' of all these subsystems. Instead they have tried to simplify by claiming the semantic subsystem serves where the syntactic system would serve in adult language. However, although Brown claimed to be offering a semantic classification, he in fact appealed, and needed to appeal, to syntax, to morphology and to pragmatics. (He simply takes phonology for granted by virtue of the fact that he assumes the strings of sound produced by the child are indeed the words represented on the page.)

Let's look again at some of Brown's examples. In the second example under 'nomination' in the summary of Brown's categories above, he assigned 'Here baby' to the simple naming category. The accuracy of this assignment depended on us presuming that, in asking 'Where's the baby?', the adult did not mean 'In what exact spot is the baby?', but rather 'Do you know which is the baby?' or 'Can you point out the baby to me?'. If the child understood the utterance to mean where exactly is the baby, and responded with 'Here baby', and knows the meaning of the word 'here', then we would have to say the meaning of the utterance is location–object. The problem is that in order to decide which, ostensibly semantic, category to apply, we have to make a determination as to the pragmatic function of the utterance and the context in which it occurs before we can do so. Thus pragmatic analysis is there, despite appearances.

I have already mentioned another problem with Brown's categories in my summary of his definitions. Several items must be categorised as agents, even though they really are not. This error is forced by the fact that Brown did not acknowledge the status of words such as 'Mommy' in 'Mommy kitchen' and 'biscuit' in 'Biscuit fall' as subjects along with 'Mommy' in 'Mommy write' and 'Daddy' in 'Daddy go'. The point is that there are semantically two categories of words (agent and non-agent) but syntactically only one (subject). By using only one system (a semantic one), terms must be applied inappropriately, and a distinction is lost. Those using a purely semantic analysis might say there is no evidence that children have the distinction. I would say, however, that there is no evidence that they don't.

A final criticism of the one-dimensionality of Brown's system (and other systems like it) is that even if it claims not to credit the child with grammatical knowledge, grammatical knowledge is not only reflected in the data, it is used by the researcher to classify the utterances semantically. How do researchers decide that 'Throw ball' is action–object? They do it by presuming that the child knows that 'throw' is a verb, that 'ball' is a noun, that the ordering 'throw' first and 'ball' second is not accidental, but reflects the deliberate putting together of words in an utterance. In other words, the researcher must assume the child understands, and thus has a system that includes, word classes and word order, i.e. a grammatical system.

Where does that leave us? I would argue that it is certainly legitimate to try to describe early utterances (one- and two-word) in semantic terms. However, if you only describe them in those terms, you are going to miss much of the richness of even the earliest utterances. Conflating semantic categories with each other, and with categories from other systems (pragmatic and syntactic), leads to some serious problems. As we will see more clearly in Chapter 7, when we look at the acquisition of languages other than English, when the language to be learned has more (arbitrary) syntactic and morphological features (e.g. the grammatical gender of languages such as French which lead to the sun being classified as masculine, but the moon as feminine!), children show much clearer evidence of working with a grammatical system that *cannot* be reduced to a semantic one. Even their one- and two-word utterances contain markers of this kind, a fact that cannot be explained very easily if one takes only a semantic approach.

Another problem that arises from a purely semantic approach has to do with how children could figure out that they need a syntactic and morphological system. This is an example of what is known as the *continuity* problem. Remember the 'logical' approach discussed in Chapter 1? There I said that if children know something later that they don't know earlier, they had better have some very clear evidence to teach it to them. If that evidence is lacking, then it must be presumed that they actually knew it from the start. The problem of inventing, or learning to put in place, a grammatical system at the two- or three-word stage is a problem of this kind. There is some evidence, as we will see in Chapter 5, that children can learn some of the syntax from understanding the semantics, but not that they invent, or deduce, the basic design features of natural language syntax.

OK, so let's presume that children do operate with a set of subsystems from the start, and let's end this chapter by looking again at Brown's examples and developing an analysis that will, I hope, more successfully capture the richness of what the child knows. I'll take three examples from Brown and provide each with a possible coding in (a) syntactic terms, (b) morphological terms, (c) semantic terms and (d) pragmatic terms. (I am leaving out phonology because Brown's utterances are presented in standard orthography rather than in a phonetic transcription. However, you must certainly include considerations of sound choice and pronunciation in any full analysis of children's utterances.)

1   The adult says, 'What's this?', and the child answers, 'This doll'. (Brown: nomination)

   (a)   This is a noun phrase, made up of a demonstrative 'this' and a noun 'doll'. A more mature speaker might produce a longer utterance, such as 'This is a doll', in response to the same question. On the other hand, 'This doll' could form part of a well-formed adult sentence, such as 'This doll is over here'. (Note that the latter would not be a pragmatically well-formed response to the question the adult asked. It would sound odd.)

   (b)   Morphologically, this utterance consists of two uninflected words. English is not a particularly rich language from a morphological point of view, and children seem to make it even less so when they first attempt to use it, so a lack of inflections is not surprising. (Quite a different story emerges when we look at the acquisition of highly inflected languages, as we will see in Chapter 7.)

   (c)   Semantically, 'This doll' refers to a particular object to which an appropriate name has been given. The 'this' indicates that a particular doll is being identified, and (probably) that it is one close to the speaker (cf. the contrast with 'that doll'). It is always a little difficult to determine precisely where semantics leaves off and pragmatics takes over. I will assume that the semantics of the utterance guides the hearer to look for a doll close to the speaker. The pragmatics then takes this utterance in context (both the physical positions of speaker and hearer, as well as any and all prior knowledge they each have about each other's experience, attitudes, etc.) and assigns a reasonable and relevant interpretation to it.

   (d)   Pragmatically, then, this utterance serves to identify, name, or, in Brown's words, 'nominate' an object at the request of an adult. Thus the utterance is also a relevant answer to a question that requests information. (Note that it is unlikely that the adult is truly asking for information that he or she doesn't already have. It is not known whether or not the child knows the adult is simply testing her, rather than truly asking for information.)

2      Mother is writing a letter. She asks her child 'What's Mommy doing?' Her child answers 'Mommy write'. (Brown: agent–action)

   (a)   Syntactically, 'Mommy write' is a noun subject followed by a verb. The verb is uninflected, that is, it does not have any of the endings that might be possible. We might expect a more mature speaker to say 'Mommy writes' or 'Mommy is writing', but this young child is not doing either. That tells us something about his or her stage of development. (Ken Wexler has suggested that all children go through a stage where verbs are optionally in the infinitive form.)

   (b)   Morphologically, this utterance contains two uninflected words as in the first example (unless you count the 'y' on 'Mommy' as a diminutive marker of some kind).

   (c)   Semantically, this utterance refers to an individual (the mother) and to an action she is performing. In both cases, the word choice appears to be appropriate according to the adult system of word meanings. The combination of the two words is also appropriate semantically. Mommies can and do write. In a semantic analysis, we might also make reference to the fact that both the mother and the child refer to the mother as 'Mommy', as if she were some other third person in the context. In a conversation that did not involve a young child, the mother might have said, 'What am *I* doing?', and the child might have answered, '*You* write'. The avoidance of pronouns tells us something about the child's semantic (or pragmatic) system. He or she probably is not using pronouns yet in situations such as this.

   (d)   Pragmatically, 'Mommy write' is a response to an apparent request for information. As above, the request is unlikely to be genuine, since the mother clearly knows what she's doing, she is simply testing the child. However, the child willingly plays the game.

3      An adult asks a child, 'Where did you put your socks?' The child answers, pointing, 'Put there'. (Brown: action–location)

   (a)   Syntactically, this is a verb plus a pronominal that expresses location. In the adult language, the verb 'put' cannot appear with only a locative expression as here. There must also be a direct object. So, we can say, 'I put *the book* on the table', but not 'I put on the table'. What the child has said is equivalent to the second of these, and thus is ungrammatical from an adult language point of view. Alternatively, we can say the child's linguistic system has yet to categorise the verb 'put' as one which requires a direct object in all cases, and thus in the child's system, 'Put there' is completely grammatical.

(b)   Morphologically, the utterance contains two uninflected lexical items.

(c)   Semantically, 'Put there' can be seen as expressing an action and a location, just as Brown has described it. 'Put' could also describe an end state of an action of 'putting'.

(d)   Pragmatically, the pointing gesture must be used to disambiguate the location expression 'there'. Without it, the utterance is what we call 'infelicitous'. It does not allow the hearer to interpret it. However, with the pointing gesture, the expression 'there' can be seen as an effective substitute for 'there under the couch' or whatever.

Each of Brown's examples, and each example of young child speech you hear, can be analysed as I have shown in these examples. The context of the utterance is important in order to disambiguate possible analyses, and each utterance can be looked at from each of a variety of vantage points: syntactic, morphological, semantic and pragmatic. (Also phonological, although I did not do that here.) In the next chapter, we'll look further at these aspects of children's sentences and at more complicated syntactic constructions. In the meantime, try the following exercise, as well as the activities presented at the end of the chapter.

### Exercise 3

---

Write your own brief analyses of the following two-word utterances from Brown's data, following the pattern of the three I have just done. (Suggested solutions are given at the end of the chapter.)

1   Mother is busy making bread. Child looks at her and says, 'Mommy bread'.
2   Child looks at empty breakfast plate and says, 'Allgone egg'.
3   Child points to his or her father's place at the table and says, 'Daddy chair'.
4   Adult says to child, 'Bring me a book to read to you'. Child brings a book about animals and says, 'Animal book'.

## To be or not to be a language

Using a minimum of technical terms, this chapter has tried to show you that very early utterances can be viewed from the perspective of all the major subsystems of language that are also needed to describe adult language. So, is early child language then 'language'? My answer is emphatically 'yes'. And I have a number of reasons for saying this: reasons I have raised in various places above, but which I want to bring together here in summary form.

1   Any attempt to look at early language from a severely pared-down perspective (e.g. as only a semantically structured system) results in failing to recognise distinctions children are almost certainly already making (e.g. between nouns used as agents and nouns used as subjects).

2   If children don't have all the systems in place from the beginning, then they have a severe learning task ahead of them which it is not clear they can solve. If language were solely structured by semantics at the early stages, what kind of evidence would teach them to add the other systems? (The force of this argument will become clearer later in the book.)

3   As researchers trying to assign interpretations to child utterances, we automatically use all the subsystems. Attempts to argue that children use only a semantic system confines children themselves to trying to interpret adult utterances with an impoverished system. And in fact the high degree of success children exhibit in understanding us suggests that their system is in fact as complicated as ours. (We will revisit this later when we talk about comprehension versus production in Chapter 4.)

## Discussion of in-text exercises

Exercise 2

I made up these examples of child utterances to illustrate how context affects utterance interpretation, but they are typical of real data. You might have thought without the context that, in data sample (1), 'Go' could mean the child was telling someone to go, or asking to go somewhere, or commenting that an outing was imminent. The context I gave you supports the last of these most easily, but the child could be still asking to go out, even though to an adult eye it may look as though the decision has already been taken and is being acted upon.

In the second example, 'Up' could have meant 'I want to go up' or 'I want someone else to go up' or 'something is up there' or 'something is coming up', the possibilities are actually endless, even supposing that the word 'up' in the child's vocabulary means more or less what it means to an adult. Given the context, the options narrow to, arguably, a request to go up or a comment that someone else is going up. The addition of phonological information such as whether the 'up' was said in a whining/wheedling intonation, or simply said calmly and contentedly, would help resolve some of this ambiguity.

Example (3), 'Waddat?', was included to show that child pronunciation does not always help us to know what has been said. Is this 'What's that?' or 'Want that' said with a rising intonation (intended to be signalled by the'?')?. The fact that there is an accompanying point rather than a reach probably indicates that it is 'What's that?' rather than 'Want that', but we can never completely rule out the other possibility.

Example (4), 'No more', was printed for you with normal spacing to make you think, independent of context, that it meant the child did not want any more of something already possessed, or eaten, or that he or she wanted somebody to stop something (perhaps teasing or tickling him or her). The context, however, is intended to make you think of an interpretation in which 'no' and 'more' have a different relationship, perhaps one that could have more helpfully been presented to you as 'No! More!' or 'no . . . more'. (Yes, I know refusing dessert in favour of mashed potato is unlikely, but children prefer odd things sometimes.) The point is that it is extremely important not to lose phonetic and phonological information such as pitch, timing, and voice quality when transcribing children's utterances. If you ever collect your own data from children, you must have a tape recorder, or at the very least use an extremely efficient and reliable system of transcription conventions so that if anyone challenges your interpretation, you have some assurance you can defend yourself. (Those who have tried to analyse utterances such as 'No the sun shining' have found themselves embroiled in just such debates over whether it is 'No, you're wrong, the sun is shining' or 'The sun isn't shining'.) (See Appendix I for some suggestions for transcription conventions.)

Exercise 3

(1) 'Mommy bread'. On the assumption that the child means 'Mommy is making bread', the analysis in Brown's system of 'Mommy bread' would be agent–object. *Syntactically*, however, we would describe this as a noun–noun sequence with the grammatical relations of subject–object. As in the adult system, neither noun is *morphologically* inflected. *Semantically*, the utterance refers to an individual and to an object she is creating. Note that we supplied the verb 'is making' between 'Mommy' and 'bread', but there are other options with corresponding

differences in the analysis of the semantics of 'bread'. If we had chosen 'is kneading', then 'bread' would be an object acted upon, rather than created. In fact, if we chose 'is looking at', we not only change the semantics of 'bread' but also the semantics of 'Mommy', who is no longer an agent, but an observer. There is no way to be sure of the correct analysis from the information we have here. *Pragmatically*, this utterance is likely to be an observation on a state of affairs, although it could be a preface to a request for, say, some dough to play with. Without more contextual information, we cannot go further.

(2) 'Allgone egg'. This is described by Brown as expressing non-existence. From our point of view, it is a more complex and more interesting utterance. What exactly is the relationship between the two words? How should we flesh it out into an adult utterance? It could be, 'The egg is all gone' or 'Look, allgone egg!', meaning egg that has been finished, or 'I have made allgone with my egg'. Notice that in 'The egg is all gone', the order of words of 'egg' and 'allgone' is the reverse of what the child said. It also represents 'all' and 'gone' as two words. This would be an inadvisable move from an analytical point of view. First, the spelling of 'allgone' as one word indicates that the stress pattern is as a single word. Second, children make very few word order errors, even at this stage, so if an interpretation that does not change word order (and thereby accuses the child of having made an error in word order) is possible, it should be taken. You need to know also that in the US parents often say things like 'Come on, make allgone with your breakfast' and 'Can you make allgone with that?', so there is quite a strong likelihood that an analysis which assumes 'I have made allgone with my egg' or more simply 'Look, allgone egg!' is appropriate. Taking the latter option, let's say that, *syntactically*, we can analyse the utterance as an adjective–noun sequence, where the adjective is derived from a past participle. *Semantically*, it expresses a description of the outcome of a process. The egg is 'allgone egg' because the child has 'made allgone' with it. *Morphologically*, there is nothing of particular interest beyond the observation that 'allgone' is one morphologically complex word, as argued above. *Pragmatically*, one can assume the child is making an observation, drawing attention to an action well done, requesting approval from the mother, or perhaps (depending on the intonation, which is not available) lamenting that there isn't any more egg. Without

more contextual information, a more precise pragmatic analysis cannot be given.

(3) 'Daddy chair'. This is possessor–possessed in Brown's system. Assuming this is the correct semantics for this utterance, it is simply the same as the adult form, except that *morphologically* it does not have the '-'s' inflection. Children learning English routinely leave out this inflection at first, and in fact treat such expressions like adjective–noun combinations, which have the same kind of attributive semantic relationship, and the same word order. Thus, what is *syntactically* a noun–noun combination, may be viewed *semantically* as a relationship of attribution. *Pragmatically*, we can say little without further context, but perhaps it is part of a listing of which chair belongs to which person, perhaps it is an accusation that someone else has been trying to sit in Daddy's chair who shouldn't . . .

(4) 'Animal book'. In Brown's system, this is classified as object–attribute, and here we see a radical difference between his system and the one I am advocating. For Brown it doesn't matter whether the order is attribute–object (as in 'Animal book') or object–attribute (as in 'Microphone hot'). They are still the same semantic relationship. *Syntactically*, however, they are quite different. In fact, Brown's object–attribute category covers at least three different syntactic analyses. One is assigned when there is a noun–noun combination, as there is here in 'Animal book'. This is a very common construction in English ('golf course', 'clock tower', etc.). A second is assigned when the first word is an adjective ('old book'), and an adjective–noun analysis is appropriate. A third is used when the order of object and attribute is reversed, e.g. in 'Microphone hot', where 'microphone' is the subject of a sentence with 'hot' in the predicate ('microphone is/seems/looks hot'). (We might include the possessor–possessed category of the example above as a fourth category in this framework.) Thus, Brown's single semantic category obscures a range of syntactic possibilities only one of which the child has chosen in this particular utterance. If there is evidence that, on other occasions, other structures can appear, it is a shame to obscure that diversity by placing all the variants into a single category. *Morphologically*, 'Animal book' needs no inflections to be the adult form. And *pragmatically*, we might assume from the context that the child is informing the adult of the type of book he or she has chosen to have read to him or her.

# Questions for discussion

1   What are the difficulties inherent in trying to determine what children mean by what they say? How do we draw the line between healthy creative interpretation and unreasonable over-interpretation?

2   This chapter has tried to make you think about what children might 'know' about language at the very earliest stages. It has contrasted Brown's semantic approach with a more multi-faceted one. What do you think about these two approaches? What are the advantages of each? What are the disadvantages of each?

3   In preparation for a later chapter, think about the nature of the child's task when a semantic system must be replaced by a full system of subsystems around the end of the two-word stage. Assuming, as Brown and others do, that there is not automatic (genetically triggered) emergence of the adult system, what kinds of things would the child have to notice in the input in order to deduce how the adult system works? Here's a hint: If children are used to recognising certain words as applying to agents of actions ('Mommy', 'dog', etc.), how are they going to put in the same syntactic category (namely 'noun') words for abstract entities, such as 'truth' and 'beauty'? (Chapter 5 of Hyams (1986) will help you see the difficulties, as will Atkinson (1982).)

## Some activities

1   Table 3.3 shows Avi's productive vocabulary at 1;3, represented as if all the words had adult pronunciation. Your task is to consider, discuss, and provide an analysis of this vocabulary.

Table 3.3   Avi's productive vocabulary at 1;3

| hair | door | go | outside | heehaw |
|------|------|------|------|------|
| dog | kitty | bottle | book | (donkey) |
| mama | papa | rabbit | hi (phone) | out |
| diaper | peepee | bear | frog | bath |
| car | sock | hat | Avi | shoe |
| Randy | nose | eyes | Mouse (Mickey) | Odette |
| bye | flower | tower | hi (hello) | mouse |
| plane | Big Bird | Ernie | turtle | ball |
| toy | fish | duck | watch | tiger |
| shit | booger | water | pupup (hen) | moo (cow) |
| milk | clown | key | yogurt | water |
| spider | baby | peach | nana (fruit) | shower |
| chair | bike | backpack | spoon | people |
| no | yes | balloon | apple | bird |
| rock | again | | | animal |

As indicated, his word for a donkey was 'heehaw'. You should also know that he used the word 'hi' both as a greeting and as the word for a telephone; his word 'mouse' was used both to identify a particular mouse (Mickey Mouse) and for mice in general; his word for cow was 'moo', for fruit was 'nana' (Why, do you suppose?); and his word for hen was 'pupup' (any guesses about this one?). Otherwise, his words were all clear attempts at the adult words indicated.

What sorts of things does he have words for? What do these words suggest about the world he inhabits? Do any of the words cluster together into subgroups in any obvious ways? What part(s) of speech would you assign each of the words (which are nouns, adjectives, verbs, etc.)? In combination with the types of gestures we discussed in the previous chapter, what kinds of messages could Avi get across with this vocabulary? What other information would you have liked about Avi at this stage in order to do your analysis? (Hint: Do you think he comprehended more than just these words?) (See the end of the chapter for some suggested responses to this activity.)

2    When Avi was one year and nine months old (1;9), I collected from him the utterances shows in Table 3.4. They were all collected at the same time in a conversation with me and my husband one day at home while none of us was doing anything special. (Note: ( . . . ? . . . ) means I could not transcribe what he said here; ( ) round a word means I think he said what is inside the brackets, but cannot be sure.

You may use this data set in whatever ways you would like, both in connection with the discussion in this chapter and in other chapters. In connection with the current chapter, I would like you to discuss ways of analysing these early utterances, focusing both on what they can tell you about Avi's linguistic system at this time, and what they cannot tell you. I would like you to focus carefully on the latter issue, and to list what other information you would ideally have liked to have about the data I have given you.

Besides being the inventor of the major-meanings approach to analysis, Roger Brown also devised a way of measuring the morphological complexity of early utterances by counting and averaging the number of morphemes across a sample of utterances. You may also wish to calculate Avi's Mean Length of Utterance (MLU) for this sampled point in his development. The instructions (from Roger Brown, adapted by Philip Dale) for how to do this are given in Appendix 1. (The solution to this calculation is given below.)

Table 3.4   Data set for Mean Length of Utterance (MLU) calculation

| | | | |
|---|---|---|---|
| 1 | back-pack | 39 | I try it |
| 2 | back-pack | 40 | Oh cinnamon roll |
| 3 | lap | 41 | peanut butter |
| 4 | right now | 42 | doodoo |
| 5 | right now | 43 | have a look |
| 6 | right now | 44 | here, Papa bite that |
| 7 | Hi | 45 | Papa bite that |
| 8 | Hi | 46 | (de) diaper change |
| 9 | peekaboo | 47 | Here Papa |
| 10 | peekaboo | 48 | break a piece Mama |
| 11 | bottle | 49 | thank you |
| 12 | here mama | 50 | here |
| 13 | by lap Aja | 51 | here |
| 14 | I sit down here | 52 | here |
| 15 | I sit down here | 53 | here |
| 16 | I sit down here | 54 | here Papa |
| 17 | I sit down here | 55 | here Mama |
| 18 | I read that | 56 | hey! |
| 19 | I get it | 57 | hey! |
| 20 | corner | 58 | hey! |
| 21 | here Mama | 59 | hey! |
| 22 | by corner | 60 | here you go |
| 23 | by corner | 61 | here you go |
| 24 | throw it | 62 | here you go |
| 25 | I throw it | 63 | in the pockets |
| 26 | throw it | 64 | one |
| 27 | here Mama get that | 65 | yessir |
| 28 | see you later alligator | 66 | have it |
| 29 | under there | 67 | have it |
| 30 | I pooted | 68 | have it |
| 31 | (..?..) a clown | 69 | have it |
| 32 | a hooks | 70 | have it |
| 33 | I reach that | 71 | flush |
| 34 | get that | 72 | I flush |
| 35 | get that | 73 | have it |
| 36 | kick it | 74 | shut de door |
| 37 | yessir | 75 | yessir |
| 38 | powder | | |

## Solutions to and comments on discussion questions and activities

Activity 1

You have probably worked out that Avi was/is a child exposed to various cultural icons of the twentieth century, Disney and Sesame Street being the obvious ones from his early vocabulary. He also has a healthy number of words for animals, the result mainly of looking at books. Shortly after the stage shown here, he acquired the word 'booby', having been rather taken with a photo of a blue-footed booby in a book about the Galapagos Islands. He has his own name, and that of his immediate family including his baby-sitter (Odette, pronounced /odɛtʃiː/ in the Brazilian Portuguese way). He also has words for body parts and bodily functions, things talked about freely in our house. And he has words for things in the house, and everyday activities of washing, eating, etc.

Some of the parts of speech are easy. He mostly has nouns at this stage, such as 'diaper', 'sock', and 'hat'. There are also a few social words, such as 'hi', meaning 'hello', and 'bye'. Then there are words that are more difficult to classify, such as 'out', 'shower' and 'go'. The last of these is probably safely a verb, 'shower' could be either a verb or a noun, and 'out', could be a preposition in principle, but is more likely to be a word indicating location. Until these words are combined with others in two-word constructions, we cannot be very sure. In combination with gestures such as reaching, pointing and showing, Avi was able to comment on his environment, demand more food, request to be with friends and family, and so on. (See Chapter 2.) Finally, Avi most definitely comprehended more than he said, as we could tell from a variety of situations, e.g. the way he followed commands to look at the 'door' or 'window' even though he had neither of these words in his productive vocabulary.

Activity 2

I threw out utterance (31) because it contained an untranscribable portion, and (28) because it is a recitation. I did not count the 'oh' on the front of utterance (40) although I did count the rest of the utterance. I treated both 'peanut butter' (41) and 'cinnamon roll' (40) as one morpheme, since they behave in the adult vocabulary as individual lexical items. Similarly 'back-pack' (1,2) was treated as a single morpheme. In

(63), 'pockets' contains two morphemes resulting in a total of four for the utterance. (30) 'pooted' contains two morphemes resulting in three morphemes for the utterance. (32) contains three morphemes. I treated 'yessir' as a single morpheme because of the way it is pronounced as a single word by (American) adults. That gave me a grand total of 150 morphemes spread over 73 utterances. That gives a Mean Length of Utterance of 2.05.

## Further reading

Several technical linguistic terms have been introduced in this chapter. If you are new to linguistics, you may find it hard to juggle so many new terms at once. To help you, you might like to consult the introductory books on linguistics mentioned in the 'How to use this book' section on page 12. Particularly relevant to this chapter is O'Grady, Dobrovolsky and Katamba, *Contemporary Linguistics: An Introduction* (1997).

Brown (1973) is a marvellous book, full of fine observations of the peculiarities of early speech. From our vantage point more than twenty years after its publication, his analysis of earlier scholars will seem dated, but many of the arguments and observations still pertain, and the book is still important for the serious student of child language, not least because a careful reading of it will help in understanding the roots and origins of child language study in the twentieth century.

Chapter 5 of Hyams (1986) discusses the issues involved in moving from semantically based grammars to syntactically based grammars in more – and more technical – detail than I have done here. If you are interested in pursuing this issue, you might find her discussion interesting.

The analysis I gave of how a hearer recovers information from the utterance (of either a child or an adult), as well as all my comments about pragmatics elsewhere in this chapter, are informed by Relevance Theory, as proposed by Sperber and Wilson (1995) and in a variety of other papers.

## CHAPTER 4

# How do young children think language works?

## Chapter summary

This chapter examines four representative samples of children's language from four different ages, all under five. It then uses these samples to discuss the major developments in language structure (phonology, morphology and syntax) and function (semantics and pragmatics) over this age span.

## Looking at children's language

Let's begin by getting a feel for the kinds of language that are produced by two-, three-, four- and five-year-olds. We'll do that by examining some actual examples of speech produced by children at those ages. We must be careful, however, not to put too much store by the chronological ages of the children doing the talking. Children vary greatly in the pace at which their language develops, so characteristics of language represented here as being spoken by a three-year-old may be equivalent to the language of another four-year-old, or even of a two-and-a-half-year-old. As we will see, there are more linguistically appropriate measures of development than chronological age.

After I have presented the speech of the children, we'll see how much it can tell us about the system that the children seem to be operating with. That system is the unconscious 'knowledge' or set of assumptions they have about the language they are speaking: their *competence* in the special sense of that word that we met in Chapter 1. The discussion will also use the data samples as a springboard for discussing other relevant research.

## Data Set I: Two-year-old speech

SAMPLE 1

Ross at two years and six months. Ross was a little boy I studied as part of my dissertation work in the 1970s. I video-taped him at home with his mother as they went about their normal daily activities. I will present two little dialogues from my data. In the first one, Ross and his mother have just sat down for lunch. I had rearranged their usual seating arrangements in order to get both mother and child on the video screen at the same time. Ross's speech is represented in a fairly rough rendition of what he actually said, using the International Phonetic Alphabet symbols. An ordinary orthographic version of what he said is provided in [ ] afterwards. The interpretation of each of the symbols is given in Appendix B at the back of this book.

R:   /dæʔ mʌmɪ ʃeə/ [That Mummy chair]
M:   Yes, I usually sit over there don't I? This is where Daddy sits isn't it.
R:   /rɔs ʃeə ovə dɛə/ [Ross's chair over there]
M:   That's right you sit there.

SAMPLE 2

In the second example, Ross and his mother are sitting talking. Ross is describing what he does at night when he is supposed to be in bed.

R:   /sʌmtaymz rɔs kʌmɔʔ bɛd bɛd kʌmɔʔ maɪ( )/ [Sometimes Ross comes bed bed come out night]
M:   What are you talking about? What about that bed at night? Sometimes you what the bed at night?
R:   mmm
M:   What did you say?
R:   /ɪnə 'dɔk/ [In the dark]
M:   In the dark!
R:   /rɔʃ əŋ rɔs rʌnz ɪn ə daːk/ [Ross em Ross runz in a dark]
M:   Run in the dark!
R:   /rɔs rʌnz/ [Ross runs]
M:   You get out of the – you get out of the bed in the night did you and ran around in the dark. That sounds a daft thing to do.

SAMPLE 3

Christilei is the daughter of one of my students in a language acquisition class I taught at Portland State University in 1990.

Christilei is in conversation with her mother, as part of an assignment I gave the students to tape the language of a small child. They are talking about Christilei's friends, and she has just mentioned that she has a friend called Maggie.

M:   You have a friend named Maggie! And what kind of games do you like to play?
C:   Uh. . . . /yuː əv fɛnz/ [You have friends]
M:   Oh, I have friends? Yes, I have lots of friends in Hawaii, don't I?
C:   uh huh!
M:   Ya.
C:   /yuː æv pɛntiː yuː æv yuː ə æv/ [You have plenty . . . you have . . . you a have]
M:   Ya, what do I have?
C:   /ə yuː æv/ [uh you have]
M:   I have friends?
C:   uh huh!
M:   Ohooo!
C:   /ay æv fɛnz tuː/ [I have friends too!]

Data Set II: Three-year-old speech

SAMPLE 4

This data sample is reprinted from Judith Wells Lindfors' book, *Children's Language and Learning* (1980: 244). The excerpt was originally collected and published by Joan Tough (1974: 21).

Two three-year-old boys are discussing the kind of garage they will make out of a shoe box.

A:   Well, you know, garages have to have doors.
B:   Sometimes they don't.
A:   Garages have to have doors that will open and shut.
B:   My grandad has one and he puts his car in and that hasn't doors.
A:   But a garage has doors – and you lock the door so nobody can take it – the car you see.
B:   My grandad has a car thing and it hasn't doors on. It just keeps the rain off you.
A:   Oh – well – shall we make a garage or a car thing like your grandad's?
B:   Well, I don't know how to put doors on.
A:   I would think of glue or pins or something like that.
B:   No – put it this way up see – and cut it.
A:   Yes, that might be all right.
B:   Right – Mark – right – I'll get the scissors.

## Data Set III: Four-year-old speech

SAMPLE 5

This sample comes from another of my students in the language acquisition class at Portland State University. The student was talking with his niece, who was 4;8 at the time of the recording. In this particular transcription, pauses are notated using ( . . ) if they are less than one second, and with the number of seconds indicated if longer than one second, e.g. (3) = a three-second pause. Words that were unclear to the transcriber are placed in [ ]. Overlapping utterances are italicised in the parts that are said simultaneously.

A:   Do you go to school?
C:   Yep, I go to pre-school.
A:   Oh, really? Is that the same school that (S) goes to?
C:   No, S goes in *kindergarten*
A:   *kindergarten*. OK. (3) What d'you do in pre-school?
C:   We-e-e-ell, I made a snowman (laughs) a army snowman today.
A:   An army snowman! You had snow at your pre-school?
C:   No, it didn't – we – te   made it out of paper, we teared it with our hands.
A:   Ooooooooh, OK.
C:   Yeah, I made a-u-u-h, ( . . ) my-uh-snowman's body ( . . ) [first?] shaped like a triangle.

SAMPLE 6

This sample comes from Judith Wells Lindfors' book (1980: 144–145) (Mr B is the school bus driver).

M:   What did you do at school today?
C:   Working – just was working. Teacher has a magnet game. Some things are magnet and some things are not. The ones that are sticky stick and the ones that are not sticky don't stick.
M:   Did you play on the jungle gym today?
C:   No, I'm a watcher.
M:   What's a watcher?
C:   I watch everybody fall off and if they do, I go and get the teacher.
M:   Did you have a nice ride on the school bus?
C:   Yes. Do you know what Mr B says?
M:   No, what?
C:   'Shut up, R___' and he turns the radio up real loud.

## Data Set IV: Five-year-old speech
In the following samples (also taken from Lindfors (1980: 307–308), who owed them to Debbie Strasmick), the same boy is

seen in three different conversations. In the first, he is talking with another five-year-old. In the second, he is talking with his mother about the tape recorder. In the third, he is talking with his infant sister.

SAMPLE 7

Two five-year-olds eating lunch.

E: Do you like pickles?
B: What?
E: Do you like pickles on your hamburger?
B: Pickles?
E: Yes.
B: Yes.
E: Not me. My mommy took 'em off.
(Now they are playing.)
B: I need a big block like that.
E: Here – because you can use those medium ones.
B: Okay, now.
E: Hey, look at this! My trailer's gonna park in here with my truck.
B: So is mine.
E: I need some medium ones (i.e. blocks). These are mine, right? Here, you need these? You have to put it just like mine. You see how I put it there?
B: How? Where are the mediums?
E: You see, there are a lot of mediums.
B: I don't have enough blocks
E: You don't? Oh my gosh! Here's a little one. Now look! Look how many cars I have!

SAMPLE 8

E is talking with his mother about the tape recorder.

E: What is that star? (Refers to the microphone on the tape recorder.)
M: What is what?
E: The star.
M: Where? Right there?
E: Yes.
M: That's the microphone.
E: It is?
M: Uh-huh. Isn't that neat?
E: But if people are far away from it, how will they talk through it, and will it still be loud?
M: Yes, because this little dial over here can make it louder or not over here. So that's what we have to do.

E:   Where's our other tape recorder what we used to have – ours?
M:   A long time ago?
E:   Yes.
M:   I don't know.
E:   Can we ask Daddy? He might have took it somewhere.
M:   Maybe. We'll have to find out.
E:   Now?
M:   Not now.
E:   If he doesn't know where it is, then you know what we are just going to do?
M:   What?
E:   Buy another one, and it's gonna be mine!

SAMPLE 9

### E is talking to his infant sister, M.

E:   You are my beautiful M____. You're a beautiful bye, you're
     a beautiful bye. I will get you somewhere else. Beautiful pie,
     beautiful pie. Beautiful girl. M____, how are you doing? Yes,
     you're beautiful. They are records in there. Do you know what
     records are? Do you know? Do you know what this is for?
     They are things that we listen to. Did you know that? M____,
     records are the things what we listen to with our ears.
     (Baby babbles.)
E:   M____, hi there! M____ da-da-da! Da-da-da-da-ya-ya-da da-
     da-da! Say 'da-da,' M____. (Sings) Hello, sweetie pie. We'll put
     some fancy sock on and you will look so pretty, my little
     M____. (Baby coos.)
E:   M____, how are you doing this morning? That's my beautiful
     pie, that's a beautiful bye, right, M____? This is a sweet li'l girl.
     (Baby whines.)
E:   . . . Don't cry, my sweetie baby girl. Don't cry, sweet as apple
     pie. (Sings) I like you, my sweetie pie, pretty girl. Do you want
     to go to school sister? It's a beautiful day outside.

**Exercise 1**

Before we go on, try to decide for yourself how these data samples
differ from each other. Think in terms of the linguistic divisions we
have been making: phonological (as far as you can tell from the
transcripts), morphological, syntactic, semantic and pragmatic
features. Try to make a list of at least ten points of interest in these
transcripts.

## Analysing children's language

Now that you have had a chance to think about the samples,
I will spend the rest of this chapter focusing on what *I* think

each of the samples above tells us about the path of development in children's language. You or your teacher may have
different ideas about the data. That's OK. As we have already
seen, child language researchers do not all agree about how to
analyse children's language, and so they don't all come to the
same conclusions either. And while I have declared my own
position openly in Chapter 1, if you come to different conclusions on the basis of careful analysis, and reasonable premises,
then that's perfectly acceptable.

I will divide the discussion into two parts. First, we'll look at
the structural features of the language at each age (phonology,
morphology and syntax), and then we'll look at the functional
aspects of the same language (semantics and pragmatics). It is
always a little hard to decide where to place semantics in a
structural versus functional division, since it has characteristics
of both. I have decided to put it together with the discussion
of pragmatics because it can be argued that both contribute to
the interpretation of what the child intended each utterance to
communicate; but be aware that the placement is not without
its problems.

We also need a preliminary word here about the term 'functional'. I am using it here to cover those aspects of language
analysis which are concerned with what an utterance 'does'
– what it means/how it functions (as opposed to how it is
constructed). I am making no claims at this point about how
these different aspects of language are learned or developed by
the child. You will, however, read in the child language literature about 'functional' explanations for language development.
These are explanations which explicitly reject any genetic (innate) component for language development, and argue (in the
strong version of functionalism) that the entire linguistic system is structured the way it is *because of* how it functions/what
it does. I do not agree with this latter view (see my basic tenets
in Chapter 1), and this is not the sense in which I am using the
term 'functional' in this discussion.

## Structural aspects of two-year-old speech

In Data Set I (two-year-old speech), the utterances are, as far
as can be determined from what the children actually said:

(1)   'That Mummy chair'
(2)   'Ross chair over there'

(3) 'Sometimes Ross come out bed bed come out nigh(t)'
(4) 'In a dark'
(5) 'Ross erm Ross runs in a dark'
(6) 'Ross runs'
(7) 'You have friends'
(8) 'You have plenty . . . you have . . . you er have'
(9) 'Er you have'
(10) 'I have friends too'

In representing the utterances as above rather than as the child actually pronounced them, I have deliberately obscured one aspect of structure: the pronunciation used, and the *phonological system* these pronunciations reveal. Doing so makes it easier to talk about the *morphological* and *syntactic* aspects of the utterances, but let's talk for just a minute about the phonology.

### The phonology of two-year-old speech

Since the previous chapter covered phonological development in some detail, I will simply make a few observations about the pronunciations shown in the data above. Moreover, since only the two-year-old data give any indication of the children's pronunciations, in this chapter, only this section will address issues in phonological development directly.

If you look at the transcribed utterances between // in the samples at the beginning of this chapter, you will see that they are not pronounced with the kind of adult pronunciations suggested by rendering them as in (1) through (10) above. The word 'chair', for example, is not actually pronounced /tʃeə/ as it would have been by an adult British English speaker; rather the first sound is /ʃ/ rather than /tʃ/. The child produces a fricative rather than an affricate. However, otherwise the sound is appropriate. As adults we have no trouble adjusting for the slight difference and interpreting the word as intended.

In (3) above I have interpreted Ross as saying 'come out'. However, I did that on the basis of /kʌmɔʔ/ in the original transcription. It is possible that it should be rendered 'come off'. I decided 'out' was more likely because the glottal stop he produced at the end (/ʔ/) is more likely as a version of the phoneme /t/ than of the phoneme /f/. In fact, as adult speakers we use a glottal stop for a /t/ in the same position. (Listen carefully to how you say 'out'. Only if you are being ever so careful are you likely to pronounce the final sound as a /t/.) On the other hand, the vowel /ɔ/ in what Ross said is closer to the vowel in 'off' than to that in 'out'. So, if we interpret him as saying 'out', as I have done, then we must come to terms with the lack of fit of the vowels. (Remember my comment about the instability of Avi's vowels in Chapter 3?)

Apart from dropping the /h/ on 'have', which adults do too in running speech, it is the avoidance of consonant clusters that stands out in Christilei's speech. As we saw in Chapter 3, this is typical of young children, and Christilei gives us two examples in the short extract in Sample 3: /pɛntiː/ for 'plenty' and /fɛnz/ for 'friends'. The adult pronunciations of these two would be /plɛntiː/ and /frɛnz/ respectively. So, it is only in the consonant clusters that there is a difference. Christilei has reproduced only the first consonant in the cluster, omitting the second.

While all the samples of the older children's speech have been rendered in the standard orthography of English, thus giving no indication of phonological development, it is unlikely that, in fact, all pronunciations are completely adult-like until at least the age of five, and for many children until quite a bit later. See Chapter 3 for further discussion of phonological development.

### The morphology and syntax of two-year-old speech

Let's turn now to the evidence we can glean from the ten utterances about the morphological and syntactic systems they are operating with. We can see that Ross can produce the sequence of nouns needed for a possessive construction: 'Mummy chair' and 'Ross chair'. We can also see, however, that (just like the child who produced 'Daddy chair' analysed in the previous chapter), he does not appear to have acquired the final '-s' morpheme on the first noun that, in the adult language, signals the possessive; unless, of course, he has, but for phonological reasons he is not actually producing it. Actually, it is quite feasible that the lack of an 's' is a question of pronunciation in 'Ross chair', since even adults have a hard time inserting an 's' after a word that already ends in an 's', but the fact that it is also missing from 'Mummy' suggests that the problem is a question of Ross's morphological system rather than his phonological system. The analysis can then proceed along exactly the same lines as for 'Daddy chair' in Exercise 3 in Chapter 3.

The utterances numbered (5) and (6) show that Ross has acquired the third person singular '-s', and 'In a dark' shows he can construct a prepositional phrase, although it is not clear from his pronunciation that he has acquired the distinction between 'a' and 'the' (the indefinite and the definite article respectively). An adult would use 'the' in this utterance, but he seems to have produced the indefinite 'a'.

Deciding when a child has acquired the articles is rather tricky, particularly in the case of the indefinite, because it is just the vowel /ə/ on the front of a word. For a while I thought my son didn't understand what he was doing with that little sound, but then he showed me he did. At about 1;1 he started putting a schwa (the name for that /ə/ vowel) on the front of nouns. Since almost all his words were nouns at that stage I decided to listen and see if he really knew it could only go on the front of nouns or whether he would try to put it on the front of something that wasn't a noun. If he did the latter, then I'd have a case for saying that he didn't really know anything about the article, and was adding schwas to the front of words for some other reason. (As we saw in Chapter 2, several researchers have found children using 'filler syllables' in early utterances.) So I listened, and after a day or two I heard him say /əmɔɪ/ as he reached for some more food. Ah ha! I said, he doesn't know that 'a' is an article and can only go on nouns, because, look, he said 'a more' I dutifully wrote that down in my diary. Then a few days later he reached towards his bag and said 'a more, a more'. 'A more what?', I asked. I couldn't see what he was wanting. He insisted, 'A more! A more!' Finally, I realised he was reaching towards a spoon stuck in the pocket of his diaper bag. I gave him the spoon, and he said 'a more' contentedly. So there went my analysis. 'More' was a noun after all. He thought 'more' meant 'spoon', and was thus a noun, presumably because I had offered a spoon full of food and said, 'Do you want more?' so often. And so he *was* putting /ə/ only on the front of nouns. Of course, he didn't know that 'a' is indefinite and is used in contrast with both zero and 'the', but he did know where this little vowel is supposed to go.

Turning to the syntactic structure of the sentences in our data samples, we can see that the sentences in the two-year-old sample above are all very short and very simple. They are also all declaratives (statements). There are no questions. This is actually not typical of two-year-old speech. In other situations, we find children producing questions such as the following, from my son at 1;10: 'Where's a cup?', 'Who's that?' (or perhaps it was 'Whose that?' without the 'is' copula verb),

'What /ə/ dis one?', 'What /ə/ dese tings?'. A little bit later he produced questions such as these:

'Are you ready for eat?' (2;0)
'Are you gonna get dressed Naomi?' (2;5) meaning 'Are you (mother)
    going to dress Naomi?'
'I wonder the yoghurt's pink' (2;7) meaning 'I wonder why the
    yoghurt's pink' (an embedded question)
'Did I eat all it?' (2;11)

In the data from Ross, there are no complex sentences containing more than one clause. However, as can be seen from the list of questions from Avi above, they do occur during the third year:

'I *wonder* the yoghurt'*s* pink'

has two main verbs (italicised), and thus consists of two clauses, and in the transcript of Christilei from which Sample 3 was taken, I found:

'Er . . *get up* and then *read*'

which is a complex sentence consisting of two clauses joined by 'and'. (Alternatively, we can look at it as two verbs joined by 'and'. Either way, it is grammatically complex because it has two main verbs.) Towards the end of the year, we find children moving into much more complex clause linkages such as the following:

'I'm gonna share with Joe 'cause he gots the horse next year' (2;11)
'You didn't make enough room for I to come in' (Avi, 2;6)
'I think you should have monkey earrings so they can come out at
    bedtime' (Avi, 2;11) (A colleague of mine with particularly
    luxuriant hair had recently told Avi that she had little monkeys
    who hid in it, and came out at night to play.)

At 2;6, Ross was able to combine ideas only with help. In his description of what he does in the night (Sample 2), he is trying valiantly to produce a sentence that contains more phrases than he is capable of stringing together, and has to content himself with letting his mother put it together for him. Although she can combine clauses, Christilei also seems to be struggling with trying to produce 'You have plenty of friends' in Sample 3. In the section below on functional development, we will see how her mother helps her overcome her shortcomings.

# Structural aspects of three-year-old speech

The morphology of three-year-old speech

The sample of three-year-old speech shows quite clearly that there is a significant difference between speech at this age and speech from two-year-olds. Perhaps the most obvious difference is in the length of the children's utterances. Three-year-olds produce significantly longer utterances. Look at speaker B's second utterance in Sample 4, for example. It is 14 words long; and if you count it by morphemes, it is 17 morphemes long!

Assessing the complexity of children's language by counting the number of morphemes in each utterance (and then averaging them) turns out to be a much better way of gauging children's structural development than looking at their ages. This method was first suggested by Roger Brown (1973) and has been used ever since. (In Appendix 1 you will find Roger Brown's detailed instructions for how to make the calculation, and there is an activity at the end of the previous chapter for you to practise this widely used method of language assessment.)

MLU measures average length of utterance (see Chapter 3, Activity 1, and Appendix 1), but as children develop their language, not only do their utterances get longer, but the number of different morphemes they use increases. In the utterance we have just been examining, there is a third person singular '-s' morpheme on the end of 'put'. There is also a plural '-s' morpheme on the end of 'door'. In addition, the verb 'have' appears twice in its (irregular) third person singular form 'has'; and pronouns in possessive form appear twice: 'my' and 'his'. There is also a negative morpheme 'not' appearing here in its contracted form attached to the second 'has' in the utterance. All of this morphological complexity provides evidence of the sophisticated system with which the child is already operating.

So far, I have only focused on the bound morphemes (those that must be attached to something such as '-s'), together with specially marked forms such as 'his' and 'has', but we can also look at the free morphemes, which are the vocabulary words. These children demonstrate a range of vocabulary items that they employ in this short exchange ('doors', 'open', 'shut', 'grandad', 'rain', 'scissors', etc.). However, in Sample 4, there is also a problem with vocabulary. If either of the children possessed the word 'carport', there would probably not be so much confusion over the type of garage they were trying to build.

Young children of this age do not use only words they have heard. They also *create* words by recombining the pieces of adult words to make new ones or by offering new interpretations for existing words. Here are a few of my favourites from Avi:

'Oh you have jelly on you, now you're jealous' (2;11)
'We're Jewish. We don't eat hamster food' (2;11) (The fictitious 'ham' morpheme in 'hamster' created this interpretation of a kosher diet.)
'Hold this end of the ho' (2;11) (He is referring to a 'hose', but thinks that the final '-s' is a bound morpheme.)

**Exercise 2**
_____

Here are two examples of creative analysis by a child aged 3;11. Try to explain exactly what the child has done.

1    Mother is trying to persuade child to eat and is playing the age-old plane-into-the-mouth routine.
     M:  This is a cargo plane.
     C:  Cars go into it. (a few seconds elapse)
     C:  Let's make the next one a peoplego plane.
2    As part of a discussion about my various roles, as mother, teacher, daughter, sister, Avi suggested I was also an 'officer' because of *where* I do my work.

A third example is a little different. How would you describe what is going on?

3    Avi (3;4) looking at the logo for 'Fruit of the Loom' underwear, which shows a pile of different kinds of fruit: 'Look, Papa, a food group!'

(My analysis of these samples is given at the end of the chapter.)

The syntax of three-year-old speech
Let's turn now to the syntactic features of the children's utterances. We'll start by looking at the expression of negation, which actually involves both morphological and syntactic factors. I have already mentioned the presence of 'not' in the sentence from Sample 4 that we looked at in detail; and the same form appears later, in 'and it hasn't doors on'. There are several other instances of negation in this sample. In B's first utterance, there is a negative morpheme in contracted form – 'don't' – and there is another one later in the sample, when B says 'I don't know how to put doors on'. There is also a bare

'No' in 'No – put it this way up see – and cut it'. And there is a negative in the word 'nobody' in 'so nobody can take it'.

The morphology and syntax of children's negatives have been studied extensively over the years (Bellugi 1967; Bloom 1970; de Villiers and de Villiers 1979; de Villiers 1984; Klein 1982). There is some consensus that the first expression of the negative is via a separate 'no' or 'not', usually at the beginning of an utterance. It is a matter of some controversy, however, whether that 'no' or 'not' is genuinely part of the utterance, or a comment that precedes it, as, for example, when B says 'No – put it this way up see'.

**Exercise 3**

---

Look carefully at the utterance 'No – put it this way up see' in the data from the three-year-olds, and at the context in which it appears. If you view the 'no' as part of the utterance, would it mean that the child was saying the same thing as if you viewed it as a separate utterance? What does your conclusion tell you about how important accurate transcriptions are? (See the end of the chapter for a possible response.)

Later, contracted negatives appear, such as 'don't' and 'hasn't'. Later still, the contracted negative begins to alternate occasionally with uncontracted ones, as in 'I am not going to do that!', although there are actually very few places where an uncontracted negative is called for. However, it is probably safe to assume that the three-year-olds in Sample 4 are capable of using an uncontracted negative even though they don't in this sample. The consequence of this remark is that we feel confident in claiming that these three-year-olds know (at an unconscious level) that 'don't' is made up of 'do' and 'not'. And that 'hasn't' is made up of 'has' and 'not'. At earlier stages of language development, this is much less clear, and several researchers have claimed that 'don't', 'can't', 'hasn't' and so forth are *unanalysed* (are regarded by the child as single-morpheme words) when they first appear.

In English, the negative morpheme 'not' almost always appears next to or attached to an auxiliary verb ('is', 'have', 'can', 'could', 'must', etc.). So, we cannot really look at the development of negation in children's speech without also looking at the development of auxiliary verbs (again both a morphological and a syntactic issue). In Sample 4, there are several different auxiliary verbs appearing. They include 'do' in 'Sometimes they *don't*'; 'will' in 'doors that *will* open and shut'; 'might' in 'that *might* be all right'; and 'will' in 'I'*ll* get the scissors'. (In the British English these children are speaking, it is also possible to attach 'not' to a main verb if that verb is 'be' or 'have', so B says 'it *hasn't* doors on'. In American English (and some other British dialects), while 'isn't' is a possible form, 'hasn't' is not possible in this context, and would have to be rendered as 'It *doesn't* have doors on' or 'It hasn't got doors on' where the '-'nt' is attached to the auxiliary verb.

When we look at the clausal structure of these children's speech, we see that they have acquired several of the basic syntactic devices for linking ideas together. The simplest way of linking two clauses together is by using 'and', and we see an example in, 'My grandad has one *and* he puts his car in *and* that hasn't doors'. By 2;6, my daughter Naomi was already producing the likes of 'You get me cereal and then you shout me eat and I will eat'. Another device is the use of an adverbial clause introduced by 'so', as in 'and you lock the door *so* nobody can take it' in the sample here. Naomi produced, 'You hafta leave the light on so I can see my way to bed' at 2;6. Still another device is the use of a relative clause, as in, 'Garages have to have doors *that will open and shut*'. The (italicised) relative clause modifies the word 'doors' by providing additional information, in this case specifying the kind of doors that are required (they must be working doors). A particularly advanced device appears in the use of a wh-clause in 'I don't know *how to put doors on*'. Here a clause introduced by one of the so-called wh-words (because most of the words in this class (in English) do begin with 'wh', e.g. who, what, where, when, although 'how' is an exception) acts as a modifier of the verb 'know'.

Overall these three-year-olds have achieved a noticeably higher level of structural complexity when compared with most two-year-olds. They are using morphologically complex utterances with syntactically complex structures, and they are doing so accurately by adult standards.

## Structural aspects of four-year-old speech

The morphology of four-year-old speech
Although most of the action in four-year-old language development is in the syntax, there are still some interesting things going on in the morphology. An example can be seen in Sample 5, when the child says, 'we teared it with our hands'.

The problem for the child here is that 'tear' does not have the regular past tense form 'teared', but rather the irregular form 'tore', but she does not yet control that form.

Children systematically ignore exceptions to rules as part of their language development. When they realise a rule exists, they almost always go through a stage of using the rule every-where where it might apply, even if it does not. This some-times gives the impression that they have regressed in their language development. For example, the four-year-old in Sample 5 might very well have produced the correct past tense 'tore' a few months earlier, at a stage where she did not realise how the regular past tense rule worked. At that point she would have simply been imitating the form 'tore', and using it in appropriate places, perhaps not even realising that it was related to 'tear'. Once she realised that the vast majority of past tense forms have the '-ed' ending, she would have started applying it to all verb forms and started producing forms such as 'teared', as she does here. Later she will recognise that 'tear' is an exception to the rule, and the irregular form will re-appear. Such apparent regression followed by a reappearance of the correct form is very common in a variety of different aspects of language development, and is usually referred to as U-shaped development because of how it looks when you plot the number of correct forms on a two-dimensional graph (high–low–high).

### The syntax of four-year-old speech

The samples from four-year-olds show both a continuation of the developments we saw with the three-year-olds and some new constructions emerging. In Sample 6, for instance, the child uses a conditional construction: 'if they do, I go and get the teacher'. Conditionals begin to emerge soon after 2;0 (Reilly 1982), but are often not recognisably adult in form until around the age of 4;0. Notice that the four-year-old in Sample 6 is able to combine the conditional construction with another sen-tence using 'and': 'I watch everybody fall off and . . .' It would seem that this is this child's way of coping with a double conditional, because clearly what is meant is 'I watch to see if people fall off, and if they do . . .' The child only managed to produce the second of the two, however, showing that know-ing a construction does not necessarily mean that it *can* or *will* be used appropriately in every situation in which it is needed; at least at first.

Another complex construction is the nominal clause in 'Do you know what Mr B says?', produced by the child in Sample 6. This involves correctly recognising that the verb 'know' is one which can take a clausal complement, and producing a grammatical clause of the right type. Notice that to do this, the child must recognise that the complement clause [what Mr B- says] has a form similar to a question [What does Mr B- say?] in which the wh-word ('what') appears at the beginning of the clause, and the verb 'say', which would normally have an object following it ('say something') has nothing following it. In other words, there is a systematic relationship between the two sentences below:

Mr B said 'Hello'
What did Mr B say [e]?

(The [e] shows where the missing object of the verb 'say' is.) Linguists argue that a kind of movement has taken place which moves the object of the verb 'say' to the front of the clause, where it appears as the word 'what'. This kind of movement, called wh-movement, is a very important aspect of the English language (and many other languages, though not all), and getting all its subtleties right is an important part of language acquisition, requiring some time to accomplish.

Researchers who have looked at wh-movement in questions, most notably Klima and Bellugi (1966), have argued that children go through a sequence of stages in their development of wh-questions. The first stage involves simply placing the wh-word at the front of the sentence and making no other adjustments. At this stage, such questions take the form of the following: 'Where Ann pencil?', 'Who that?', 'What book name?' At the second stage, more of the sentence components begin to appear; specifically, auxiliary verbs such as 'can' and negative particles such as 'not'. These are the sentence elements that, in adult sentences, invert their order with the subject of the sentence to produce a well-formed sentence. For example, we don't say, 'Why *he can't* come here?' We say, 'Why *can't he* come here?' When these elements first appear they often do so without inversion, so Klima and Bellugi found sentences such as 'What I did yesterday?' and 'What he can ride in?' in their data. In these, the auxiliary verb appears to the right of the subject, not the left. In 'Why not me sleeping?', the negative particle does seem to appear to the left of the subject (assuming that 'me' is the subject of the sentence), but without the supporting auxiliary verb that the adult form requires ('Why *aren't* I sleeping?').

As the third stage of question development unfolds, the correct order begins to appear, although not always with the right tensing on the verb: 'What did you doed?'. And often the older forms, without the correct subject–auxiliary order, persist throughout this pre-final stage of development ('Which way they should go?'). Interestingly, the wh-complement clause in 'Do you know [what Mr B says]?' requires wh-movement but no subject–auxiliary inversion, so it is perhaps easier, and acquired earlier.

While wh-questions are evolving, the development of yes/no questions (questions which demand an answer 'yes' or 'no') is unfolding along similar lines. At the first stage of these, rising intonation alone marks the utterances as questions: 'Sit chair?', 'See hole?' In the second stage, auxiliary verbs begin to appear, but in the uninverted order: 'You can't fix it?' In the third stage, the subject and auxiliary begin appearing in the adult order, but, as with the wh-questions, often without the correct tensing of the verb: 'Oh, did I caught it?' Finally, the order and the verb forms are correct: 'Can't you get it?' Some researchers have suggested that the correct order of subject and auxiliary shows up in yes/no questions before it shows up in wh-questions, but this is a matter of some debate. What is clear is that the development of questions is intimately tied not only to the emergence of 'movement', i.e. the rules that govern the placing of the wh-word and of the subject and auxiliary verb (see above), but also to the development of the verb forms themselves.

## Structural aspects of five-year-old speech

The three samples from a five-year-old child presented at the beginning of the chapter (Samples 7–9) were largely chosen to show how children vary the way they use language depending upon the person they are talking to. This is a sociolinguistic or pragmatic aspect of language, and is discussed below in the section on functional aspects of children's language. However, there are several indications of the continuing structural sophistication of five-year-old language in these excerpts.

The morphology of five-year-old speech
The five-year-old in Samples 7-9 is still having a tough time
with verbal morphology. In Sample 8, he says, 'He might have
took it somewhere'. What he is doing here is double marking
the tense on both the auxiliary 'might' and the main verb
'take'. In adult language, only the first verb in the verb group
carries the tense. What this child has done is to put it correctly
on the modal auxiliary ('might'), but also to put it on the main
verb as well, which ought to be in the past participle form.
Since the adult system involves a complicated chaining of forms,
depending on which auxiliary verbs appear, it is not surprising
that many children struggle with these forms well into late
childhood.

The syntax of five-year-old speech
In Sample 9, in which the boy is talking to his baby sister, the
sentences are short and simple, and we cannot really tell how
advanced his system is. It is important to remember that if we
are interested in the complexities of the syntactic and morphological system, we must observe children in situations where
they are most likely to demonstrate the extent of their knowledge. Clearly, a child talking to a younger child is not one of
those situations. More profitable are situations where the child
is speaking to a more advanced conversational partner, or where
an experimental situation explicitly demands that the child produce or show evidence of comprehending complex forms.
    As we might expect, therefore, the structurally most com-
plex language occurs in Sample 8, when the boy is talking to
his mother. There we see the use of a complex conditional:
'But if people are far away from it, how will they talk through
it, and will it still be loud?' This is a two-clause conditional
followed by another clause introduced by 'and'. He also uses a
relative clause: 'Where's our other tape recorder *what we used
to have?*' There's an interesting issue here. According to the
rules of so-called standard English, this is not a correct adult
form. However, adult speakers of many dialects of English
allow this form. So, whether we see this as a child form of
the relative clause that will be replaced later, or whether we
see it as a successfully acquired adult form, depends entirely on
whether the adults around this child use the form he is using
or not. Incidentally, using 'what' to introduce a relative clause
is entirely logical if we assume that the underlying form of a
relative clause is 'the tape recorder [we used to have a tape

recorder]' and wh-movement has occurred in the relative clause. If it were a main clause, such movement would lead to 'what did we used to have?', so if the same movement occurs in a relative clause, it is not surprising that a 'what' gets used instead of 'that', either in the child's speech or in the adult dialects that do it.

This concludes our survey of some of the structural (morphological and syntactic) aspects of children's language during the period from two to five. Now let's look at the functional (semantic and pragmatic) aspects of the same samples of language.

## Functional aspects of two-year-old speech

In the first data sample, Ross produces two related contributions to the conversation. If his linguistic resources had been greater, and his mother has been less quick off the mark, he might have said, 'That's Mummy's chair and Ross's chair is over there'. As it was, he produced each of the two propositions in a separate utterance. This is very typical of two-year-old speech, as is the type of joint construction of a long utterance we see in Sample 2. There Ross is trying to convey something longer and more complex than he is currently capable of. However, his mother steps in and reframes what he has said. It is interesting that in response to her first attempt, he appears to think he has succeeded. She reframes as much as she could glean from what he said, but with gaps still present (What about that bed at night? Sometimes you what the bed at night?). She repeats back to him so much of what he said that he seems to think she's got it all, and just says 'mmm'. His mother then has to back-track and ask him to try again. He doesn't seem to understand that he should repeat the previous information. Instead, he simply adds more information, leaving his mother to construct the picture using what she made of the first part and second parts combined. Amazingly, she appears to manage it! This kind of constructing of a story with the help of someone else is often called 'scaffolding' (Wood *et al.* 1976; Bruner 1974).

Christilei also seems to be trying to put together a more complex idea than she is grammatically capable of in Sample 3. She, however, receives less help from her mother, who does not help her put the idea of 'plenty' together with the idea of 'friends'. None the less, her mother encourages her by helpful prompt questions, and, towards the end of the extract, offers a possible completion to an utterance her child is trying to produce:

C:    uh you have
M:    I have friends?

A difference between Ross and Christilei can be seen in the fact that Ross uses names instead of pronouns. He refers to himself as Ross and to his mother as Mummy. Christilei, on the other hand, uses 'I' and 'you'. Often the use of pronouns is regarded as more sophisticated than the use of names, although this is disputed by others.

All the utterances in the two-year-old selection happen to be simple statements, which gives rather a false impression of the range of different types of expression possible at this age. Not only can two-year-olds give information using statements, they can also request information, using either rising intonation on an otherwise declarative form, e.g. 'Fraser water?', or by using a question form such as 'What cowboy doing?' (Brown 1973). In addition, they can use both questions and imperatives in order to influence the actions of others.

**Exercise 4**

Here's a selection of Avi's demands and requests for action and information. For each one, decide whether it is (a) a demand for action, (b) a demand for information, (c) a request for action, or (d) a request for information. What further information would you like to have to be sure you have coded them correctly?

1    'No Mama, not hit it!' (i.e. don't hit it) (1;9)
2    'Where's a piglet?' (1;9)
3    'Bring a milk!' (1;9)
4    'How 'bout this one?' (1;10)
5    'See dis?' (1;10)
6    'What in the mouth, Mama?' (i.e. what's in your mouth, Mama) (1;10)

(See the end of the chapter for a possible set of responses.)

## Functional aspects of three-year-old speech

The whole of the three-year-old sample is a negotiation. These two boys show they are well able to negotiate a joint activity through language, and even negotiate about the language itself. An important part of this sequence is the discussion of the definition of a garage: whether it has doors or not. Speaker A is sure the definition of a garage includes having doors for the security of the car. Speaker B is confused because he knows that there is something he thought was a garage that does not have doors. He concedes, however, that it may not be a garage in the face of his friend's firm definition. The boys don't appear to know the word 'carport', so they are forced to use a circumlocution: 'a car thing like your grandad's'.

It is interesting to note that both the beginning and the end of the difficulties with the definition of the garage are marked by 'well'. In both cases, the word seems to indicate some attempt to be definite about what is going to happen, but yet acknowledge that there may be some opposition from the other speaker looming. These 'well's also seem to mark shifts in topic, the thing being discussed. The first 'well' appears to mark the beginning of talking about 'garages have doors', and the second marks the shift to 'which type of garage we will make'. B's use of 'well' in the next line seems to be an expression of diffidence or uncertainty, rather than the certainty expressed by A's uses here.

Overall, these two children can handle a smooth flow of topics, discuss language as an object – a skill that depends on 'metalinguistic awareness', to be discussed in Chapter 8 – and are able to use language to negotiate differences of opinion. Along the way, they make subtly different uses of discourse markers such as 'well' to indicate certainty or uncertainty and the boundaries of topics of conversation. Other linguistic devices, such as relative clauses and clauses joined by 'and', allow them to express the complex ideas central to their exchange.

## Exercise 5

The pragmatics of language use demand that children learn how to interpret pronouns such as 'he', 'she' and 'they' in context. Sometimes the results are comical. Here's an example from Avi, just before his third birthday. Look at what he said, and try to explain what the problem was. You may feel that there is also a lexical problem involved here.

When we had visitors to stay once, Avi wanted to go in and see John (the father) first thing in the morning. I tried to suggest this was not a good idea.

Me:    He doesn't want a little boy poking his nose in while he's trying to get dressed.

Avi:    I won't poke his nose. (2;11)

(My analysis is given at the end of the chapter.)

## Functional aspects of four-year-old speech

The four-year-old speech samples contain particularly clear examples of the ability to understand what other people might be thinking, often referred to as the 'theory of mind'. Having an adequate 'theory of mind' is a prerequisite to functioning fully in a conversation. In Sample 5, the child is asked whether there was snow at her school when she claims to have made a snowman at school. She doesn't only deny that there was snow at school, but also recognises that the adult is requesting an explanation of how she managed to make a snowman without any snow. The fact that she does not find the adult request odd, suggests that she fully understands the adult definition of 'snowman' as something (usually) made out of snow, and recognises the need to explain the apparent contradiction. In Sample 6, the child is asked whether he or she played on the jungle gym. The response is not simply 'no'. The child provides an explanation of the job he or she had to do that prevented him or her from playing. The child interprets the adult's question not just as a question about playing on the gym, but as a general request for information about what he or she did that day. Similarly, when asked about the bus ride, the child uses the opening the adult provides to relate a story about something that happened on the bus.

The way the child in Sample 6 begins the story is interesting, too. He or she first checks that his or her mother shares the appropriate background knowledge. Rather than simply beginning with 'Mr B told R to shut up', the child begins with a pre-question which functions to check that the mother knows whom he or she is referring to when talking about Mr B, and to ascertain that she is going to be interested in hearing what Mr B had to say. Being able to presume that your conversational partner shares the background knowledge you want to presuppose and that he or she is interested in pursuing a particular topic is crucial to successful conversation, and addressing these requirements head-on in a pre-question to a statement, in the way the child in Sample 6 does, shows considerable sophistication in pragmatic development.

### Exercise 6

---

Look at the data sample below. What does it tell us about Avi's knowledge of the functional aspect of questions? After listening to the 'three little fishes' song several times, Avi finally expressed his puzzlement over the chorus which goes, 'Dib bab diddum waddam why don't you?'

'What do they want the dib dab diddum waddams to do?' (3;4)

(My analysis is given at the end of the chapter.)

## Functional aspects of five-year-old speech

The same child appears in Samples 7-9; in each he modifies the way he speaks depending on the type of person he is talking to and probably the type of topic he is talking about. It is difficult to disentangle person from topic since the type of topic that can be talked about is, to a degree, dependent on the type of person being talked to. This boy, for example, cannot talk about the intricacies of the tape recorder with his baby sister, although he does try to talk about records. However, it is clear from the way he approaches the 'records' topic that he knows his sister must be assumed to lack even basic knowledge of what they are ('M____, records are things we listen to with our ears'). This is actually a very good example of a child giving a semantic definition, a skill which is highly encouraged in formal education, and one which requires a high degree of metalinguistic awareness and sophistication (see Chapter 8), although, as we saw in the three year olds' discussion of the word 'garage' in Sample 4, quite young children can begin to give definitions.

The length of the sentences clearly varies depending on whom the child is talking to. The shortest sentences appear in Sample 9, where the boy is talking with his baby sister, the next longest appear in Sample 7, when he is talking with another five-year-old, and the longest in Sample 8, when he is talking with his mother. In the section where he is talking with his sister, the sentences are short and simple. He uses the younger child's name very frequently to attract her attention and to keep it. He also repeats himself quite frequently, again possibly as an attention-securing device. He plays with the sounds of the language, producing nonsense by adult standards ('You're a beautiful bye . . . beautiful pie'), but appropriate as a sing-songy way of entertaining the infant. He also asks her a lot of questions. It is clear, however, that he doesn't expect her to answer him because he doesn't wait for the answers; rather he answers them himself.

The way this boy talks to his infant sister contrasts sharply with the way he talks to his five-year-old friend. Here there is some true conversational sparring going on. E draws B into his statement about not liking pickles by finding out whether B likes them and then announcing that he (E) doesn't. Depending on the relationship between the boys, this might be a more meaningful disagreement than it appears. If B always likes to agree with E, who might be a stronger, more forceful, personality, then B has been drawn into disagreeing with E because he has been forced by the conversation to state his opinion first. Evidence that B is indeed the follower rather than the leader comes from the way he allows himself to be steered by E into using medium-sized blocks, and the way he copies E in wanting to park his trailer where E parks his.

In talking with his mother, E is less in command. Here he asks questions, first to find out what the microphone is, and then to discuss how it works. He solicits information about the name of the thing, exactly how people at a distance can be recorded, what happened to the tape recorder they used to own, and so forth. Notice, however, that he is still steering the conversation. In fact, in the section with his peer, he used questions to steer at least the first part (about the pickles), but his question there was a preface to a statement, whereas in the section with his mother, he seems genuinely to be seeking information he wants or needs.

These three samples reflect an ability to modify language according to interlocutor (the other person in the conversation) and purpose. This kind of sociolinguistic competence is extremely important to being a successful member of society, and requires paying attention to relevant dimensions of interactions and the people in them, as well as being able to select from the storehouse of linguistic expressions the ones that will serve the purpose most appropriately. This five-year-old seems to be doing a fine job.

There is always more to say about the kind of data we've looked at in this chapter. However, I hope it's clear how one can go about examining even the simplest utterance and tease out the developmental aspects. It is better if one has a video tape of an interaction and if one were there taking notes when it was recorded, but even transcribed aural data can be quite revealing about certain aspects of children's language. It does not tell us *how* children develop language, but it does allow us to see the kinds of things that need to be explained. The next chapter tackles the *how* of language acquisition.

## Discussion of in-text exercises

Exercise 2

In (1), the child analyses the word 'cargo' into fictitious component morphemes, and then generalises the pattern of word formation to create a new non-existent, but perfectly logical, 'peoplego'. In (2), Avi extends the use of the very productive morpheme '-er', which expresses an agent who does something, and which normally attaches to verbs ('farm'/'farmer', 'teach'/'teacher', 'help'/'helper'), by attaching it to a noun ('office'). That he should take such liberties is hardly surprising since there are many examples of words for people which, although they have an '-er' ending, do not express the agent meaning ('mother', 'daughter' and 'sister', among them). In (3), Avi has probably heard the expression 'food group', particularly as a standing joke in our family involves listing the five major food groups as 'fresh, frozen, spoiled, junk and chocolate'. However, it is highly unlikely that he has a conception of the abstract notion of 'food group'. To him it is most likely to be a group of food, so when he sees the cornucopia logo, he uses what to an adult is an abstract expression to describe the concrete collection of items.

Exercise 3

If the 'no' is separated from the utterance by intonation, then it cannot be considered to be part of the syntactic construction that follows it. The difference is very important, because 'No put it up this way' (presumably meaning, 'Don't put it up this way') would be a genuinely deviant utterance when compared with the adult language, whereas 'No, put it up this way' is not. In the context shown in the data, the first interpretation (where the 'no' is not part of the following utterance) is a more likely interpretation, given speaker B's response. Since the transcriber is often the only person to hear or see the original tape, whatever decision the transcriber makes about the placement of commas, dashes, full stops, and other clues to structure beyond the words spoken, affects all uses of that transcript from then on.

Exercise 4

1    'No Mama, not hit it!' (i.e. don't hit it) (1;9) [demand for ceasing a particular behaviour]

2　'Where's a piglet?' (1;9) [request for information]
3　'Bring a milk!' (1;9) [demand for action]
4　'How 'bout this one?' (1;10) [request for information]
5　'See dis?' (1;10) [request for information/action]
6　'What in the mouth, Mama?' (i.e. what's in your mouth, Mama) (1;10) [request for information]

I have coded 'See dis?' as either a request for information or a request for action, since I was remiss in not recording the surrounding context. In order to tell whether the request was simply to provide some name for an object (an appropriate response to a request for information) or whether it was a request to come and do something to some object he was holding (an appropriate response to a request for action), you would need to know what Avi was doing at the time, and how he reacted to whichever interpretation I gave. When you do your own recording, be sure to take good field notes about what's going on at the time, and preferably use a video camera.

Exercise 5
When I said, 'He doesn't want a little boy poking his nose in . . .', I intended 'his' in 'his nose' to refer back to 'little boy', but Avi took it to refer back to the 'he' at the beginning of the sentence. His lack of familiarity with the reflexive idiom 'to poke one's nose in' (one doesn't poke someone else's nose in) led him to interpret the sentence as if it did not contain this idiom; and, under those conditions, either the subject 'he' or the object 'little boy' could serve as the antecedent (the coreferent) for 'his' in 'his nose'.

Exercise 6
Avi apparently understands that the question 'Why don't you?' is incomplete. In the adult system, what is missing may either be present in the sentence, as in 'Why don't you close the door/come with me/etc.', or is presupposed by what has gone before. (For example, when children have been told that someone doesn't want to do something, they often demand, '[But] why don't you?', with stress on 'why'. Either way, the version in the song is incomplete, and Avi is puzzled over what exactly is missing, assuming it must be some action. He also assumes that the nonsense 'dib dab diddum waddam' is a group of creatures being addressed, on a par with 'Avi, why don't you . . . ?'. So, from a functional point of view, we can say that Avi knows that questions are addressed to people,

often by name, and that 'Why don't you?' requires the hearer to be able to recover what is presupposed in order to be able to understand what is being asked.

## Questions for discussion

1    This chapter has assumed that when children correctly produce an adult-like utterance, they possess adult-like knowledge of that structure. Similarly, it has assumed that when a child produces a child structure which varies systematically from the adult one, this reveals the system the child possesses, i.e. what the child knows. What problems are there with this assumption? To help your thinking, consider the following:

(a)    Do you know anyone who can say just a few words in a language, but says them well enough that native speakers assume they are fluent?

(b)    Have you ever had the experience of trying to speak a foreign language and having something you did not intend come out of your mouth? (See below.)

2    Much of the work in child language acquisition leaves the impression that children have mastered the language by the age of five. What evidence do you have, or could you get, that this is not the case? (See below.)

## Some activities

1    Read carefully through the data samples given below. Analyse the structural and functional characteristics of each sample, and comment on the relationships between the samples. What are the differences you see between one and the next? What do the differences tell you about the development of linguistic expression? I have also deliberately not given you ages for the children, and have not presented them in chronological order. So, one of your tasks is to put them in the developmental order you think makes sense, and to justify your order. I also want you to learn from these transcripts about some of the difficulties of getting revealing data. What kinds of problems did my students, who collected this data, run into in fulfilling my assignment?

SAMPLE 1
P is in conversation with her baby-sitter (C).
C:    Who gave you that Frances book? This one?
P:    Your Janet did.
C:    You don't know Janet do you?
P:    Well, she gave me that book.

C:   Oh, Janet that I don't know?
P:   Nooo, Janet gave me the book.
C:   Oooh, I see. I understand.
P:   And Janet gave me this doll to AJ (AJ is P's sister.)
C:   Oh, that's where she got it. I understand. I understand.
     She's a very pretty doll.
P:   An', An' Janet gave me these dolls for sharing.
C:   And you are very good at sharing, aren't you? And the,
     and the bouncy horse, too.
P:   I'll share. I'm gonna share with Joe 'cause he gots the
     horse next year.
C:   Next year?
P:   Yes . . . It's my house and I'm not gonna share with
     anyone.

SAMPLE 2
Andy and his father are performing for a student in my Portland
State University class. The tape recorder is running. They are
looking at picture books.
F:   What's this?
A:   Bambi!
F:   Bambi, yeah!
A:   Wasdat?
F:   That's Johnny Appleseed.
A:   Dani abosi:d. Wasdat?
F:   Those are Indians.
A:   'S Indians. Wasdat?' As a wolf.
F:   Yeah, a wolf, that's right. Very good.
A:   Wasdat?
F:   Dont' climb on the table please. What's this?
A:   I dinno.
F:   It's a big bird.
A:   Is a . . I dinno.
F:   You didn't know that?
A:   A big bird. Is a bird.
F:   Mmm. Two birds.
A:   Two birds. Wasdat?

SAMPLE 3
Jeremy and my student Gene are playing with blocks.
G:   Come on Jeremy . . . sit down.
J:   I need a road like this with sides going up.
G:   OK.
J:   I'll go ge-, I'm going to get some other ones, the other
     ones.
G:   No, you don't have to. You don't have to.
J:   (inaudible talking in the distance)

G:   How many cars have we got now?

J:   I'll count 'em let's see, one, two, three, four, five, six.

G:   Six. OK.

J:   (Bak)

G:   You want to make a garage for the, er, cars?

J:   Na, there's supposed to be a bunch of little garages.

G:   Where are the garages, over here?

P:   Yeah (unintelligible utterance).

G:   That's OK, listen we'll make some more, we'll make some other garages, don't go away, don't got away.

J:   Let me get other, other cars 'cause its gonna be a bunch of them.

G:   Well I tell you what, let's build the building first, and then we will get the garages, OK we'll get the cars, what's this?

J:   It's, it's some books in case you want to build a liberry.

(Some brief remarks on this activity can be found below.)

2   One of the parts of the linguistic system which young children often have difficulty with involves the pronouns. Here are some samples from Avi. He produced these at the same time as he was getting many other instances of the same pronouns right. I have only shown the errors here, but don't forget that a full description of this stage of his language development would include many error-free examples.

(a)   Me:   Did Papa wash his 'bunda' in the bath? (In our house, we use a version of the Portugese word for one's rear end.)

       Avi:   I. (Said with emphasis, and apparently meaning, 'No, he washed mine'.) (1;11)

(b)   Me:   Where's Avi?

       Avi:   Here me is. (2;0)

(c)   'That's she's Mom.' (2;1)

(d)   'Look at I.'
       'Open you legs so her can sit.'
       'Let I do it.' (2;2)

(e)   'Let's go same as we. . . . . let's go same as us.' (2;3) (He appears to be searching for a way to express 'let's both crawl on our hands and knees the same way as each other'.)

(f)   'Look at he, Mama.' (2;2)

(g)   'I want a bite of him's.' (2;3)

(h)   'You can carry we both at once.' (2;5)

(i)   'I gave she a toy.' (2;5)

(j)   'You didn't make enough room for I to come in.' (2;6)

Try to describe what you see here. Is there any pattern to these 'errors'? A preference for one kind of error over another? Can you see how some of these 'errors' might have come about? What do you make of the fact that my daughter, just two years younger, when she entered this age/stage of development made in my hearing at most *three* 'errors' of this kind, whereas Avi made all of the above and many, many more that I was not quick enough to get down in my diary. (See below for discussion of these data.)

## Solutions to and comments on discussion questions and activities

Discussion question 1

There is always the possibility that data will lead to false conclusions, but this is a problem common to all science. The usual way of dealing with the problem is to make sure you have enough data from which to draw generalisations, and, when you try to determine underlying knowledge, to triangulate data from a variety of sources.

Discussion question 2

You have seen in this chapter that five-year-old speech contains a number of non-adult features. If you have any experience teaching or observing children in school, you will know that there are a number of linguistic skills, particularly those connected with reading and writing, which have to be learned laboriously throughout the school years. Classrooms and playgrounds are fertile places to see what is learned later. Chapter 8 of this book deals specifically with later language development.

Activity 1

'P' in Sample 1 is 2;11. Andy in Sample 2 is 2;2. Jeremy in Sample 3 is 5;0. You should be able to see the differences between the samples in terms of utterance length, some phonological changes (within the limits of how the utterances are represented here), morphological and syntactic development, and the increasing complexity of the ideas expressed and conversations engaged in. My students, who collected these data, had trouble deciding when to represent an utterance in standard spelling and when to try to give a version of what the child actually said. They also had to decide how to represent hesitations and false starts, such as when Jeremy says, 'I'll go ge-, I'm going to get . . .', and what to do when there were unintelligible utterances. In each case, they solved the problem by providing a representation that stayed as true to the original as possible, allowing you to get more of a sense of the original than would have been possible if you simply had a list of complete utterances to read.

Activity 2

You might start your analysis by noting that Avi seems to be having trouble with possessive pronouns. He says 'she's' for 'her', 'him's' for 'his' and 'you' for 'your'. The first two of these suggest he understands the possessive morphology, but does not have the special possessive pronoun forms. He also seems to be reversing the subject and object pronouns, putting 'I' and 'he'/'she' where 'me' and 'him'/'her' should go and vice versa. The fact that there seems to be a frequent systematic reversal means that it is not a question of a haphazard choice of pronouns, but rather that, for some principled reason, he thinks the system can work the way he is using it. One of the simplest possibilities would be that it is a lexical problem, in which he has matched the wrong sound sequence (word) with the wrong meaning. However, he doesn't *always* make the errors you see in this exercise. Many times he gets the pronoun correct, so it is unlikely that sometimes he thinks the subject pronoun is 'I' and sometimes he thinks it is 'me'. A more likely possibility is that there is something about the contexts in which the errors appear which make him think that, for example, a subject pronoun is required, when in fact it is an object. For example, in 'Let I do it' under (d), perhaps he thinks 'I' is the subject of 'do', when in fact it is the object of 'let'. These are the sorts of lines along which productive thinking about a data set such as this can proceed. Some very interesting work on accounting for these kinds of errors is being done by Matthew Rispoli (e.g. Rispoli 1994). If you are interested in pursuing this issue, you might like to read what he has to say.

## Further reading

Because the bulk of the child language literature has focused on the 'what' (as opposed to the 'how' or 'why') of language acquisition, 'further reading' is, in a sense, *any* of the myriad descriptions of early child language available. In Chapter 1, I mentioned Naomi Baron's book. I recommend it again here. More detailed descriptions of the acquisition of English than I have given here can be found in a couple of excellent chapters by Jill and Peter de Villiers. One of these appears in the first volume of Dan Slobin's survey of language acquisition in different language communities (Slobin 1985). The other chapter by the de Villiers appears in Bornstein and Lamb (1992). I have published a survey of the acquisition of pragmatics as Foster (1990b). Finally, I recommend Jean Stilwell Peccei's language workbook (1994). It has a whole chapter of language acquisition projects you might find useful.

## CHAPTER 5

# What influences language development?

## Chapter summary

Now that you have some familiarity with *what* is learned in language acquisition, it is time to start asking *how* it all happens. Steering a course between 'nature' and 'nurture', we will examine the evidence for the roles of various influences on language development. In particular, we will see to what extent language development is either influenced or caused by the language spoken around and to the young child. We will also see what evidence there is for language development being either affected or effected by forces from within the child, language-specific innate knowledge, and developing cognitive and social skills.

## What is input and how much is enough?

If you ask most parents how their children learned language, you will probably find they think either that they taught the language to them, or that the children somehow 'picked the language up' from hearing it and from being spoken to. As it turns out, neither of these suppositions is true.

Now, obviously, a child must hear (or see, in the case of a sign language) a language in order to learn/acquire it. If a child is not exposed to a language he or she will not learn it. This very obvious statement belies the complexity of the issue of what constitutes exposure. How much is needed, of what kind, and *when* must the exposure occur? What happens if children do not get sufficient input? And what happens if children are not exposed to language at all as young children? Let's begin by addressing the timing issue.

## Input at the right time: the 'critical period'

The notion of a 'critical period' for language was first suggested in the late 1960s by the psychologist Eric Lenneberg
(1969), who proposed that a number of human developments,
among them language and walking, emerge according to a
genetic schedule that is only partially specified, requiring experience to trigger the entire process. One of the most dramatic
demonstrations of the critical period is provided by the case of
'Genie', who will be discussed in detail in Chapter 6. Genie
was a child who was so abused and neglected that she did not
receive sufficient input to learn language until she was more
than 13, at which point all the evidence suggests it was too
late, and she never acquired genuine language (Curtiss 1977).

Other data that show children need early exposure to sufficient language come from cases involving deaf children of hearing parents who do not know sign language. These children,
forced to learn a spoken language they cannot hear properly (or
at all), are noticeably similar to Genie: they are often communicative, but they lack those grammatical features which characterise real language (see Chapter 6). Severely deaf children
trained in spoken language are deprived of input because they
cannot receive enough of the oral/aural input to make sense
of it. They are thus often no better off than Genie because, in
fact, they have *not* been exposed to language at all. The adults
around them only *think* they have. Sadly, when such children
are eventually exposed to sign language (if they ever are), they
are often beyond the 'critical period' and the long-term effect
of the delay in language exposure is to deprive them of a chance
to learn real language.

I have been talking about the critical period as if it were a
clearly bounded period, and as if a child could wake up one
day and it would suddenly be too late to learn language. This
is probably not the case. Elissa Newport (1990) argues that language learning skills only gradually get worse as the child's ability
to process more and more of the input increases. She argues
for a 'less is more' hypothesis in which younger children are
better learners than older ones because they don't pay attention to everything all at once and so have a simpler task. She
prefers to argue against a purely linguistic critical period and for
a more general decline in processing ability. However, whether
we view the critical period as specifically linguistic or not, other
issues remain:

1    Do children need to actively communicate with a language in order to learn that language?
2    Do children need to hear only simple, clearly articulated sentences in order to acquire the basic structure of their language?
3    Do children need the input to increase in complexity as they move through the stages of language acquisition, so that they are effectively guided through the stages of acquisition by the input?
4    What aspects of language can children *never* learn from the input?

Tentative answers to these questions will emerge in the sections that follow.

### Exercise 1

Before continuing to read this chapter, you might like to stop and write down your intuitive answers to the questions above. Then, as you read on, you can compare your answers with those that researchers have come up with.

## Is active communication necessary?

Much has been written about the importance of adults receiving children's first attempts at communication and treating them as meaningful. Adults in many cultures treat infants, from the beginning of life, 'as if' they were behaving with intention to communicate, 'as if' those gurgles and coos and smiles were intended to solicit a reaction from an adult. Newson (1979) has suggested that 'human caregivers programme . . . intention into babies'. In other words, babies become human because adults behave as if they already were. At a later stage, children's vocalisations and gestures (reaching, pointing, head-shaking) are treated 'as if' they communicated such expressions as 'Look at that', 'I want that' and 'I don't want that'. The adults' reactions act as a 'scaffold', allowing children to work out what their behaviours must mean (Wood et al. 1976; Bruner 1974). And once (hearing) children understand that they can communicate with vocalisations, and that those vocalisations are joyfully received by parents, caregivers and others around them, they usually need little encouragement to continue communicating. In fact, parents (even one as passionately interested in child language as myself) often have the feeling that they would like to find the voice 'off switch' at the end of a long day!

Children in linguistically supportive environments continue to receive feedback on their communications, and learn thereby how to design messages so that they communicate what the children intended. And the very act of communicating gives practice in producing utterances. In other words, being active as a communicator builds functional (pragmatic) skills of message design, and gives practice in fluency. In the terms of Chapter 4, it helps develop functional skills; it does not, however, necessarily help develop structural aspects of language.

Evidence that structural language development is to some degree independent of active communication comes from a variety of sources. One of them is cross-cultural comparisons of children's linguistic environments. White, Western, middle-class children usually grow up in an environment which (as I've already said) treats them almost as full conversational partners from the time they show the barest signs of interactional ability. In other cultures, this is not the case. In Samoa, for example, children are not regarded as plausible conversational partners until they have produced quite a large number of words. In fact, not until they have produced the word for 'Shit!'. (See Chapter 3 for discussion of the difficulties of recognising first words.) In this and many other cultures, children are not spoken to in a special 'register'. People do not use 'Baby Talk' to them. However, this does not appear to affect the pace or order of structural language development. Let's look further at the kind of input children receive.

## The nature of Baby Talk

'Baby Talk' is the term applied to that way of talking that parents and others use when they are addressing young children.

### Exercise 2

Before I describe Baby Talk, stop for a minute and try to list features of this particular way of speaking that you have observed. Think through the various levels of language from phonetics/phonology to pragmatics to help you recall the features.

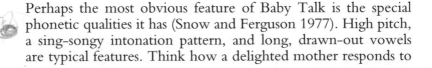

Perhaps the most obvious feature of Baby Talk is the special phonetic qualities it has (Snow and Ferguson 1977). High pitch, a sing-songy intonation pattern, and long, drawn-out vowels are typical features. Think how a delighted mother responds to the smile of her young infant: 'Heloooooooooo' starts very high, then drops down and rises again to the height of the original pitch, or nearly so. Another phonological feature of Baby Talk is reflected in adults preferring to use words or versions of words with a simple structure, such as consonant–vowel–consonant–vowel, which results in 'horse' becoming 'horsie' for example, or 'train' becoming 'choo-choo'. Adults seem to be aware that some sounds, such as /l/ and /r/, are difficult for children and often avoid using them, although sometimes adults end up avoiding sounds their children have actually mastered! (More than once, for example, my husband and I adopted one of our children's words and went on using it long after the child had substituted the adult version. Eventually, we realised how silly we sounded, and stopped!)

Adult substitutions mimic the kind of substitutions we saw in children's phonological development (Chapter 3). They result, for example, in 'little' becoming 'ickoo', 'rabbit' becoming 'wabbit', and 'water' becoming 'wawa'. 'Wawa' not only avoids a final /r/ (in dialects where it would have been pronounced), it also has the preferred CV syllable shape, repeated identically to give what linguists call a reduplicative structure (cf. 'choo-choo', 'dai-dai' (diaper), 'moo-moo' (cow)). Other languages show the same processes. So, in Japanese, for example, 'kutsu' (the word for 'shoe') becomes /kukuː/ in Japanese Baby Talk, and 'mushi' (the word for 'bug') becomes /tsitsi/. All these are features typical of talk *by* babies and talk *to* babies.

At the level of syntax, Baby Talk is often, but not always, characterised by short, grammatical utterances. Several researchers have argued that an adult talking to a child tends to be more grammatical than an adult talking to another adult. (By the way, among adults, academics are among the least grammatical and the most wordy!) Another feature of adult speech to children is that it almost all pertains to the 'here and now' of the conversation that both child and adult are engaged in. This reflects semantic and pragmatic features of Baby Talk. Adults are most likely to label objects the children are already paying attention to, to try to direct the children's attention to items in the immediate environment, and, if they do stray from the concrete to the abstract, it will still be anchored in the here and now. So whom a particular object belongs to might be talked about, or who gave the child a particular toy, or where a certain person is who is intimately connected with a visible object, etc.

So, that's what Baby Talk is like. But why do adults use it, and is it of any use to the child learning the language? We'll try to answer these questions in the next section.

## The value of Baby Talk

You may have got the impression that Baby Talk is a particularly clear way of talking, designed for children to be able to understand most or all of what is being said to them. While this is a plausible hypothesis, there are several reasons for thinking otherwise.

First, although highly exaggerated intonation and a slow delivery of speech might seem to make the language clearer, some recent research suggests that, from an acoustic point of view, speech to children (aged 1;10 to 3;0) is actually less intelligible than speech to adults. Secondly, Baby Talk vocabulary is far from obviously helpful. How could 'horsie' be more helpful than 'horse'? Let alone 'wawa' more helpful than 'water', not least because these words would get little or no reinforcement outside the family. It almost seems like a conspiracy to keep children from learning the proper names for things. There is perhaps some information carried by the '-ie' on horsie; perhaps it signals that the word is a noun, and perhaps the extra phonetic length makes the word easier to process. But 'choo-choo' and 'Baba want go nigh-nigh?'?

So why do adults do Baby Talk, and why does it come so naturally to so many adults? While we do not have an entirely clear answer to these questions, one factor seems to be that adults recognise that understanding language is difficult for children (which it is), and recognise the need to make some changes, but they do not know what changes would be helpful. Just as many people faced with a foreigner will shout (not a very helpful reaction), so adults with small children do not actually know what changes to make. The attempt to make some sort of change, however, is perhaps inborn – a natural nurturing reaction akin to the genetically programmed caring response we have to the widely spaced and large eyes of an infant in relation to the overall size of its face. (That's why we find rabbits, koalas and other animals with the same features so 'cute', by the way.) But why do we use silly words and intonation patterns?

A possible answer is that it is because we heard our own parents do it to us, and other adults do it to their children. In other words, it is a culturally perpetuated style. The fact that all cultures do not do Baby Talk would seem to support this idea. Still, when you think that Baby Talk with very similar features occurs across the globe in lots of different communities speaking languages as different as Arabic, Comanche, French, Japanese and Serb-Croatian, we still have to ask the question, What suggested to all these different language groups that this was the way to modify their language?

Perhaps they do it because they are mimicking the language used by children themselves. After all, as we have seen, several features of Baby Talk seem to match the vocal productions of small children themselves. But there's a problem with this suggestion: How could mimicking children explain why adults use Baby Talk to dogs and other pets?

Perhaps the best we can say is that Baby Talk reflects adults' best attempts to produce comprehensible input, based on a teaspoonful of observation of the kinds of productions the children use, combined with a faint memory of how they were spoken to, and more recent observations of how other adults speak to other children. The effect is certainly to produce a 'register' (a special way of talking) which, in the cultures that do it, says very clearly to a child 'I'm talking to *you*, and I care enough about you to speak in this special way which *shows* I care about you.' Perhaps that explains the extension of the use of this style to animals (and sometimes one's most intimate partner).

Another point to make is that Baby Talk may not be as simply structured as many people think it is (Newport 1976). Yes, it highlights words in ways that might help a child learn those words, but it also contains lots of questions (in which wh-words appear at the front of utterances and must be linked back with the appropriate position elsewhere in the sentence), complex sentences with embedded clauses, and other constructions which could not be called simple. So, if children are going to make good use of the Baby Talk input, they must sift that input for the things that are simple enough for them to make sense of. This is the idea behind Newport's 'less is more' hypothesis (see above) in which the input to children does not need to be simple because the children themselves simplify it by only paying attention to certain parts of it (Newport 1990).

## Exercise 3

Here are some dialogues between children and their mothers. (These data come originally from Brown and Bellugi (1964), and are reproduced in the following form by Dale (1976).) In each case, the child produces an utterance and the adult expands on it. Ask yourself the following questions:

(a)    What kind of linguistic information is the mother filling in each time?
(b)    How is she able to do this?
(c)    When children hear the expansions, what kinds of things might they learn from them?

1      Child:    Baby highchair.
       Mother:   Baby is in the highchair.
2      Child:    Mommy eggnog.
       Mother:   Mommy had her eggnog.
3      Child:    Eve lunch.
       Mother:   Eve is having lunch.
4      Child:    Mommy sandwich.
       Mother:   Mommy'll have a sandwich.
5      Child:    Sat wall.
       Mother:   He sat on the wall.
6      Child:    Throw daddy.
       Mother:   Throw it to daddy.
7      Child:    Pick glove.
       Mother:   Pick the glove up.

(There is some feedback on this exercise at the end of the chapter.)

Newport's position suggests that the input does, in fact, contain what children need to learn language, even if they have to go and find it for themselves. But I want to endorse a position which says that Baby Talk is not by itself going to allow children to learn language, no matter what features it has. No account in which the child must figure out language from the input (distorted or not) will be successful. In the next section I'll lay out the problem, so that we can analyse exactly why input accounts cannot work.

## The poverty of the stimulus

Borrowing the terminology of behaviourist conditioning, the problem of Baby Talk and all other input-based accounts of language development has been dubbed the problem of the 'poverty of the stimulus'. The basic hypothesis is that while there is no doubt at all that children learn a great deal from the input, the input (the stimulus) which children receive from their environment is not able to do the whole job of teaching language to a child who has no preconceptions about language ahead of time. This notion of the 'poverty of the stimulus' is securely attached to the 'logical' approach to language acquisition (see Chapter 1), and is quite opposed by many in the 'observational' approach. A little history might be useful here, but, remember, it is *not* being claimed that input is no use – of course it is of use – only that it cannot be the whole story.

The first claims about the inadequacy of the input for language acquisition were made by Chomsky in 1965 in his book *Aspects of the Theory of Syntax*. Here, Chomsky suggested that the 'primary linguistic data' (i.e. the input) is seriously inadequate in a number of ways. Since what he actually said is frequently misunderstood, let's look at exactly what he said:

> Consider first the nature of primary linguistic data. This consists of a finite amount of information about sentences, which, furthermore, must be rather restricted in scope, considering the time limitations that are in effect, and fairly degenerate in quality (cf. note 14). For example, certain signals might be accepted as properly formed sentences, while others are classed as nonsentences . . . (Chomsky 1965: 31)

And in note 14 we find:

> It seems clear that many children acquire first or second languages quite successfully even though no special care is taken to teach them, and no special attention is given to their progress. It also seems apparent that much of the actual speech observed consists of fragments and deviant expressions of a variety of sorts. Thus it seems that a child must have the ability to 'invent' a generative grammar that defines well-formedness and assigns interpretations to sentences even though the primary linguistic data that he uses as a basis for this act of theory construction may, from the point of view of the theory he constructs, be deficient in various respects. (*ibid.*: 200–201)

What jumped out at (observationally motivated) child language researchers when they read this was the claim that the speech to children was fragmented and deviant. They were pretty sure it wasn't, and set out to document just how unfragmented and grammatically perfect the language to children was (see the section above on Baby Talk) (Snow and Ferguson 1977). They then said, 'See, you're wrong. Language to children is not deviant and fragmented. Therefore you are wrong about children needing to have "an ability to 'invent' a generative grammar" (where a generative grammar is simply a fully explicit representation of the knowledge an adult has of a language).' In other words, they were convinced that by showing Chomsky's characterisation of the input to children to be wrong, they had successfully shown that his claim for innate knowledge of language (this ability to 'invent' a generative grammar) must also be wrong.

Unfortunately, this argument from the 'observationalist' camp fails because it does not respond to Chomsky's points about the other ways in which the input data was insufficient. Let's look at what he actually said. In the first of the two quotations above, Chomsky pointed out that input to language acquisition is *finite*. It must be. Children learn language in a specified amount of time. Whether that's three years or five matters not. What matters is that in whatever span of time it takes, children will have heard only a subset of all the possible sentences in the language. They could listen to adults all day and all night, and they would still have heard only a subset of the sentences of the language they are being exposed to.

Chomsky is also saying here that some of the sentences a child hears will not be sentences of the language. Even if, by and large, the utterances to children are complete, there will still be utterances which are not. Performance factors will always lead to some false starts, some ungrammaticalities of one kind or another. The problem is not so much that they are there but rather that the child has no clues as to which ones they are. Imagine watching a game you have never seen before and being asked to figure out the rules. You might manage it if no one cheated. But what if, from time to time, someone cheats without indicating they are cheating. Your job becomes virtually impossible. The same is true for children. If they must figure out the rules of language from observing the input, and people cheat (producing ungrammatical sentences from time to time without marking them as such), the task becomes impossible.

Finally, the problem of limited data is that children are not exposed to the full range of linguistic facts which they actually come to know. And here the observationalists' rush to prove Chomsky wrong about the degeneracy of the input backfired. Remember how we saw in the previous section that Baby Talk generally consists of short, simple sentences? Well, if that's the case, then how do children learn to produce and comprehend complex structures? Surely, if language input really 'teaches' children, it had better have all the structures in it that the child needs to acquire the language fully. And if it contains only short, simple sentences, it won't.

The observational response to this was to look very carefully at the developmental relationship between language input and child development of structures, because a plausible hypothesis would be that adults increase the complexity of their language to children so as to stay just ahead of them. In other words, the language to very young children may not contain complex sentences (with relative clauses, noun complements, and the like) but the language to slightly older children – those ready to learn such things – might. The results of this approach reveal, interestingly, that adults seem to follow children's lead, not the other way round. In other words, adults start producing more complex language because their children do (Shatz 1982; Gleitman, Newport and Gleitman 1984)!

So, adults' abilities to provide the right input when needed seems not to be up to the task of 'teaching' language. And, in any case, this line of research actually misses the point. Even if it had turned out that adults were able to lead children through the path of development in this way, there is still much that an adult, no matter how sensitive, could never teach a child. These are things which adults themselves don't know about the language they speak, and so could not control in their speech to children even if they wanted to.

Among the most spectacular of these things we 'know' without knowing we 'know' them are the things we 'know' you cannot do! I gave some examples of these kinds of things in Chapter 1. Here's another one:

(1)    I saw John.
(2)    Who(m) did you see?
(3)    I saw John and Mary.
(4)    *Who(m) did you see John and?

The sentences in (1) and (2) show that one can ask a question to which the answer is the object of a verb (in this case, 'John') by placing the appropriate wh-word at the front of the sentence and leaving the object position 'empty'. However, as (3) and (4) show, if the object of the verb was part of a complex noun phrase involving two nouns joined by 'and', then it is not possible. There is no obvious reason for this. Sentence (4) is understandable, and there *is* an almost identical structure which expresses, grammatically, what (4) expresses ungrammatically, at least if you are prepared to accept a sentence ending with a preposition:

(5)   Who(m) did you see John with?

And one can always clean up the horror of the dangling pre-position (only a horror to prescriptive grammarians such as English teachers, by the way; not a problem for linguists) and get:

(6)   With who(m) did you see John?

but you cannot say:

(7)   *And who(m) did you see John?

The point is that there seems to be no obvious reason why one cannot say (4) or (7) above. They fit the pattern of (1) and (2), and they convey a perfectly understandable message. You just can't do it, that's all. Why not? Well, it turns out that you cannot take all sorts of things out of noun phrases that are not simple. John Robert (Haj) Ross noticed this back in the 1960s, and dubbed complex noun phrases as one of a series of 'islands' in the grammar of English (Ross 1967). You can move the whole 'island' (as in (2) above or in the 'with whom' version in (6)), but you cannot move part of one (as in (4) or (7)). Since then, it has been found that languages across the world exhibit this same property of 'islands'; and now the thinking is (by many in the logical camp) that such cross-linguistic simil-arity cannot be accidental; that, in fact, since no one has ever heard anyone trying to do constructions such as (4) or (7), and certainly never heard a child doing it, it must be one of the pieces of innate knowledge – part of a child's inborn under-standing of how the languages of the world work.

   'OK', says the observationalist, 'so you think that because children apparently do not make mistakes on a feature of lan-guage that seems to be universal, therefore, that part of linguistic knowledge must be innate. But there's a simpler explanation: children don't make mistakes such as (4) because they don't hear adults saying anything like (4).' 'OK', I say, 'but what about children saying things such as "I didded it" or "That's she's Mum". Children never hear adults saying those either. How come they make some errors and not others when they are learning language?' It is *this* question which, to my way of thinking, is not answerable without appeal to *a priori* (i.e. ahead-of-time) 'knowledge' of language.

As Ray Jackendoff acknowledges in his excellent book on this topic, *Patterns in the Mind* (Jackendoff 1994), while the poverty of the stimulus argument is a 'How else could it happen?' argument, it is not an attempt to jump to innate ideas without paying due attention to the possible teaching function of language input to children. Rather, it stems from genuine logical problems with input being the sole guide to children forming the grammar of their languages. In the next section, I'll provide a brief description of what linguists think the knowledge children bring to language acquisition must look like, and then in the final section of the chapter, we'll see how the acquisition of first words involves both innate knowledge *and* experience with a particular language.

## Universal Grammar

Before I try to explain what linguists mean by Universal Grammar (UG), let's think for a minute about the necessary features of the knowledge children bring to the language acquisition task.

### Exercise 4

Here's the problem. What kind of mechanism of language acquisition can accommodate the kinds of variation in experience exemplified by the five children described below? Think it through for yourself for a minute before we go on.

1   Chan was born in London to Chinese-born parents who have learned English as a second language, but who believe that only English is of use or importance to Chan. At home they therefore exclusively use English to him, although they speak Chinese to each other. When Chan is six months old, he starts going to a day care centre where the predominant language is English, although there is one child who speaks Tamil at home, and occasionally tries to use Tamil with his day care centre friends.

2   Eric is a deaf child born to deaf parents who are users of French sign language. He spends most of his time at home because there are no other speakers of sign language in his neighbourhood. When he is three, he starts going to a special school for the deaf, which uses French sign language as its means of communication.

3   Marya is a Navajo child born on the Navajo Reservation in Arizona. She is raised mostly by her grandmother, a monolingual Navajo who speaks only a few phrases of

English. Marya spends much of her time silently watching her grandmother as she weave blankets, helping her grow and harvest corn, squash and beans, and listening to her tell stories about the Holy People in the evenings.

4    Lela is a child born on an island in the South Pacific. Her parents make sure she is clothed and fed, but do not believe that it is worthwhile talking to children until they can talk. She spends most of her time, as soon as she can walk, with her older brothers and sisters, and with cousins and other children in the village. They spend whole days together roaming around the village area, the oldest children taking care of the youngest.

5    Don will discover, when he goes to school and gets tested, that he has an IQ considerably lower than the normal population. He will have immense trouble learning to read and write, and his teachers will in the end give up trying to make him numerate. He does not have a particular syndrome that any of his doctors can identify, but his mother noticed that although his language is normal, he started to speak later than she expected.

These children are all very different, with different kinds of experiences, and yet they all (with the exception of Don) started to produce their first words (whether spoken or signed words) during the second half of their first year. Don produced his first word after his first birthday, and was behind the other children in each of the stages of language development. However, his stages were none the less the same as theirs, just slower to appear.

All the children produced shorter utterances before longer ones. All tried to make rules apply across the board, even to what are in fact exceptions. None wrongly assumed that one can move words around to make questions without paying attention to the structure of the sentence. Those learning languages with lots of morphology (Eric, Marya and Lela) quickly started paying attention to it, and using it. Those learning languages with little morphology (Chan and Don) left most of it out at first. Even though the children were learning language with radically different word orders (e.g. Marya's language has the order Subject–Object–Verb, and Chan's has Subject–Verb–Object), they made hardly any mistakes. Even though Eric was learning a sign language, he went through the same stages as the children learning a spoken language. Even though Lela received hardly any input from adults, and certainly no Baby Talk, she learned language according to the same schedule as the others.

What kind of mechanism is it that can allow for these kinds of similarities in the face of these kinds of differences of experience?

Clearly, whatever UG is, it must be very flexible. It cannot contain information about any *particular* language, or we would be led to the obviously silly position of saying that children are born 'knowing' all the world's languages. Clearly, the form of linguistic knowledge children possess must be abstract. It must be able to recognise the specifics of particular languages once they are presented, and to cope with what appear to be pretty extreme differences between languages. So, for example, if UG is to cope with languages that are heavily dependent on word order to convey their meanings (such as English), as well as languages which have highly free word order (such as the Australian aboriginal language Walbiri), UG must allow for an equal ability to recognise these two options.

Without going into too many of the details here, let me simply present the idea of UG (for further detail, see Chapter 7). Universal Grammar is not the grammar of any particular language. Rather, it is a *propensity* for acquiring language which embodies within it representations of certain abstract facts about human language. Some people see it as a 'device' for acquiring a language (Chomsky himself originally called it a Language Acquisition Device (LAD)), others think of it as a set of representations of linguistic knowledge with options built into them and gaps to be filled in by experience. The options are known as *parameters*, and the information that tells the system which option (which setting of the parameter) to choose is known as a *trigger*. When all the open options within UG have been set by input triggers, we say that a 'core' grammar of the language being acquired has been established. Unlike UG, a core grammar is the grammar of a *particular* language (English, Navajo, French, etc.), consisting of a combination of invariant principles of language (such as that languages have a lexicon, that their rules are structure-dependent, etc.) together with the parameter settings.

We can't actually observe UG directly, and there are some who think we'll never get beyond speculation until we can tie innate knowledge of language to specific neurological structures in the brain. That's as may be, but we now know enough about what appears to be constant across the world's languages as well as what seems to vary to make some fairly specific claims about what UG must encode.

The establishment of core grammar completes the work of UG in language acquisition. It does not, however, complete the work of language acquisition itself. There's a lot more to be done – lots more to really *learn* from the input: all the vocabulary of the language, the bound morphemes, the idioms, etc. The list may be very long. Language acquisition is thus a cooperative effort between UG and learning from the input, both in the sense of the input triggering the parameter settings and in the sense of the input providing language forms from which rules can be deduced by general learning mechanisms not special to language. In the next section, we'll see a bit of that cooperation in action in the acquisition of words, and we'll return to the issue of parameter setting in Chapter 7.

## Words are more cunning than they let on

Humorist Ivor Cutler declares that socks are more cunning than they let on because they are able to be both around one's foot and inside one's shoe: two places and two shapes. Words are similarly cunning. Although a word appears to be a simple thing, it actually has several roles to play and can be viewed from several different perspectives. Words are simultaneously phonetic strings which carry semantic meaning, members of a small set of structurally defined groups (nouns, verbs, adjectives, etc.) and players of defined roles in sentences (such as subjects, objects, heads of phrases, etc.) So, for example, a concrete noun such as 'dog' refers (in a way which is itself more complicated than it might appear) to the appropriate animal. It is a noun, and as such behaves in the way most other nouns do: you can put a plural '-s' on it, you can put a 'the' before it, and so on. And, as a noun, it can serve as the subject of a verb, as the object of a verb, as the object of a preposition, and so on. A verb such as 'hit' or 'sleep' has an identity as coding some kind of activity, state or event (again this is not simple), a morphological identity as a verb, and a syntactic identity in terms of the words and phrases it can or must have around it. 'Hit' and 'sleep' differ, for example, in that the first must have a noun phrase object following it (it is a transitive verb) whereas 'sleep' normally must not have a noun phrase object following it (it is intransitive).

Now, the question is how children learn all this. Do they learn it from analysing the input using general (non-linguistic-specific) analysing abilities, or are they given a leg up in the process by expecting certain things in advance? Well, it makes no sense to say that children are expecting the particular phonetic strings of their language, otherwise we would be in a position of having to say that children are born knowing all the words of all the world's existing (and possible) languages.

This is a position we have already said is clearly absurd. They could, however, have certain phonological expectations, for example that a 'raspberry' is not going to be a speech sound, or that certain distinctive features of the sounds of the language are unremarkable and thus assumed to be present in speech sounds, while others are perceived as more unusual, or marked (see discussion of phonetic features in Appendix 2 and Gierut 1996). But most of the acquisition of the phonetics of words will progress via learning, using the highly sensitive and attuned mechanisms we saw in Chapters 2 and 3. (Whether categorial perception is a linguistic skill or a general perceptual one for humans is still in debate, as you will remember from Chapter 2.)

Now, what about figuring out the meaning of words? What are the possibilities? We know that children largely operate in the here and now for their early years, and that the input they receive from adults and others focuses on the immediate situation. So, it is not unreasonable to suppose that young children do not need to worry at first about abstract nouns (e.g. 'justice', 'freedom', 'peace', 'beauty'). Instead, they can focus on the concrete ('cookie', 'milk', 'teddy') and get the words for those things first. Some researchers would say that the way talk to children isolates separate words, and the way those words are produced exactly when the child is paying attention to an object, will provide enough clues to the relationship between early words and the things they refer to. So, if a parent says, 'That's TEDDY', with marked stress on 'teddy', when the child picks up his or her teddy, that probably makes the connection pretty easy.

Although this is a reasonable hypothesis, it is not as simple as it appears. The philosopher Quine (1960) has pointed out that the child would in principle be at liberty to think that the word 'teddy' could apply to all sorts of things that it doesn't: the bow round the teddy's neck, its ears, the quality of its fur, the smell of its stuffing, the bit of food stuck to its nose from last time it was cuddled, etc. What is it that tells the child that the name for an object is the name for an object and not for some sub-part of the object, or some peripheral or abstract feature of the object? Children seem to have an automatic preference for hooking words onto *whole* objects (Markman 1990). Is this innate? And, if so, is it a specific linguistic ability, and thus a candidate for UG, or is it part of a more general perceptual mechanism? These are still unanswered questions, and there are arguments on both sides.

Here's another wrinkle. Children seem to detest synonyms. When given a word for something they already have a word for, they will assume that the new word does not mean the same as the one they already have. They may decide that the new word is for some sub-part or quality of the object, or they may decide it is a term at a different level, a superordinate, perhaps ('tree' is the superordinate for 'birch', 'larch', 'oak', etc.; 'furniture' is the superordinate for 'sofa', 'chair', 'bed', etc.). Now, this preference for avoiding synonyms is pretty clever on the child's part, because there really are very few real synonyms in languages. Words such as 'child' and 'kid' may appear to be synonyms, but they have different connotations and cannot appear with equal appropriateness in every context. So, an automatic preference for avoiding synonyms would seem to be very useful in learning language. Is it an innate preference? And, if so, is it a specifically linguistic preference, or is it part of a more general avoidance of completely overlapping categories? Again the jury is still out (Clark 1993).

A further consideration arises from research by Gopnik and Meltzoff (1984), who tried to find out whether children's understanding preceded their word use or followed it. They focused on words such as 'gone' and 'down' and tried to find out whether children come to use these words only when they have understood the ideas behind them. It turns out that there is no clear progression from understanding the concept to using the words. In fact, children often reverse the order, using the words before they apparently understand the concept. While this research can be interpreted in a number of different ways, one possibility is that the acquisition of words progresses along a separate path from cognitive development, and that the two paths intersect with each other when children work on similar linguistic and non-linguistic issues at the same time. Insight into whether there are separate developments is offered by work with blind children. Blind children cannot see the world, and yet, as Leila Gleitman and her colleagues have shown, blind children's word learning is remarkably similar to that of sighted children (Landau and Gleitman 1985). They even use words such as 'see' and 'look' appropriately, even though 'look' appears to mean 'explore with the hands' rather than 'explore with the eyes'. (See Chapter 6 for further discussion of language acquisition in blind children, and for some other perspectives on the 'normality' of language acquisition by blind children.)

On the basis of her work, Gleitman argues that children learn new words through using the syntax of the utterances that contain them as clues to what they mean. So, for example, a child will learn the different meanings of 'laugh', 'smack' and 'put', not by observing these words used in isolation (which in fact would be very hard), but rather in syntactic context:

(8)   Arnold laughs.
(9)   Arnold smacks Gloria.
(10)  Gloria puts Arnold in his place.

From these contexts, and the observation of the absence of a noun phrase after the verb in (8), its presence in (9), and of both a noun phrase and a prepositional phrase in (10), the child grasps that laughing is something Arnold can do by himself, smacking involves acting on something or someone else, and putting involves an actor, an object and some place. This view of word learning, Gleitman has called 'syntactic bootstrapping'. Knowing the syntax allows children to pull themselves up by their own (syntactic) bootstraps and discover the semantics of what is said to them. This implies that very early on (innately?) children can use their knowledge of syntax and the possible syntactic behaviours of individual words to acquire the lexicon of their language.

Syntactic bootstrapping can be contrasted with 'semantic bootstrapping', a position advocated by Steven Pinker, among others. Here the idea is the opposite: when children understand the meaning of words, they can discover their syntactic behaviour by observing in which positions in sentences adults use the words children already know. If children are doing semantic bootstrapping, perhaps they can 'discover' the syntactic behaviour of words (as nouns, as subjects, etc.), although they may not do so without any preconceptions of what grammar is like. For example, why is it that children make almost no errors of word order? If their use of words is semantically driven at first, wouldn't we expect them to offer words in whatever order reflected their attention to them, so 'Cookie want' ought to be as common as 'Want cookie'? But it isn't. As we saw in Chapter 3, children obey the word order of their language just as soon as they start producing more than one word at a time. And if their word order is consistent, they must have some conception of syntactic structure. But how did they get that? One answer, of course, and the one I favour, is that they already know what to expect. On the basis of very little input, they realise that English is a subject–verb–object language, and, once they realise that, they can use that fact to structure their own utterances and the interpretation of those of others. And with that information, they can, as Gleitman suggests, use their syntactic knowledge to discover the meaning of more words.

This area of research is ongoing and lively. I have tried to make it clear that the assumption that children are operating with no notions of linguistic structure, while not impossible as a hypothesis, makes the child's task at least extremely difficult. Moreover, the data suggest that two- and three-year-old children make far fewer errors than would be expected of a mechanism which is 'unprimed'. Rather, the evidence suggests that early word learning is aided by expectations set up by UG, and triggered by information from the input.

## Discussion of in-text exercises

Exercise 3

The mother respects the word order the child uses each time and fills in mostly function words such as 'her' and 'it', together with semantically lightweight main verbs such as 'is' and 'have' which allow her to flesh out the child's utterance to make a complete adult one. The mother's choice of tenses (e.g. 'Mommy *had* her eggnog' versus 'Eve *is having* lunch') and pronouns (e.g. '*He* sat on the wall') depends on her contextual knowledge of the child's experience and current activities. It is possible that these fuller versions of the utterances (provided they do, in fact, match what the child intended to mean) provide the child with immediately relevant input which he or she can, in principle, make use of. In particular, if the child is able to compare in some way what he or she said and what was said to him or her, the child could pick up at least the surface elements of phrases. Whether the phrases teach the underlying system remains to be seen. In other words, it could be that these expansions build what can be called collocational memories (what words routinely go with what others), as opposed to 'teaching' the child how the grammatical system works.

## Questions for discussion

1   An issue that is currently under debate is the idea that triggering of UG is intimately tied to the *absence of negative feedback*. The

claim is that children do not receive much useful negative feedback. In other words, children are rarely corrected for the form of what they say (although they are corrected for the truth). Thus, parents may ignore the fact that their children use an incorrect past tense such as 'I goed there yesterday', the parents saying in response, 'No, it was last week we went there, honey'. This absence of negative feedback, or 'negative evidence' for how the language works, means that if children are operating with a UG, it must be set up in such a way that children will not be forced into corners by the data they encounter. In other words, all the false assumptions they make about how the language works must be overcome on the basis of positive input, i.e. the language naturally used by those around them.

What do you think of the 'no negative evidence' idea? Are there any ways that children could receive correction other than via overt statements from parents that they have said something wrong? How would you try to investigate the existence of negative evidence, the effect it might have on acquisition, and the possible consequences of its existence for the viability of the UG hypothesis? (Some thoughts on this question are presented below.)

2    Most acquisition researchers in the 'logical' camp have assumed that children cannot pay attention to how often a form appears in the input, and so cannot recognise errors in the input from the fact that they are rare. The main reason it is assumed to be inaccessible information is that it seems to be impossible to specify any given number as a threshold for teaching a particular aspect of language. Does it take ten exposures to learn a word? 20? One? What do you think of this idea? Can you think of any evidence that children *do* pay attention to frequency of experiences? Perhaps in other arenas than language? We know that in order to acquire the vocabularies they do, children must learn about nine new words a day. In second language teaching, it is sometimes assumed one needs about a dozen exposures to learn a word. Could a similar number be calculated for first language learners? What about syntax acquisition? Could that be equally sensitive to frequency? What problems would such an account encounter? (Some thoughts on this question are presented below.)

## An activity

If you have access to a mother from a culture other than white, Western, middle-class culture, try to find out what the Baby Talk register is like. (See page 98 for a discussion of Baby

Talk register.) There are a number of ways of doing this that would be revealing. You might begin by asking the mother whether she thinks of her child as a conversational partner, what she thinks her child can communicate, whether the child 'needs' any special speech addressed to him or her, and, if the answer is positive, what sorts of language the mother *thinks* she uses. You might couple this interview data with some direct observations of the mother interacting with the child. If you can do the direct observations before you ask the mother questions, so much the better, as you will avoid any effect of the mother deliberately modelling the behaviours she *thinks* she does – just in case her perception of her own behaviour is not, in fact, accurate. (A discrepancy between the way people *think* they speak and the way they *do* speak is a common occurrence in all sorts of linguistic research.) If you are able to tape and then transcribe the language the mother uses, try to describe the differences you see between language to her child and language to other adults (perhaps to you), and try to see what systematic features there are in those differences. (See Appendix 1 for discussion of transcription conventions.) Can you see phonological simplification, for example? Can you see a preferred word shape? If the language you are observing is not English, and is not a language you speak yourself, you are going to have to work with the mother, or another native speaker of the language, in order to do this activity.

## Solutions to and comments on discussion questions and activity

Discussion question 1
The 'no negative evidence' claim is undergoing considerable discussion at the moment. There is no doubt that children generally respond poorly to direct correction except on small straightforward points such as particular morphological forms (e.g. irregular past tenses), and, even then, correction rarely leads to immediate acquisition. However, other kinds of behaviour might be considered negative evidence, for example, lack of comprehension on the part of the adult, expansions of the kind we saw in Exercise 3 above, or the persistent absence of forms and constructions so that certain child assumptions are simply not reinforced. The existence of any of these can be determined with any reasonably sized corpus from adults in

conversation with children of the right age. However, deter-mining whether the child uses the input or not is much more difficult, and would have to be done with controlled experiments since you need to know exactly what the child heard, what he or she did with it, and when. The problems in such experimentation are legion. As far as the UG story is concerned, the child's ability to use any of these behaviours to move from one stage of the grammar to the next would only affect the UG story if they are used for parameter setting, since the UG account allows for the fact that other aspects of the language may be learned in other ways. If negative evidence turns out to be used by children to get irregular past tense forms right ('bought', 'taught', 'sung'), for example, this will not have an impact on the UG story as currently conceived because it is not argued that the acquisition of past tense morphology falls under UG.

Discussion question 2
The issue of frequency is a tricky one, not least because sometimes children seem to be able to learn on very minimal exposure, and at other times no amount of exposure makes a difference. Vocabulary acquisition clearly involves rapid learning with low frequencies of exposure, at least during the period of rapid expansion. In general, however, no amount of exposure is going to make a difference if the child is not ready to learn, i.e. if the current system is not ready to receive the new input; and this is equally true of all areas of language. Saying that children learn a particular aspect of language because they have 'heard enough evidence' for its existence (or non-existence, see the previous discussion question), however, remains problematic because it is virtually impossible to know how many times a child has been exposed to an item in anything other than experimental conditions, or to know the exact disposition of the system to know when it is ready to receive the new input and use it after X numbers of exposure. Therefore, determining the value of X is extremely difficult.

## Further reading

The classic paper on Baby Talk register was written by Charles Ferguson and appears in Snow and Ferguson (1977). One of the very best presentations of the poverty of the stimulus argument is presented by Lightfoot (1982). My discussion owes much to his presentation, and his book, though more technical later on, is accessible enough to be worth looking at in connection with this chapter. In his book, he goes on, as I have done, to describe what Universal Grammar must be like in order to fill in the logical gaps between the input and the learner's knowledge. You will find it a useful complement to my discussion, I think.

I highly recommend Goodluck (1991) for a detailed introduction to language acquisition seen through the lens of Universal Grammar. She goes into much more linguistic detail of how exactly innate knowledge prepares the child for acquiring a language than I have attempted here. Her book requires more knowledge of linguistics than I have assumed, but if you read carefully, you will find it accessible. You might also find a paper of mine useful (Foster–Cohen 1995).

Bloom (1994) covers a number of the key debates in child language studies at the moment. Of particular interest in connection with the current chapter is the section on word learning, which contains a paper by Leila Gleitman presenting the position I have summarised above. Steven Pinker's position on this and other issues is presented in Pinker (1994), a volume designed for a general audience. The non-UG position is well presented in Clark (1993).

## CHAPTER 6

# Do all children learn language the same way?

## Chapter summary

In the previous chapters, I have tended to stress the similarities among children in the ways they learn language. However, even children learning the same language do not approach it identically. Within the range of what is regarded as normal development, there are variations due to individual learning styles, learning strategics, gender, intelligence, etc. Within the range that is regarded as disordered, there are differences generated by problems with gaining access to language (e.g. deafness, blindness, abuse), and by problems of brain development and organisation (e.g. specific language impairment). This chapter deals with variation in language development in both normal and disordered children in the belief that understanding all sorts of variation helps develop a more accurate picture of how language develops. (Differences due to experiences with different languages are discussed in Chapter 7.)

## Types of variation

Linguists have proceeded on the assumption that all speakers of the same language share more or less the same body of knowledge about that language. And language acquisition theorists have assumed that all children proceed more or less in the same way when they learn their language. This approach has allowed us to generate reasonably reliable descriptions of the path of language development such as that presented so far in this book. However, those descriptions come at the cost of ignoring the data from those children who appear not to fit the mould. In this chapter, we will take a look at these data, and try to articulate the kinds of variation that exist.

The discussion in this chapter will focus on three types of difference:

1     differences in the endpoint of language development, i.e. the grammar children end up with as adults;
2     differences in the path of language development, i.e. divergences from the patterns outlined in the previous chapters;
3     differences in the rate of development, i.e. the pace at which children move through the various stages.

It perhaps calls for some justification to include normal and disordered variation in the same chapter. My reasoning is that while some of the boundaries between 'normal' and 'disordered' are clear, many others are not. Thus, while we tend to dichotomise deaf versus hearing or blind versus sighted, in fact many children show degrees of deafness or degrees of blindness with corresponding greater or lesser degrees of affectedness of language development. Similarly, while extreme cases of abuse result in a child being unable to learn true language at all, milder forms of abuse have been shown to affect just the pragmatics parts of the linguistic system. There are, of course, more clear-cut cases. Particularly where genetically controlled syndromes are concerned (e.g. Williams syndrome or Specific Language Impairment (SLI)), there seems to be a cluster of symptoms which characterise the syndrome. However, it still remains the case that even children diagnosed with a certain syndrome vary in the severity of their symptoms, and while children with extremes of the disorder may be very different from children without such syndromes, there are others at the other end of the continuum who are quite similar to normal children. So, I suggest that it is better to take in the whole range of variation, identified as disordered or not, as we try to get a better understanding of how language development works. Let's begin with differences in the endpoint of language development.

## Different endpoints

### Language change

There is a strongly held assumption in linguistics that all children, unless seriously disordered or seriously abused, learn their first language to completion. Moreover, people who speak the same language have been assumed to be relatively homogeneous in their grammatical knowledge. But, it cannot be true that each generation of children acquires exactly the same grammar as the previous one. If they did, languages would stay stable and never change. However, languages do change – quite radically sometimes. Old English, for example, had a basic word order of subject–object–verb, whereas Modern English has a basic word order of subject–verb–object. Old English had a much more elaborate morphological system than Modern English. For example, whereas Modern English marks case only in the pronoun system ('he', 'him', 'his', etc.), Old English marked case on regular nouns as well. These case endings marked the role that the noun was playing in the structure of the sentence (subject, object, etc.). In modern English, we rely on word order to indicate those roles, so 'The horse bit the ox' means something different from 'The ox bit the horse.'

The interesting question in connection with language acquisition concerns how these changes came about. Although linguists are not in complete agreement, it is plausible that change occurs because children come to slightly different conclusions about the way the language works than their parents did. (Another possibility is that teenagers deliberately make changes which they carry into their own adulthood, and then pass on to their children. Parents of teenagers, frequently mystified by their failure to understand their own children, are often more receptive to this hypothesis than others.) However the changes come about, the issue is, how do generations continue to communicate during a period when, for example, the basic word order is changing from Subject–Object–Verb (SOV) to Subject–Verb–Object (SVO)? Clearly, the endpoints of acquisition for children in subsequent generations must have been importantly different from the endpoints for previous generations. David Lightfoot (1982, 1991) has discussed this question at some length, and he concludes that the problem is not as difficult as it might at first appear, because normal variation in Old English allowed SVO to appear in main clauses even when the basic order was still SOV. So it was more a question of slowly, over four centuries, locking that order in as basic and then allowing subordinate clauses to 'catch up', which they did quite quickly. So, as the change happened, the important structures for communication from one generation to another (simple, single-clause, sentences) changed only gradually, from a stylistic preference to a syntactic requirement, not interrupting communication; and by the time the base system actually changed, it was only embedded clauses that had to change on the surface, and this could be achieved without creating a problem for communication because the main clauses in both systems already matched.

This word order change is an example of gradual cross-generational changes in which the endpoint of grammar development shifted for everyone. But what about variety in endpoints within a generation?

## Different competences

In Chapter 1, I made quite a lot of the fact that in linguistics the term 'competence' is not an evaluative term, and that linguists avoid talking about people being more or less competent at language. Instead, linguists are interested in the system that any native speaker has in common with any other native speaker, and a fiction is maintained that the endpoint of acquisition is shared by all native speakers of a language at any given point in time. However, we need to reconsider this fiction.

Something that teachers have known for centuries, but which linguists have been much slower to acknowledge, is that people vary in their control over the language. Some people – perhaps the more highly educated, more widely read, more intelligent by certain measures – have larger vocabularies, and access to a wider range of expressions. Others have specialised vocabularies and ways of speaking for specific subfields of human endeavour: computers, skateboarding, mathematics, cuisine. Others still are more fluent at using their language, more persuasive, more elegant, more precise. Some view language as more central to their lives than others and pass their attitudes and linguistic practices on to subsequent generations (see Shirley Heath's wonderful book *Ways With Words* (1983) about the language used by two different communities in the American South).

As already indicated, part of the reticence of first language researchers and, particularly, of linguists studying adult language to face these differences is that they lead inevitably towards evaluative statements about language abilities. Thus, looking at very advanced structures, and their effective use, while natural territory for a language teacher, is less natural for a descriptive linguist. However, one indication that there is now interest in this sort of variation can perhaps be seen in the relatively new interest in children's later language development (see Chapter 8).

## Lack of input

At the opposite extreme from those who develop highly skilled uses of language are those who fail to develop language at all because of a lack of input. These are children whose endpoints look very different from those we have seen so far. One population that is seriously at risk in this respect comprises profoundly deaf children of hearing parents who are not given access to the natural languages they can acquire easily, namely sign languages (see Chapter 7). Although there are now more schools teaching sign languages than ever before, there still remain many which attempt to teach either oral language or a simplistic gestural version of that oral language to children who do not have enough hearing to make sense of spoken language, in the belief that absorption into the hearing world is in the children's best interests. These children are, in my view, seriously mistreated, given that there are many true sign languages which, if presented during the critical period for language acquisition, will be learned naturally and effectively, and will stimulate the brain of the deaf child to develop language normally. They may then acquire a spoken language (perhaps in written form) as a second language, if they wish. Without a sign language as a first language, however, they will not 'know' language in the crucial sense used in this book, and so will be prevented as surely as by any more obvious kind of abuse from developing their full linguistic potential (de Villiers *et al.* 1994).

'Feral' or 'wild' children are children who appear to have been abandoned and yet have survived. Some of these cases have been quite celebrated. Two cases have been particularly well documented: the case of Victor, the 'Wild Boy of Aveyron', about whom Harlan Lane has published an account that is both accessible and exciting (Lane 1976), and 'Genie' (Curtiss 1977). Let's look at these cases in turn.

Victor was discovered living like a wild animal in the French countryside at the end of the eighteenth century. A young French doctor named Itard took over the task of attempting to train Victor for normal life, and subjected him to a strict training regimen. It is particularly noteworthy, therefore, that despite this regimen, Victor did not progress very far linguistically. With great effort, he apparently mastered the concept of word reference, initially treating the words he learned as names which could only be applied to the objects on which he had been trained, and then gradually coming to extend them to any of a class of similar objects. He even over-generalised creatively in the way normal children are known to do.

Having mastered some nouns, Victor was then taught a few adjectives (e.g. 'petit' ('small'), 'grand' ('big')) and some action verbs (e.g. 'jeter' ('throw'), 'toucher' ('touch')). This highly skeletal communication system appears to have been the height of Victor's linguistic achievement. He did manage to learn to write the words in his system, but the system itself does not appear to have become any more complicated: no pronouns, no auxiliaries, no embedded clauses. As we will see, this same pattern characterises Genie's linguistic efforts.

Genie's story takes place more than a century after Victor's, and yet there are some striking similarities between the cases. Genie was 'discovered' at the age of 13 in November 1970, and admitted to Los Angeles Children's Hospital for evaluation and therapy. She had been severely neglected and abused, having spent much of her young life strapped to a potty chair alone in a room, deprived of human contact, natural movement, and light. She was unsocialised, and had no language.

Susan Curtiss was among the team of professionals who tried to help Genie learn language, and who followed her progress eagerly. Genie was a natural experiment, like Victor. She held the key to the question of whether a child can learn a first language after the age of puberty. Curtiss found that although Genie neither spoke nor, apparently, understood more than a few words of spoken language at first, within a few weeks, 'she could differentiate the sounds constituting speech from other sounds around her, and could, furthermore, scan that stream of sound for familiar patterns constituting words she recognised ('Mama', 'Genie', 'red')' (Curtiss 1977: 53). Gradually she became able to produce speech herself, although her pronunciations remained idiosyncratic and very variable in comparison with normal adult or even child speech. Often she preferred to use a sign system, part of which she made up and part of which she was taught, and which in many ways was an easier medium of expression for her to master. (In fact, she continued to use both signs and speech together even after she could speak.)

The extent to which Genie learned to comprehend English is hard to evaluate. She was particularly bad at formal language tests, which require attention to decontextualised utterances; she was much better at informal conversations. Curtiss suggested that in the latter case a range of non-verbal and contextual information allowed Genie to get round her lack of a proper linguistic system. It is possible that she was relying, in fact, on right hemisphere communicative skills, rather than left hemisphere linguistic ones.

Assessing Genie's verbal production was equally hard because she talked so little. However, Curtiss assembled evidence that, like a normal much younger child, Genie went through a two-word and then a three-word stage, producing utterances such as 'Want milk', 'Like powder', 'Genie love M' and 'Mike mouth hurt', leading Curtiss and the rest of the team to an initially optimistic outlook on Genie's ability to develop normal language. However, the lack of morphology that is clear from these utterances was never remedied, and, after an initially strong start, it became clear that Genie was not going to develop normal language. Frustratingly, a number of grammatical morphemes did make brief appearances in Genie's utterances. But they did not stay. It was as if, having produced them from memorisation at first (as normal children do), they then made no sense to her, and were dropped. So, for example, 'ing', plural markers, '-ed' and possessive '-'s', made very brief appearances before disappearing. Third person singular '-s' only ever appeared in the form 'has', and then only very infrequently. A few irregular past tenses appeared ('made', 'gave', 'bought'), but were very limited. The contractible copula only appeared in uncontracted form, and only as 'is' and 'am': 'Car is wet', 'Teacher is boss at school'. The uncontractible copular (e.g. 'Is she going?') never appeared because she could not do the subject–auxiliary inversion which calls for the uncontracted auxiliary. Of the three English auxiliary verbs (modal, 'be', 'have'), only 'be' emerged in Genie's speech: 'Boy is dropping penny', 'Mama is riding bus', 'I is sitting'. The only subject pronouns to appear were 'I' and 'you' and the latter only appeared twice in the data. She never produced either relative pronouns or wh-words spontaneously, although she did manage the latter in training sessions. She never produced demonstratives ('that', 'these') or dummy subjects ('it', 'there').

Other aspects of Genie's grammar show similar failure to develop. For example, Genie made some attempts to use the definite article ('the'), although she never really got the hang of it, and it remained present but very restricted in its use in her system. The indefinite article was similarly used on occasion; and Genie used 'nother' in order to request more ('Nother penny', 'Nother big prize'). Possessives expressed in noun–noun combinations reflecting possessor–possessed ('Mike mouth') were

common from the beginning of two-word utterances, and she
later became able to express possession through clausal structures: 'Bathroom have big mirror', 'Mr B have flu'.

### Exercise 1

Here are the data from Genie that show her attempts to acquire
negation. Describe what you see. How different is her development
from that of normal children (see Chapter 4)?
Genie's negatives began to emerge around the beginning of the
second year after she was 'discovered'.

Stage 1:   'No more elevator'
           'No more meat'
Stage 2:   'No like hospital'
           'Not have floating chair'
Stage 3:   'Curtiss not sick'
           'Genie not learn PE at school'

(See the end of the chapter for a suggested response.)

Genie used both transitive and intransitive verbs ('Curtiss
come', 'Shake hand') as soon as she could combine words.
'As time passed, Genie's verb phrases grew in complexity, but
she continued to delete direct objects, even when required for
grammaticality and communication ("not have", "Genie bite")'
(*ibid.*: 156). Genie also produced what Curtiss referred to as
'serial-type verb phrases' such as 'Want buy dessert', 'Like go
ride yellow school bus' and 'Want go ride Miss F car'.
    Around the end of 1972, about two years after her 'discov-
ery', Genie started to use verb complement structures, such as
'Tell door lock' used to mean 'Tell M the door was locked',
and 'Ask go shopping' used to mean 'Ask M to go shopping'.
These are different from the more simple serial verb structures
because the subjects of the two verbs are different ('(*You/I*)
ask *M* to go shopping'). 'As time passed, Genie's complement
structures grew more elaborate: "Beth help save money" =
"Beth helps me save up money", "I want Curtiss play piano",
"I want think about Mama riding bus"' (*ibid.*: 159). Another
form of complex sentence is shown by the use of direct reported speech: 'Mr W say put face in big swimming pool',
'Dentist say drink water', and 'Teacher said Genie have temper
tantrum outside'. A structure that Genie 'invented' for herself
seemed to function like a relative clause and involved the deletion of a noun phrase where it was identical to another. An

And, finally, there is SLI: Specific Language Impairment. SLI is a term applied to children who have observable linguistic problems, but no problems with IQ, hearing, vision or emotional/behavioural development, and no other obvious symptoms of already identified syndromes. The general observation is that these children have problems with grammatical morphology. Various SLI children, learning various languages, have been found to have problems with subject–verb agreement, auxiliary and modal verbs, case marking, gender marking and tense marking. Some children have been found to have problems with noun plurals, though not all, and several researchers are sceptical that noun plurals are indeed part of the SLI problem. In fact, current research suggests that SLI is either a problem with verbal morphology (Clahsen 1992; Rice *et al.* 1995) or a general problem with grammatical dependencies between items such as subjects and verbs which must be coordinated (van der Lely 1996).

So, what can we say about this cluster of language disorders? Many of them show a dissociation between language and cognition; but within language, some show a separation between pragmatics and the computational aspects of language, and others do not. Others show dissociations within the grammar. I think that all these dissociations provide a window on the boundaries between modules within the linguistic system, and between the linguistic system and other cognitive systems. In normal children, these modules are coordinated, but in disordered children, they break apart at the natural seams, and offer us an exceptional glimpse at the inner workings of language development.

## Differences in path of development

In this discussion of different routes to successful development, we will look first at different ways of approaching the syntactic structure of the language, the vocabulary and the phonology. Then we will look at blindness and language development, where we will see that a finally successful acquisition path starts out being rather different from that of sighted children.

Before we go on, try the following exercise.

### Exercise 2

Look at the data samples below. They were all produced by a single child known as Minh, and described by Ann Peters in her 1977 article in the journal *Language*. They come from a period when Minh was around 1;4 to 1;7. (I have played fast and loose with the much more accurate transcription provided by the original report of these utterances in order to give the sense of what the child said without creating problems for those not familiar with the International Phonetic Alphabet.)

/ɔbɛ dʌtuː/   'Open-de-door'
/a lər ri gu mu nyai/   'I-like-read-Good-Moon-Night'
/mani ma mani/   'Mommy-where-mommy?'
/hɔsi/   'horsie'
/gayi/   'doggie'
/gʊgʊ/   'cookie'

Look at this collection of utterances. Does anything strike you about the first three in contrast to the second three? Read on in the chapter once you have come to a conclusion.

## Analytic versus gestalt approaches to syntax

For many years it was convenient to assume that all children begin with one word at a time, and then move to two-word utterances, then three-word utterances, and finally multi-word utterances. This step by step approach reflected the typical path of most of the pre-schoolers studied, particularly those whose pronunciations are clear and easy to transcribe. However, as many readers will readily recognise, there are those children who appear to be producing whole strings of run-together words, many of which are seriously hard to understand. Ann Peters was the first to provide a systematic description of a child who produced a sizeable number of these kinds of utterances. She suggested that the run-together strings reflected a different approach to language acquisition, and called for a revision of our thinking. In her work, Peters (1977, 1983) identified some learners as more 'gestalt' in their strategies, and others as more 'analytic'. An 'analytic' strategy is in evidence when children analyse the language they hear into the component parts – words and morphemes – and then set about producing words one at a time, and then in combination both with other words and with bound morphemes (see Chapter 3). A 'gestalt' strategy is evident when learners pick up large chunks of the language they hear and use them to communicate, initially without understanding much, if anything, about how they are composed. They may, for example, produce strings that correspond to 'What do you want?' (Nelson 1973), or the first three utterances in Minh's sample Exercise 2 above, at a time when the analytical counterparts produced by the same child are like the last three utterances in the sample from Minh. Often the pronunciation of these long strings is indistinct, although the intonation pattern is likely to be very clear. For this reason, Peters called the children who tended to speak this way, 'mush-mouthed kids'.

It is important to recognise that these two styles of language analysis are not sharply differentiated, and most children use both strategies, albeit in different proportions. There are children such as Minh who have a sizeable number of gestalt utterances, and who could be said to favour this as an acquisition strategy. Other children (such as my son) are overwhelmingly analytical learners, but have a few gestalt expressions in their repertoire. Avi had a mush-mouthed version of 'I don't want it'. He said it more like 'Aoowaait', with heavy nasalisation of the whole phrase. He used it for quite some time. It was so 'mush-mouthed' an expression that at times I couldn't tell if he was saying 'I want it' or 'I don't want it'. The gestures (and actions) that went with it were crucial to understanding what he meant. After a while he began to modify its use, initially by putting an object word on the end of the whole phrase (e.g. 'I don't want it ball'), and then by substituting in the object word (e.g. 'I don't want yogurt'). At least that's what he seemed to be doing. Again the poor articulation of the phrase often left me wondering whether he hadn't said 'I don't want a ball' rather than 'I don't want it ball'. Shortly thereafter, however, the phrase just disappeared. 'No' took its place, followed by 'Don't want it/object name' and 'No want it/object name', and finally 'I don't want it/object name'. The phrase had been rebuilt through the analytic system he favoured, even though he had earlier made use of it in a gestalt way. (At the end of the next chapter, you'll see second language learning children doing something very similar.)

What makes children prefer one strategy over the other? That's hard to say, but it is probably genetic. One reason for saying that is that similar preferences show up elsewhere in language learning, particularly in the way children treat vocabulary. Let's look at this now.

## Referential/Expressive vocabulary

Katherine Nelson is the leading researcher of individual strategies of first language acquisition, and the first to identify a difference between referential and expressive uses of vocabulary by very young children. Her paper (Nelson 1981) is an excellent presentation of the issues involved, and my presentation here owes much to her article.

Before we go on, try the following exercise.

## Exercise 3

Look at the vocabularies of the two children shown in Table 6.1 (artificially constructed to make the point). How would you characterise the difference? Look particularly at the kinds of words each child favours, in terms of what they refer to, or if they are referring words at all.

Table 6.1   Constructed vocabularies of two children

| Lisa | Rachel |
| --- | --- |
| 'dog' | 'kitty' |
| 'Mama' | 'doggie' |
| 'hi!' | 'please' |
| 'bottle' | 'allgone' |
| 'duck' | 'Mama' |
| 'kitty' | 'don't!' |
| 'recorder' | 'bottle' |
| 'car' | 'bye!' |
| 'bye!' | 'yeah!' |
| 'up' | 'duck' |
| 'baby' | 'hi!' |
| 'mine' | 'thank you' |
| 'brother' | 'stop it!' |

Read on in the chapter once you have come to a conclusion.

In her work, Katherine Nelson has noted that young children differ in the make-up of their early vocabularies. Those that she calls 'referential' children have early vocabularies that consist of mostly object names, with some verbs, proper names and adjectives. Those that she calls 'expressive' have these categories of word, but also have a large number of imitated social routines or formulae (gestalt phrases) such as 'thank you', 'stop it', and 'don't do it'. Clearly this distinction is quite similar to the analytic versus gestalt distinction, and indeed the analytic learners tend to be referential; the gestalt tend to be expressive. The referential/analytic children tend to have larger vocabularies, but the expressive/gestalt children have more diverse

vocabularies because their utterances include many more pronouns and relational terms such as 'allgone' (Bloom 1970) than
the others.

Nelson is careful to point out in her article that these individual differences 'may not be simply characteristic of individual
children across their acquisition period, but of the same children at different times and in different contexts' (1973, p. 176).
Peters (1977) suggested that Minh used his analytic strategy in
referential contexts, such as

> naming pictures in a book (horsie, doggie), labelling a quality
> (hot, cool), and naming a desired object or action (cookie!,
> milk!, up!). Gestalt speech, on the other hand, was used in
> more conversationally defined contexts: opening conversations/
> summonses (What's that?, Uh-Oh!, Mommy!), playing with his
> brother (Airplane go up), requesting (rather than demanding)
> something (I want milk), and discussing objects sociably (rather
> than naming them) (Silly, isn't it?). (1977: 566)

Of course, this kind of differentiation by context leads one to
ask the following question: Is it the case that some children are
overwhelmingly analytic because those are the contexts they
spend most of their time in? Is it possible that other children
are overwhelmingly expressive because those are the contexts
which make up the vast majority of their experience? Moreover, it is perfectly possible that the style differences we have
been looking at here continue throughout life, and lead to differences in approaching other tasks, such as reading and writing,
learning a second language or solving maths problems.

## Phonological differences

Our discussion of individual differences up to this point has
focused on lexical and syntactic development. The definition
of 'mush-mouthed', however, is a phonological definition. It is
poor articulation that got them the name in the first place. As
a further set of examples of individual differences, let's look
briefly at variation in child phonology. Charles Ferguson (who
has conducted probably the most extensive investigation of
developmental phonology) has identified a number of ways in
which individual children appear to differ in their development of the sound systems of their languages (Ferguson 1979).

Children vary in the *paths* they take in the acquisition of
particular sounds. Some children may get to the 'th' sound in

'thick' by putting a 'd' in this position first and then a 'th', other children might put a 't' or an 's' initially in this position. Children also have different *strategies* for phonology acquisition. For example, some employ a 'preference strategy' in which they favour or avoid particular sounds or classes of sounds. For example, some children like fricatives and affricates such as 's', 'sh', and 'ch' and like to produce words that have them in ('see', 'fish', 'shoes', 'cereal', 'cheese', 'ice', 'juice'). Other children avoid saying words that have these sounds in them.

Another kind of strategy involves children trying to make words more similar than they are by making them conform to a preferred pattern. The most common strategy of this type, as we saw in Chapter 3, is reduplication in which the two syllables of a (two-syllabled) word are made similar. Typical examples are 'wawa' for 'water', 'baba' for 'bottle', and 'mama' for 'mother' or 'mummy'. Some children use reduplication in truly creative ways. Kunsmann (1976), for example, reports a child who used reduplication to express negation. Thus 'wati' meant 'water' and 'watiti' meant 'no water'; 'up' meant 'up', and 'upapa' meant 'not up' (i.e. down).

A final strategy involves replacing a variety of different (and perhaps, for the child, difficult) sounds in a word with the same invariant one. For example, Priestly (1977) reports on a child who used /dʒ/ in place of a variety of sounds and sound clusters. Thus 'basket' became 'bajak', 'candle' became 'kajal', and 'elephant' became 'ejat'. There is probably little limit to this kind of idiosyncratic variation, although use of such strategies may relate to learning style differences. Precise imitators, for example, perhaps those whom we saw earlier as analytical learners, might have less call for substitution strategies than gestalt learners.

## Blind children

All the evidence suggests that blind adults have fully comparable endpoints to sighted adults. But did they follow the same path as children? This is a hotly debated issue. There is no doubt that, as Lila Gleitman, Barbara Landau and their colleagues have emphasised, the language of blind children shows many of the same features as sighted children, despite the lack of input from vision. (For these researchers, blind children provide clear evidence for the innateness of language.) Other researchers, such as Elaine Andersen and Anne Dunlea (Dunlea

1989), however, emphasise the specific problems with language that blind children present, and see this as evidence for the power of input in shaping the linguistic system.

Landau and Gleitman (1985) studied three blind children intensively over a period of several years from the age of three up. They concluded that although blind children are slightly later on average than sighted children in beginning to talk (there is a rate difference, in other words), by the age of three, blind and sighted children are virtually indistinguishable linguistically. A delay in the acquisition of auxiliary verbs was noted, but it was not a major delay and could perhaps be explained by a lack of questions in the input to blind children. They did note, however, that the meanings of some words, specifically those related to seeing and looking, are different for blind children. Not surprisingly, blind children initially understand 'looking' to mean 'exploring with the hand'. What is perhaps more interesting is that they come to have two sets of meanings for 'looking' and 'seeing': one for themselves and one for sighted others. They come to understand that 'looking' for others does not mean 'exploring with the hand', but something else, something that is done at a distance, and that is obstructed by things (such as a soft cloth) through which exploration by touch can still continue.

What Landau and Gleitman draw from their research is an appreciation of the normality of blind children's acquisition. They conclude that despite the loss of a major source of information, blind children do build a mental representation of the spatial world around them, and they do learn and use language virtually normally. They argue that this is due both to innate constraints on language, and to the fact that linguistic input itself forms part of the contextual environment from which young children can learn. So, for example, they can learn what 'give', 'get', 'look', 'see' and 'have' mean, in large part because of the sentences in which they appear in the input. Both the meaning and the form of those sentences provide strong clues to word meaning. 'Give', for example, involves a person doing the giving (the subject, in an active sentence), an object being given and a destination (person or place). Thus, if a child who does not know the word 'give' hears a sentence such as 'John gives the book to Mary', if the rest of the sentence is comprehensible, or if the whole action is deducible from context, he or she will be able to work out what 'give' must mean. Landau and Gleitman argue that this kind of 'syntactic bootstrapping' (see Chapter 5) plays a large part in both blind and sighted children's development, and is powerful enough to make up for the loss of sight in a blind child's experience. They marvel at the fact that, 'radically different sensory-perceptual bases for induction yield a similar pattern of language development', at least in structural aspects of language, although they do acknowledge that blind children have more trouble with pragmatic aspects of language, producing sometimes bizarrely irrelevant contributions to conversations, presumably because they are not privy to unspoken communications that go on between sighted individuals.

Where Landau and Gleitman background the pragmatically bizarre, Dunlea foregrounds it. In her study of six young blind children going through the early stages of language acquisition (between the ages of 0;9 and 2;7), one child used 'You wanna go outside?' as a request to go outside. In fact, the children in Dunlea's study often used whole chunks of speech imitated from their caregivers when they first began to use utterances beyond the one-word stage. Although, as we saw earlier, sighted children vary in the extent to which they employ this strategy, Dunlea suggests that blind children do it more often, and in ways that can seem unusual.

In her study, Dunlea focused on the period of first words and very early word combinations – in fact, precisely those three years which Landau and Gleitman chose not to look at when they drew their conclusions about the normality of blind children's acquisition. In particular, she focused on lexical development and pointed to the following differences between blind and sighted children:

1    Blind children, unlike sighted ones, do not use idiosyncratic forms.
2    Words for actions, and functional terms such as 'no', 'more', and 'again', are restricted by blind children to their own actions and needs, rather than describing the actions and needs of others.
3    Functional or relational terms such as 'no', 'more', and 'again' are used to satisfy blind children's own needs rather than to describe or request states of affairs separate from their own needs.
4    Blind children engage in very little either normal extension or over-extension of words. Whereas sighted children extend (e.g. use the word 'teddy' for all the teddies in their world) as much as 95% of their first words, blind children extend only 50%. Whereas sighted children over-extend (e.g. use the word 'ball' for a grapefruit, the moon, a plate or a frisbee) 41% of their first words, blind children over-extend only 8–13%.

Dunlea suggests that these young blind children are not classifying the world the way sighted children do. They are not
constructing hypotheses for the way words work as part of a
communication system. And they are generally having trouble
understanding their separateness from the world – they are
having trouble decentring, to use Piaget's term. However, once
they get the hang of what language is for, they are able to use
it for their own specific purposes, producing more attention-
getting and requesting speech acts, since that is the way to stay
connected with a world that is not visually present.

What are we to make of these different views of blind children's language skills? It seems that Dunlea's emphasis on difference reflects a stage that blind children move through. Landau
and Gleitman's data suggest that by three, blind children have
overcome whatever early problems they may have had. Another,
and equally important point, is that because of the age differences, we are, to some extent, dealing with different modules of
language. Dunlea herself suggests that it is possible that syntactic
development in blind children may be normal, even where lexical
development appears not to be. And Landau and Gleitman's
data would certainly support this interpretation. So it may be
that a modular view of language in which lexical development
and syntactic development are in different modules receives
support from the blind children's data.

Both Dunlea and Landau and Gleitman deal with lexical
development, and yet come to different conclusions. However, Dunlea is dealing with first words, when the linguistic
context may provide far less support and evidence for word
meanings than the later development discussed by Landau and
Gleitman. Dunlea's subjects have to figure out how words work
as referents in the first place, and then they have to figure out
what individual words mean largely on the basis of perceptual
information. Remember that both Victor and Genie, whose
syntactic modules seem to have been irrevocably damaged, were
able to acquire words. So perhaps, as Bloom (1994) suggests,
early word learning is cognitively driven, while later word
learning is more syntactically driven. So, blind children seem
to have different early routes from sighted children, even though
they end up in the same place. Their lack of visual input affects
one part of the language acquisition puzzle, namely the acquisition of words, before syntactic bootstrapping becomes possible.
Again, these children provide some fairly concrete evidence for
modularity of language.

## Differences in rate of development

It is axiomatic in child language studies that attaching ages to
stages of development is dangerous. Parents are easily alarmed
by pronouncements such as 'By one year old children should
be able to . . .' because parents can be too easily frightened
into thinking their children are abnormal in some way. In fact,
there is a very wide range of paces for language development,
even where there are no indications of abnormality. Some children start later than others, and some move through the stages
of development faster than others.

Gender has often been cited as a source of variation in the
pace of language development. Boys are often thought to be
later language learners than girls, although the statistical evidence in support of this claim is mixed. Even if we could show
definitively that boys and girls did differ in this respect, it
might not be caused by gender differences *per se*, but rather
by socialisation differences. It is possible that many girls engage
in verbal exchanges with their parents and other companions,
while their male counterparts are wrestling on the carpet or
watching sports, in which language plays little constructive
part. In other words, linguistic experience could be a major
contributor rather than genetics. And there are certainly many
clear exceptions to any purported advantage for girls. My son
was a very early and very fast language learner. But perhaps
that was because all the people he interacted with are highly
verbal, from his parents to the (mostly female) set of inter-
locutors at day care. Who knows?

In second language acquisition research, factors which are
suggested to affect the rate of language development include
intelligence, aptitude and motivation. While, as I suggested
earlier, there may be a link between high-level oratorical skills
and intelligence, the dissociation syndromes, as well as cases
such as Genie, suggest an essential lack of connection between
first language acquisition and intelligence. It may be the case,
however, that in testing IQ, we are still too wedded to certain
kinds of intelligence, and that when we get more sophisticated
measures of intelligence − perhaps ones that recognise the range
of different types of intelligence along the lines that Howard
Gardner identifies in his book *Frames of Mind* (1983) − we
might want to reopen the question. Then we might find some
interesting parallels between type and degree of intelligence
and strategies for language acquisition or language use.

Other sources of individual variation in second language acquisition rate, such as aptitude and motivation, have not been investigated in first language acquisition, although this might prove interesting (Foster-Cohen 1993). To my knowledge, motivation has been explored only cursorily. Brown (1973) evaluates an argument that children might be motivated to move from the one-word to the two-word stage of development by a need to communicate, but concludes that at the point when children move from one- to two-word speech, their speech is equally effective in either mode. Communicative motivation is a poor argument for language development at this (or any) stage (Brown 1973: 464). The other area where I have seen motivation discussed is in connection with sibling, particularly twin, language development. The argument has sometimes been made that younger children learn language more slowly because the older sibling 'knows' what the younger child wants and takes care of his or her needs without the younger child needing to communicate. It has sometimes been argued that twins are slower to develop the language of their environment because they develop a communicative system all of their own, and are therefore not as motivated to learn the language of the adults around them. I am not aware of significant statistical evidence in favour of either claim.

Finally, personality may have something to do with variation in language development. It is at least plausible that outgoing and risk-taking children might learn language more quickly than those who are more careful and conservative in their approach to any task. However, we need to be careful here to distinguish between acquiring the system and using it. In fact we need to observe this caution in all discussions of individual differences between language learners. Children who do not talk much may none the less comprehend a great deal, and thus possess a great deal of 'knowledge' of the linguistic system. Figuring out the knowledge possessed by a child ('competence' of the language), as opposed to his or her skills in using it ('performance'), is, as has been said many times, a very difficult task. However, paying at least as much attention to language comprehension as to language production by children is certainly a sensible first step.

This chapter has focused on those differences which child language researchers think are due to inherent individual differences. There are, however, differences in language development which are due to differences in children's experiences. Perhaps the most obvious one is that children exposed to different languages will exhibit differences in the ways they learn language. In the next chapter we will look at these differences.

## Discussion of in-text exercises

Exercise 1
You should look back at the discussion of the acquisition of negation in normal children in Chapter 4. Like normal children, Genie starts by putting a negative at the beginning of her utterance and only later incorporates it into the utterance. Since she does not have a normal syntax, it may well be that when normal children do the same thing, they are not doing it with their syntax, but with the pragmatic system that is the only means Genie seems to have for structuring her utterances. Stage 1 in Genie's data seems to show an unanalysed chunk 'no more' to which she adds the communicatively appropriate noun. (Second language learning children often use the same strategy; see the next chapter.) Stage 2 shows both 'no' and 'not' appearing, and then, in Stage 3, only 'not' appears in the middle of her utterances. Genie has almost no grammatical morphology, even though the communicative structure of what she is saying is relatively complex.

## Questions for discussion

1   How do *you* think individual differences between children should be treated in the development of a fully fledged theory of language acquisition? What types of differences can and should be safely ignored? Perhaps you think that none of them should be ignored. Has language acquisition theory been pushed along the wrong track by ignoring such differences for so long? Has the restriction of the data to be accounted for been useful or counter-productive? (See below for some ideas.)

2   We have assumed throughout this chapter that children with disorders that either do or do not affect their language are accurate mirrors of the way language works in normal children. There is, however, a fundamental problem with this assumption, since we cannot be sure that the parts of the brain/mind that we are assuming are intact are, in fact, intact. They may also be disordered or they may be crucially different from normal individuals because of, perhaps, compensating for the disordered parts. Consider this dilemma. How might it be overcome? Should researchers ignore all disorder information because of

this problem? If not, how should they appropriately respond to the issue? (See below for some brief thoughts.)

3 Current theories of autism suggest that it may stem from an inability to form a 'theory of mind'. That is, autistic children don't understand that human beings (including themselves) can be said to have states of mind, to have thoughts and opinions. As a result, it simply does not occur to them to try to convey to others their own attitudes, wants or desires, to try to change the states of minds of others, or to entertain hypothetical ideas. This view is used to explain why autistic children are so withdrawn, so uncommunicative. At a very fundamental level, they do not understand the very notion of communication. What do you think of this idea? What kinds of data would support or deny such a claim? There are some very high-functioning autistics (one is even a university professor), so what modifications, if any, should be made to this 'theory of mind' hypothesis? (See below.)

## Some activities

1 Try to identify an analytical child learner and a gestalt child learner, and tape-record a five-minute segment of speech from each. Now try to transcribe the two segments (see Appendix 1). Are they equally easy/difficult to transcribe? Try to articulate what the problems and issues are with respect to gaining an accurate transcription from a gestalt child. Calculate the MLU for each. Discuss any problems that arise in trying to carry out this type of analysis. Do a count of the number of different words encountered in the transcriptions from the two children; discuss any problems that arise in doing this kind of analysis.

2 Collect a sample of data from a young child between a year and 18 months old in three different contexts designed to replicate the contextual constraints on the use of analytic versus gestalt strategies suggested by Peters (see p. 133). Transcribe the data being careful to note intonation and poor articulation where appropriate (see Appendix 1). Do you find in your data the division between analytic and gestalt utterances suggested in this chapter?

3 Look at the way the people around you use language. Can you see differences in the volubility, articulateness, vocabulary size, etc.?

4 Talk to people (or, better yet, their mothers) about how early or quickly they think they learned their first language. Many people have recollections (either real or recalled for them) of being early talkers or late talkers; of having trouble being understood; of dealing with articulation 'problems', perceived or real, such as lisps, etc.

5    Using the description and data provided in the chapter, compare
and contrast Genie's linguistic system with what you now know
of normal children's early linguistic systems. Provide data of
your own or from elsewhere in this book to substantiate the
comparison. After you have completed this exercise, you might
want to look at Chapter 10 of Curtiss (1977), in which she
provides her own comparison.

6    In 1994 American Public Television produced a documentary
on 'Genie'. If you are able to find this in your library, or by
contacting your public television station, you will find it fully
repays the effort. It is hard to convey in print what Genie is
really like. The video-tapes shown on this documentary show
Genie at various stages in her development.

## Solutions to and comments on discussion questions

Discussion question 1

No field of scientific enquiry would get very far if it tried to
cope with all the variation from the start. There are some
kinds of variation that are easy to ignore, given what we think
we know about language. We are unlikely to consider a child's
hair colour as a relevant variable, for example. In other cases,
it may be harder to decide; for example, handedness, presence
of older siblings, parental education level, the experience of
disease, and so on. Clearly, what we decide to look at as a
variable depends on our view of language: what it is, and how
it develops. However, some restriction of the data is absolutely
necessary. The field cannot progress without it. Without it,
theories cannot be built, and without theories, we do not know
what to look at next. The mark of a healthy field is empirically
falsifiable theories.

Discussion question 2

The problem of over-interpreting data from disordered children is very real. However, any variation, including disorder,
reveals some part of the complete picture. The trick is, as it
were, to triangulate the data: move cautiously with what disorder reveals and try to develop a theory which encompasses
both the disordered data and data from normal individuals.
Many people are beginning to make considerable claims for
brain imaging techniques which can perhaps show us comparisons of normal and disordered brains doing the same things,

so that we can actually see whether the intact parts of a disordered brain are indeed working normally. While these developments are exciting, they are still a long way off being able to provide answers to questions such as this with any degree of reliability.

Discussion question 3

There is a large professional literature on autism, as well as on 'theory of mind' (Carruthers and Smith 1996; Astington *et al.* 1988). There are also some very revealing autobiographies by autistics themselves which are well worth reading. One is by Temple Grandin, the professor I mentioned. Two others are by Donna Williams (1992, 1994). These books will give you a sense both of the language of an autistic and of the issue of 'theory of mind'. The title piece in Oliver Sack's book *An Anthropologist on Mars* is about Temple Grandin (Sacks 1995).

## Further reading

A useful collection of papers on individual differences in language development is the volume edited by Charles Fillmore, Daniel Kempler and William S.-Y. Wang (1979). Katherine Nelson's (1981) paper on individual differences is worth reading in its entirety.

Gordon Wells's longitudinal project in which he collected data on a large number of children learning English as their first language provides some very useful insights into the range of differences among children, and will provide you with interesting data, as well as insightful analyses, particularly into the question of differences in rate of acquisition (Wells 1981, 1985).

Both Harlan Lane and Susan Curtiss's books are worth reading in their entirety (Lane 1976; Curtiss 1977). A more recent account is Roger Shattuck's (1994). Helen Tager-Flusberg's book on atypical language acquisition (Tager-Flusberg 1994) contains many of the papers referred to in this chapter. I recommend the whole book.

Finally, neurologist Oliver Sacks writes wonderfully and accessibly about a range of disorders, some of which affect language. You might find some of his case studies illuminating in the context of this chapter (Sacks 1984, 1985, 1995).

## CHAPTER 7

# Does it matter which language(s) you learn?

## Chapter summary

This chapter aims to broaden the view of language acquisition adopted so far in this book. From a perspective that has been heavily English-based and monolingual, we move to consider the way children faced with other languages and multiple languages approach them. The chapter begins with a brief account of some of the ways in which languages can vary, and then shows how a parameter approach to language acquisition offers an explanation for how children approach such variability. This is followed by further focus both on aspects of language acquisition this approach can account for, as well as on some that it cannot (and is not intended to) account for. Next, the particular window on acquisition afforded by bilingual development is considered, along with a discussion of the nature of bilingual acquisition and bilingual language use, particularly code-switching. The chapter closes with a brief consideration of child second language development.

## Introduction

Young children don't know there are lots of languages in the world. Even young bilingual or multi-lingual children can be expected to know only that there are as many languages in the world as they themselves are exposed to. Because of this inherent provincialism on the part of children, any theory of how languages are acquired must 'work' for each child exposed to each language or combination of languages. In other words, a theory about how children learn languages cannot depend on children knowing that there are languages other than their own, and how they work. However, as students of child language, we will not be thought to have achieved very much if we come up with a theory of language development that *only* works for one particular language, but fails when anyone tries to apply it to any other language. As researchers, we must consider all the languages in the world (as far as that is possible), and make sure that our theories about how children develop their language(s) are up to the task of coping with any language.

## So what's so very different, anyway?

It is easy, if you have learned one language to complete fluency (as you obviously have done), and have not tried to learn any other language (which I hope is not the case), to be misled into thinking that the way your language works is the way all languages work (differences in vocabulary aside, of course, since these are very obvious, and clear to even the most naïve learner). However, as linguists have known for centuries, there is both huge diversity, at least on the surface, as well as startling consistency; and both the diversity and the consistency must be built into any theory of how children learn any and all of the world's languages. After all, any child born into any language community learns the language(s) of that community in roughly similar time spans, despite quite varied experiences.

### Exercise 1

Think about the languages you know or know about. What kinds of differences among them can you enumerate? Do they have the same or different basic word orders? Do they have prepositions or postpositions? Are any of them tone languages? What other differences can you identify?

So what are some of the differences between the world's languages? Well, let's start with how the messages are conveyed Most of the world's languages are oral/aural languages making use of sounds to convey meanings. However, there are a number of sign languages in the world which are acquired by children as their first language. These sign languages have the same kinds of features as any other natural language: word order restrictions, ways of combining clauses, sign morphology, etc. They are different in their modality from other languages, using action in time and space, rather than sounds in just time; but the more we learn about sign languages the more we understand their essential similarity to all the spoken languages. (It is worth noting that sign languages do not bear any special linguistic relationship to the spoken languages used in the oral communities in the same locations. So, American Sign Language is no closer to English, for example, than it is, say, to German or Chinese; and Israeli Sign Language is no closer to Hebrew than it is to Swedish.)

Let's turn now to features of languages, other than modality, which might affect their acquisition. Let's start with word order. English has a basic subject–verb–object (SVO) structure, exemplified by the sentence in (1):

(1)   The little boy smacked the dog.

Other languages, such as Navajo, have SOV order, as exemplified in (2).

(2)   'ashkii 'at'ééd yinil'i
      boy girl he-is-looking-at-her
      'The boy is looking at the girl.'

(Here and elsewhere in this chapter, non-English examples will be presented in three versions: the orginal language first, then a word for word gloss, and then a freer translation.) Other languages still are VSO or VOS; and a very few languages (for years it was thought to be none at all) are OVS or OSV. It is not always obvious what one should consider as evidence for the basic word order, given that most languages can move words around for either syntactic or pragmatic reasons (or both). Therefore, determining basic word order is not as easy as it might seem. A language such as German, for example, looks, on the basis of examining simple, single-clause sentences, like an SVO language (see (3)), but in fact German is SOV (the order that shows up in embedded clauses (see (4)) and there is an obligatory rule that moves the finite verb into the second position in the sentence in single-clause sentences.

(3)   Der Mann liest den Buch.
      'The man reads the book.'
(4)   Hans sagt, dass er den Buch liest.
      John says that he the book reads
      'John says that he reads the book.'

We know this because when the first word in the sentence is an adverb, the inflected verb still appears in second position, now in front of the subject, as in (5).

(5)   Morgen geht Hans in die Stadt.
      tomorrow goes Hans to the town
      'Tomorrow Hans is going to town.'

The question arises, of course, of when children learning German as their first language 'know' or 'realise' that German is SOV. Although there are different opinions, it seems that even very young children show evidence of understanding that German is verb-final by sometimes putting verbs at the end of simple sentences (e.g. 'Ivar buch liest' = 'Ivar book reads' (Ivar at 2;4)) even though in adult German, a rule always moves a finite verb such as 'reads' into the second position in a main clause. Children at the same age also show some evidence of understanding this 'verb second' feature of German word order by putting most of their inflected verbs in this position, but never their infinitives.

The extent to which phrases 'move around' in sentences is another way in which languages vary. For example, English has a pretty fixed word order. We can move things about a bit, as in (6) and (7) below, but in general we must stick with the basic SVO order, or our sentence ends up meaning something else (as in (8)) or is ungrammatical (as in (9)):

(6)   Yesterday, I read the book. *versus*
      I read the book yesterday.
(7)   Books, I like to read (but magazines, I hate reading). *versus*
      I like to read books (but I hate reading magazines).
(8)   The boy saw the cat. *versus*
      The cat saw the boy.
(9)   *Cat the boy saw the.

Other languages, such as Navajo, have a much freer word order and can almost scramble the order of words without it making ungrammatical sentences; there are so many other indicators on the words as to who does what to whom that it can all be retrieved no matter what order the words are in. Children learning morphologically rich languages seem to be attuned very early to that morphology; much earlier than in languages with less rich systems. Richard Weist has shown that children learning Polish, for example, start using complex Polish bound morphology earlier than children learning English try to use bound morphology. Children learning Italian and Spanish are similarly precocious in comparison with English learners.

As we saw in Chapter 4, movement of constituents is a fundamental part of question formation in English. In other languages, however, such as Mandarin Chinese, leaving the wh-word 'in place' is simply the standard way of forming a question. Compare the examples in (10) (from English) and (11) (from Chinese).

(10)   Who(m) do you like?
(11)   Ni xihuan shei?
       you like who?
       'Who(m) do you like?'

The presence or absence of movement for question formation is a basic parameter of variation between languages, and one which children seem to recognise very early, since they do not make mistakes (leaving wh-words in place when they shouldn't or moving them when they should be left in place).

Another much discussed source of variation among languages is whether all of the basic elements of sentence structure are required overtly (i.e. must be produced as a pronounced word, rather than being left as understood) in a sentence. Although in any language, items can be left out for pragmatic reasons, in some languages they are absent for syntactic reasons. In Spanish, Italian and Chinese, for example, subjects are routinely absent as in (12) and (13); and, as (13) shows, in Chinese, objects are also routinely absent.

(12)   Mangia una mela. (Italian)
       '(He/She) eats an apple.'
(13)   kanjian le (Chinese)
       (he) see (he) Perfect-marker
       '(He) saw him.'

These languages are referred to as 'pro-drop' languages because they 'drop' their pronouns (when viewed from an English-biased point of view).

There are many more ways in which languages can be shown to be different, but I hope this section has given you a general sense of how different things can be, so that you can see that whatever theory of language development we come up with, it must be able to cope with the fact that the children in each of these communities learn these languages with roughly equal ease.

## A parameter theory of language acquisition

Logically, there can be two kinds of linguistic knowledge: knowledge we are born with (often called *a priori* knowledge), and knowledge that we acquire during our lives. Distinguishing between these two types is not easy, but comparing children learning different languages can really help. As we saw in the previous section, such cross-linguistic comparisons reveal lots of aspects of languages which, although they vary from one language to another, none the less seem to appear in children's linguistic systems early on. These aspects include basic word order, whether a language allows syntactically missing subjects or not (i.e. whether it is a pro-drop language or not), and whether wh-questions involve placing the wh-word at the front of the sentence or not. How can we account for the early acquisition of these aspects combined with the variability among languages?

One possible answer is an approach which involves building parameters of variation into the *a priori* knowledge that children are born with. For example, although all the possible orders of subject, object and verb exist somewhere in the world's languages, what turns out to underlie this variation is a two-way distinction between whether languages are 'head-initial' or 'head-final'. Head-initial languages have the main word of the phrase on the left and modify it on the right; head-final languages have their modifiers preceding the main word of the phrase. So, for example, verb phrases in SVO languages are VO, with the head of the verb phrase (the verb) first, and the object afterwards, and SOV languages are OV, with the head (the verb) last. (SVO languages are often called 'head-initial' languages, while SOV language are called 'head-final'.) Children do not, then, have to learn which of six possible orders their language has; rather, they only have to learn whether it is head initial or head-final. And it turns out that once they have made that determination, other things follow. For example, head-initial languages tend, like English, to have prepositions; head-final languages tend, like Japanese, to have postpositions. So a simple binary decision reaps far more information than that decision alone might suggest.

How do children figure out how their language behaves with respect to pro-drop? Nina Hyams has worked on this problem within a UG perspective more than anyone else, and over the years has proposed a number of different solutions to the problem of why even children learning non-pro-drop languages such as English seem to go through a stage of omitting subjects and saying things such as 'Want cookie'. Her original proposal (Hyams 1986) suggested that children start out assuming all languages are pro-drop, and then children learning English have to figure out, by paying attention to the obligatory but semantically empty subject 'It' in 'It's raining', that subjects are required. A later proposal was that the parameter involved was one that divided languages into two types: on the one hand, those that are morphologically uniform by having either full verbal inflectional paradigms (e.g. Spanish and Italian) or no inflectional verbal morphology (e.g. Chinese), and, on the other hand, those which are morphologically non-uniform with some verbal morphology but not full paradigms (e.g. English). The first group are pro-drop and the second are not, so the suggestion was that realising which setting of the parameter was appropriate (+ or − uniform) led to the right conclusions for each language. Prior to such a realisation, children learning non-pro-drop languages mistakenly believed the contrary and left their subjects out. This account (put forward by Jaeggli and Hyams (1988)) unfortunately fell foul of languages such as German which are not pro-drop but have full inflectional paradigms. A current proposal (Hyams 1994c) suggests that Universal Grammar provides a default assumption that *all* languages allow pro-drop, but only those languages with rich morphology (such as Spanish and Italian) can actually work this way, because only those languages (with inflections which provide information about the subject) allow the automatic syntactic recoverability (identification) of the subject that is omitted. That children learning English also leave their subjects out is suggested to be not a grammatical effect, but a pragmatic one. (It is argued that what looks like a subject is actually a topic, attached to the front end of the sentence, and it is this topic which is deleted.) That a pragmatic element in the explanation of the pro-drop facts should have emerged in the context of highly technical syntactic argumentation (that I have only hinted at here) is interesting because parallel attempts to account for the same facts from a purely pragmatic point of view (e.g. arguing that children omit assumed information (Greenfield and Smith 1976; Allen 1997)) have continued over the same time frame, and one wonders if the two lines of research are about to converge.

Finally, a word about wh-movement, which has also received a parametric account. The syntax of a language either does or does not involve syntactic movement to form wh-questions. Once a child realises that the language does have wh-movement (like English, say), the decision is made. Again, it turns out that other things follow from that decision, including restrictions on where a wh-word can move from, what kinds of sentence parts it can move across, and whether it can ever be left in place when a sentence involves two wh-words at the same time ('Who saw what?' versus *'What who saw?').

So the parameter approach depends on *a priori* knowledge, which is activated by exposure to the language around the child. The nature of the input therefore has a major role to play in the form of positive evidence for how the language works (see Chapter 5). This positive evidence 'triggers' the appropriate settings of the parameters, and the timing of that triggering is likely to be connected to the frequency of the triggering structures in the input (in a way that we do not yet understand).

Languages vary in the frequency with which their speakers use certain structures. A case in point is the use of the passive construction. The passive construction (e.g. 'The horse was whipped by his master') falls within the domain of UG because it depends on the movement of constituents (the object of an active sentence becomes the subject of a passive), but the timing of the acquisition of the passive varies among languages because of differences in the availability of the trigger. For children learning English, the passive is a late-learned structure. In Hebrew, too, the passive is mastered very late. However, a number of studies have found that in other languages, the passive is learned considerably earlier; these include the Bantu language Sesotho (Demuth 1989), the Eskimo language of Inuktitut (Allen and Crago 1992) and the Guatemalan Indian language of K'iche' (Pye 1992).

What is going on here? Well, it turns out that in those language communities where the passive is learned earlier, it is pretty difficult to get away with not using the passive. It is used all the time by the adults in the community (unlike in English-speaking communities), and some of the most basic communications call for the passive. For example, in English one can question the subject of a sentence by saying, 'Who hit you?' In Sesotho, you cannot do this. Instead, you have to say the equivalent of, 'You were hit, by who(m)?' Simplifying somewhat, the reason for this is that putting a question word in subject position, as in English, involves putting a word that asks for new information ('who') in the subject position, and Sesotho only allows the subject position to be filled by an item which is already established (known) to the hearer; hence the need for the passive. So, here we see that an aspect of UG is activated earlier in one language than in another because of the nature of the input.

It is also important to note that individual children vary some-what even within the same language group. So, for example, Pye (1994) has found that some children learning certain K'iche' constructions (specifically, causative ones) progress faster in learn-ing than others. And Pizzuto and Caselli (1992) found differ-ences in the acquisition of Italian inflections, both in the age at which they were acquired, and in the order of acquisition of some of the inflections. Hyams (1994a, 1994b) notes that because language is complex and involves the coordination of a number of different modules or subsystems, it is likely that individual differences will occur, even though the mechanisms for acquisition are the same for all children. One child may have a triggering experience earlier than another, and so set a parameter a little earlier. Thus, while some researchers have tried to use the evidence of individual differences to argue against UG, there are very cogent arguments in favour of UG which also allow for individual differences.

Those aspects of language covered by UG are usually referred to as 'core', while all the rest, which do not fall under UG, are 'peripheral'. Despite the dismissiveness of the terminology, there is *lots* of interesting acquisition going on in the periphery. It, too, is affected by the frequency in the input, but it is also affected by the complexity of the structures involved. (Note that aspects of language covered by UG are not affected by complexity in the same way because it is precisely the com-plexity of the *a priori* knowledge which relieves the child of the burden of having to extract complex knowledge from the input.)

An area of language where acquisition is clearly affected by complexity is nominal and verbal morphology. Here, although the options or features for agreement, tense, etc. may be offered by UG, the exact manifestation of those options in individual languages has to be learned through exposure. Languages vary greatly in the number and type of distinctions they mark morpho-logically. Number (singular, dual, plural . . . ), gender (masculine, feminine, neuter . . . ), animacy (inanimate, animate, supernatural . . . ), person (first, second, third, fourth . . . ), etc. Navajo, for example, marks on its verbs whether the subject of the verb is a single individual, two individuals, or more than two, but there is no distinction made between masculine and feminine in the third person. The question is, how do children go about learning all the distinctions that their language expects them to mark, and are some of them more difficult than others?

The short answer is 'yes'. The derivational systems in Hebrew, for example, turn out to create all sorts of problems for children. In her discussion of the acquisition of the Hebrew verb conjugation system known as 'binyan', Berman (1994) suggests that a number of factors enter into the piecemeal fashion in which the system is built up. Hebrew verbs all consist of a root made up of three consonants. To these three consonants are added vowels and other consonants to make the actual words. The binyan system encodes the complexities of what is known as 'transitivity' and involves the assignment of different verbs to different categories. Crucially, however, verbs based on the same root can show up in different categories, carrying different vowels and additional consonants, and meaning related things. So, a group 1 intransitive form such as 'CaXaK', which means 'laugh', becomes a group 5 transitive form 'hiCXiK', meaning 'amuse'. The group 2 intransitive form 'niRDaM' means 'fall asleep' and corresponds to the group 5 transitive form 'hiRDiM', which means 'put to sleep'. (I have capitalised the consonants that form the root in each form to make it easier to see what is happening.)

Parts of this system are predictable and easily learnable, parts of it are relatively opaque, and parts of it are completely so, and can only be learned by rote. Children begin by not using the system at all, even though they are already using the quite complex inflectional systems of number, gender and tense. Then they start to learn some forms by rote; then they begin to pull the system together, making generalisations across the various rote-learned items; and finally they master the full system. But it takes until quite late into childhood (maybe 7;0 or so) to master the whole system.

The gender system in French is another example of a complex morphological system. Children learning French must learn that every noun has a grammatical gender (masculine 'le' or feminine 'la') and that only in a few cases does the choice depend in any sensible way on the real-word gender of the object (e.g. 'la femme' = 'a woman'). Children, in fact, pay little or no attention to the real-world correlations, apparently recognising from the start that this part of the system is arbitrary (Karmiloff-Smith 1979). Instead, they pick up on the phonology of the word with which the article is paired, since this is, to a large extent, a reliable indicator of the appropriate gender marking ('-elle' is usually feminine; '-on' is masculine). Getting the appropriate pronoun form when referring back to an item already mentioned, however, seems to be a little more difficult. The adult language requires that a masculine pronoun ('il') be used when the referent is grammatically masculine, and a feminine pronoun ('elle') when the referent is feminine. However, children reporting an accident in which the victim ('la victime') was a man, refer for quite some time to 'il', even though it should be 'elle'. Here, children have some considerable trouble letting go of the hints provided by the pragmatics of the situation and paying attention only to the grammatical aspects of the system. Notions of whether something is difficult to learn thus seem to depend on both the complexity of the system and on the particular constellations of knowledge they engage: pragmatics dictates the choice of pronoun, except where the reference is back to a noun with grammatical gender (all common nouns in French), when it is a morphologically/lexically dictated choice. The choice of article, on the other hand, is lexically dictated, with influence from phonology.

When the same child is learning two quite different languages simultaneously, we have the clearest possible evidence for the relative difficulty of subsystems of languages. A now famous comparison was made by Dan Slobin (1973) in reporting the data collected by Mikeš on the simultaneous acquisition of Serbo-Croatian and Hungarian locative expressions. Serbo-Croatian encodes locatives by using prepositions ('kuci' = 'house', 'u-kuci' = 'in the house') and Hungarian uses suffixes ('hajo' = 'boat', 'hajo-ban' = 'in the boat'), so they have quite different means of encoding the same information. Since we may assume that children understand the notion of location, any differences in the ages at which the coding of this single distinction occurs (assuming that it is indeed a single distinction) must be the result of the relative difficulties of the two types of expression. It turns out that the children used the Hungarian suffixes before they used the Serbo-Croatian prepositions, suggesting that the prepositions are harder to acquire than the suffixes. In the next section, we will look in some detail at the linguistic experiences of bilingual children.

## How do children become bilingual?

There is a general consensus in the literature that children who begin learning two languages under natural conditions before the age of three should be considered as engaged in first language acquisition in two languages, whereas children who learn their second language after the age of three should be regarded as second language learners (McLaughlin 1984). There is no generally accepted motivation for this cut-off; however, a proposal made by Andrew Radford (1990) that around the age of three genuine syntax becomes operational in children's language, might provide the beginnings of one.

A question which has provoked much discussion is whether children develop two languages in parallel or whether they begin with an initially single system. There are those who have argued that children start out treating two language systems as a single system and then separate them (Volterra and Taeschner 1978), and there are those who have argued that the languages are never part of the same system (Lindholm and Padilla 1978), i.e. that two systems develop simultaneously. One of the main reasons for the disagreement has been the prevalence of code-switching in the speech of most bilingual children and adults. Code-switching is when utterances or larger stretches of language contain elements from more than one language. The temptation has been to think that in very young children this is the result of an inability to distinguish the languages. The weight of research, however, now clearly favours the hypothesis that the languages are separate from the start. So, for example, the presence of blends such as German–English 'bitte–please' and English–French 'pinichon' (= 'pickle' + 'cornichon') has sometimes been used as evidence in favour of an early single-language hypothesis, but these seem to be little different from cross-register blends produced by monolingual children, such as 'bunny-rabbit' and 'choo-choo-train'. As Meisel (1987) suggests, this kind of mixing seems more a pragmatic problem of knowing when to use which system, rather than a problem of two linguistic systems intertwined. Bilingual children may not realise, for example, that their friends don't understand when they use a word or phrase from another language.

That children are able to build two (or more) systems simultaneously is particularly impressive when you think that, in many situations, children are surrounded by adults who are themselves switching back and forth between the languages. They could, in principle, decide that their parents are speaking a single language, and, in cases where there is no other evidence for the distinctness of the languages, this may in fact happen. In fact, something like this happens in pidgin situations where children are exposed to a stable code made up of features of two systems. In most genuinely bilingual situations, however, children are provided with clues as to the existence of two codes, and are able to recognise which phonological, lexical, morphological and syntactic features belong together.

## Exercise 2

Imagine a child of three named Lucy. Lucy has an English mother and a French father, and she lives in France. She does not yet go the *maternelle* (pre-school) although she does visit friends her own age quite often, some of whom are French speakers and some of whom are English speakers. Lucy's mother speaks English to her all the time, but speaks French to her French-speaking friends (her own and Lucy's). With her husband, she sometimes uses English, but mostly uses French. Lucy's father uses French with Lucy almost all the time, except when he playfully 'practises' his English with her. Lucy's mother has a strong accent in French and Lucy's father has a strong accent in English; both make quite a lot of errors in syntax and morphology in their non-native languages. What features of this situation make it easy for Lucy to decide what's English and what's French; what aspects make it hard? Do you think she is bilingual at three? If so, will she stay bilingual as she grows up? Try to think it through before you read on.

Lucy is almost certainly fluently bilingual in this situation, although she will need to work to prevent the loss of English as she grows up and moves more out of her mother's sphere of influence. The English-speaking friends will be crucial, because without them there is quite a good chance that Lucy will becomes passively bilingual: able to understand her mother, but not able (comfortably, at least) to use English herself.

Lucy's task of building two systems is made easier by the fairly clear distinction between the language spoken to her by Mummy versus the language spoken to her by Daddy. Even though each uses the other's language from time to time, the presence of the foreign accent and non-native errors will mark it as different from the native system. The native system for each language is reinforced by the speech of others in the context, so with her mother and her native English-speaking friends she will hear much more English spoken natively than English spoken non-natively. A similar situation exists for French, although, given that they live in France, there is even more evidence for native French than native English.

In general, many parents, teachers and researchers believe that restricting the use of one language to one situation and the use of the other to a different situation helps children maintain the separation. So, one language at home and the other on the street, or one language to mother and the other language to father, or one language when telling secrets and talking about personal things, and the other for wider communication . . . All such naturally occurring sociolinguistic variables act as markers of which language is which, together with features of the languages themselves, such as pronunciation, word order, etc., and contribute to children knowing when each language is appropriate (Meisel 1987). There are, however, many situations where bilinguals find it appropriate to switch between the languages. As Shana Poplack says in the title of her famous article, 'Sometimes I'll start a sentence in English y termino en Espanol' (Poplack 1980). Let's look at code-switching a little more.

## Code-switching

Code-switching is a hotly debated issue: How should we define it? Does it signal a high degree or a low degree of bilingual skill? Is it good for children to be exposed to code-switching in the input? Going into all the issues is well beyond the scope of this chapter, so let me just give my own view of code-switching and leave you to read further on the topic if it interests you. The definition of code-switching that I will use includes *any* use of more than one language in a single utterance or conversation (other than using fully absorbed borrowed words or phrases such as khaki or *fait accompli* in English).

### Exercise 3

Here are some examples of code-switching from bilingual children. Test your knowledge of languages. What are the languages of each example and where does the switch occur? Can you make any generalisation about the most common type of code-switching from these examples? (The answers are at the end of the chapter.)

| | |
|---|---|
| Mario (3;6) | 'Un juguete para el baby.' |
| | 'A toy for baby.' |
| Mario (6;3) | 'Yo lo voy a lokar.' |
| | 'I am going to lock it.' |
| Chr. (3;0) | 'Non, das ist ein cadeau.' |
| | 'No, that is a present.' |

Sammy (6;0)   'Rádóó lunchgo yiijah łeh.'
              'Then we usually run along to lunch.'
Isaac (4;3)   'Alikugya mubedroom.'
              'He's going into the bedroom.'

The most common form of code-switching involves the use of nouns from one language in utterances from the other, as in 'Will there be a *piñata* at the party today?' (A *piñata* is a sweet-filled, suspended paper container, often in the shape of an animal, which blind-folded children attempt to hit until the structure bursts to release the sweets.) Nouns are also the most common permanently *borrowed* items from one language to another, so it seems to be a very common process, probably because it usually does not disturb either language very much, although borrowing from a language that has inflectional endings on nouns, such as gender marking, into a language that does not, or which assigns a different gender from the source language, may create problems.

In some code-switching situations, the systematic use of words from another language has led to concern that children may not know the equivalent in the language they are speaking. For example, parents of Navajo-speaking children show concern for the number of English words that are used in Navajo. The fact is that each child and each situation may be different: some children may know the Navajo word and may be making very deliberate choices of appropriateness for the context. Other children may not know or may not be sure of the Navajo equivalent. Code-switching of nouns from one language into the sentence structure of another, therefore, need not be indicative of a lack of knowledge of either language's vocabulary. In fact, it may be indicative of high levels of sophistication in bilingual language use (Lindholm and Padilla 1978). So, rather than being a strategy for coping with a lack of knowledge, code-switching is a way of exploiting the resources of both languages, allowing speakers to be more precise in cases where one language does not have a perfect equivalent in another, to express group solidarity with other bilinguals by switching into the shared minority language, to exclude someone in the conversation by switching to a language that person does not understand, etc.

Children (and adults) may switch the spoken equivalents of whole paragraphs, of whole sentences, or of parts of sentences, as in the title of Shana Poplack's article above. A number of constraints on where it is possible to switch have been proposed, and this is currently a topic of considerable debate, both within linguistic theory and from other perspectives. The most that can be said at the moment is that, given any specified pair of languages, there may be constraints – for example, there is evidence that when the languages involved are Spanish and English, switching between a word and its bound inflectional ending is not allowed – but such constraints do not generalise to all languages. In Navajo and English, for example, English words brought into Navajo as code-switched items commonly receive Navajo verbal morphology attached, and thus reflect a switch between morphemes. For example, in the first example below, the prefix 'bi-', which means 'his/her', has been attached to the English word 'sister'. In the second example, the question suffix '-ish' has been added to the English word 'everyday'.

(14)  Da' Roy bisister?
      Q-Roy his-sister
      'Do you mean Roy's sister?'
(15)  Everydayísh nání łtééh doo?
      everyday-Q you-bring-him/her future-marker
      'Will you bring him/her every day?'

It seems that the typological relationship between the languages constrains the nature of the code-switching (Basena 1995). The extent to which such variability can ultimately be explained in terms of universal underlying constraints remains to be seen (Woolford 1983).

What seems to be clear from the debate over code-switching is that speakers of all ages do it, that it is in most cases indicative of bilingual proficiency, and that code-switching is a legitimate language use – a way of using language that is available only to bilinguals. Many children are exposed to highly code-switched input in their language experience, and yet they do seem to acquire both languages and be able to manipulate where and when they themselves code-switch. There is some evidence that children may have to learn (perhaps through not being understood at times) when they cannot switch, and there are some suggestions in the literature that when the input language involves a great deal of code-switching, the separation of the two languages is somewhat delayed; although, when evaluating a claim like this, one always has to ask how the knowledge of the two different languages is being tested, and whether code-switching is accepted as a normal feature of language use in the community.

## Exercise 4

Isaac is the son of my colleague David Basena. Isaac moved to the United States when he was four, speaking only Lusoga, the African language spoken by his parents. He started playing with English-speaking friends, and, later, going to an English-speaking school. Here are some of Isaac's early English–Lusoga utterances. Is he code-switching, or has he not separated the languages? In each case, what Isaac said is presented first, then a version of his utterance that shows the boundaries between each morpheme, then a morpheme by morpheme 'gloss' (direct translation) of his utterance, then a free translation into English, and then what the utterance would look like if it were entirely in Lusoga.

1    Alikugya home.
      A-li-kugya home
      he/she-is-going home
      He/She is going home.
      Alikugya ka.
2    Alikugya mubedroom.
      A-li-kugya mu-bedroom
      he/she-is-going to-bedroom
      He/She is going to the bedroom.
      Alikugya mukisenge.
3    Bali kuschool.
      ba-ali ku-school
      they-are at-school
      They are at school.
      Bali kwisomero.
4    Daddy, oyo ali friend we?
      Daddy, oyo ali friend we?
      Daddy, that-one is friend his/hers?
      Daddy, is that his/her friend?
      Daddy, oyo ali mukwano gwe?

(A possible response to the questions is provided at the end of this chapter.)

Bilingual language development offers a window on children's abilities to develop multiple systems, and to learn how to use them both singly and in combination. From the point of view of a UG parametric approach to acquisition, however, it raises issues which have yet to be fully dealt with. Clearly, there has to be some modification to the basic idea of a UG with a set of parameters set to particular language values on the basis of experience with language input. Are there, for example, multiple copies of the UG parameters waiting to be set just in case bilingual or multi-lingual language acquisition is called for? If there are, how many sets are there? We don't have any evidence for a limit on the number of languages that can be learned simultaneously, so it would not make sense to put any upper limit on the number of parameter sets waiting in the newborn brain. Maybe instead we should think in terms of a single set of parameters which get fixed in multiple ways, each setting being tagged with the language that that setting belongs to. So, if a child is learning a language with pro-drop and a language without, there will be two settings for that parameter: one that says (+ Italian) and the other that says (+ English), or whatever the two languages happen to be.

Finally in this chapter, let's take a slightly closer look at children learning second languages after the age of three.

## Child second language development

We know that children learning a second language are remarkably successful at it. This has suggested to many researchers that second language acquisition by children within the 'critical period' shows the same kind of success as first language acquisition. Such successful acquisition, however, is most likely in natural situations rather than unnatural ones such as language classrooms, where children often do less well than adults (at least with most methods).

In a study of the second language acquisition of school-aged children, Lilly Wong Fillmore (1976, 1983) found that Spanish-speaking and Chinese-speaking children learning English in the street from their friends used a number of strategies which seemed to work rather well for them.

### Exercise 5

Below are some data from Nora, a Spanish speaker studied by Wong Fillmore. (These data are from Wong Fillmore (1976), as presented in Lindfors (1987).) How would you characterise the strategy Nora is using and the way she moves through the various stages shown here?

Stage 1    'How do you do dese?'
           'How do you do dese?'
Stage 2    'How do you do dese little tortillas?'
           'How do you do dese in English?'
           'How do you do dese September por manana?'

Stage 3   'How do you like to be a cookie cutter?'
           'How do you make the flower?'
           'How do you gonna make these?'
           'How did you lost it?'
           'How did you make it?'
Stage 4   'How did dese work?'
           'How do cut it?'
           'How does this colour is?'
Stage 5   'Because when I call him, how I put the number?'
           'How you make it?'
           'How will take off paste?'

(A suggested solution to this exercise is presented at the end of the chapter.)

Here is Wong Fillmore's full list of strategies:

1   Assume that what people are saying is directly relevant to the situation at hand or to what they or you are experiencing.
2   Join a group and act as if you understand what's going on, even if you don't.
3   Count on your friends for help.
4   Work on big things; save the details for later.
5   Get some expressions you understand and start talking.
6   Make the most of what you've got.
7   Give the impression – with a few well-chosen words – that you speak the language.
8   Look for recurring parts in the formulas you know.

Although these strategies were deduced from watching children learning a second language, it should be obvious that they are equally valid in first language acquisition, and represent mostly social and attitudinal aspects of language learning.

The issue of what UG does in cases of second language acquisition rather than early bilingual acquisition is still much-debated. However, there are many who argue that at least some aspects of UG are available for second language acquisition. Those who argue against UG being involved in second language acquisition suggest that second language acquisition is qualitatively different from first language acquisition (monolingual or bilingual), and that learning a second language engages problem-solving and general learning strategies that could as easily be applied to the learning of mathematics or music. Frankly, I think we are a long way away from solving this particular conundrum, but you might find the debate an interesting one to enter. A few sources to get you going if you want to look further into this issue are provided at the end of the chapter.

Whether children become bilingual by dual first language development or by second language development, there are several indications that being bilingual means more than simply having access to two codes. Among the advantages that have been claimed are an increased ability to be a flexible thinker, more understanding of bicultural issues, a greater ability to think and talk *about* language (see Chapter 8), a greater facility for learning subsequent languages, and, often, an ability to translate. Ellen Bialystok (1986b, 1991), for example, has shown that bilingual children are better at certain kinds of metalinguistic tasks that require them to analyse sentences and manipulate them in certain ways. For instance, in one task, she asked children to substitute the word 'spaghetti' for every instance of 'they', so that when they heard the sentence 'They are good children' they had to say, 'Spaghetti are good children'. In another task, Galambos and Goldin-Meadow (1990) compared the ability of monolingual children with that of bilingual children to note syntactic errors, correct them and explain them. They found that bilingual children were better at both detecting and correcting errors than the monolinguals, although equally good as the monolinguals at explaining them. Since school tasks often demand manipulation of language, it is important that bilingual children seem to be better at it at a younger age. (Further discussion of metalinguistic abilities is in Chapter 8.)

The ability to translate well from one language to another requires a high degree of proficiency in both languages, as well as a high degree of metalinguistic ability. In many communities, quite young children are drafted by their elders as translators for business transactions, encounters with medical and school personnel, etc. Not all bilingual children (or adults) are naturally good translators, although they can develop their skill levels with practice and instruction; and they are often better translators in one direction than the other (e.g. better at Spanish to English than English to Spanish) (Malakoff and Hakuta 1991).

I have focused here mostly on the psycholinguistic aspects of becoming bilingual, in line with the basic approach of this book, but it needs to be stated that bilingualism is a much debated social and educational issue, so I have included in the further reading section references which will allow you to explore these issues should you wish to.

## Discussion of in-text exercises

Exercise 3

Mario is switching between Spanish and English; Chr. between German and French; Sammy between Navajo and English; and Isaac between Lusoga and English. The switch occurs when a word from one language is inserted into a sentence of the other. That inserted word may stand alone, as in 'cadeau' or 'baby', or it may have morphology attached to it from the host, or receiving, language, as in 'lokar', 'lunchgo' and 'mubedroom'. All the examples of switching here involve nouns, and that is, in fact, the most common kind of switching: the insertion of a noun from one language into a sentence of the other language.

Exercise 4

All these utterances show Lusoga syntax with words from English inserted. However, because English has the same SVO word order as Lusoga, one might try to argue that utterances (1), (2) and (3) are English with Lusoga words added. Although this might be made to work for utterance (1), in utterances (2) and (3) the fact that Lusoga morphemes actually attach themselves to English words suggests that Lusoga is, as it were, in control of these utterances. (If you try to argue that prepositions 'mu' and 'ku' are separate words, as they would be in English, then the Lusoga becomes ungrammatical because these words cannot appear alone. They must be attached to nouns.) Example (4) must be Lusoga with English words because the Lusoga possessive pronoun 'we' which means 'his/hers' follows the word 'friend', which is how it's done in Lusoga, but not how it's done in English. So, there is every evidence from these utterances that Isaac knows Lusoga syntax and morphology; he simply uses English vocabulary from time to time. This pattern of behaviour is very typical. I found exactly the same when I looked at young Navajo–English bilinguals.

Exercise 5

Stage 1 shows a fixed phrase picked up and used invariantly; stage 2 shows additions to the fixed phrase, but with no internal modification of it. Stage 3 shows the fixed phrase beginning to be analysed and independently formulated with the 'How do you' preserved, but the verb and complements creatively substituted: this stage also shows the beginning of the ability to modify the original fixed phrase by altering the tense of 'do' to 'did'. Stage 4 shows that the verbal structure of the original fixed phrase is sufficiently understood that variations in tense become possible, and stage 5 shows complete independence from the fixed phrase. Notice that independence from the fixed phrase is an advance in the learner's grammar, even though it produces errors that are not produced when the phrase is first used unanalysed. So the strategy seems to be to pick up and use a fixed form, and then gradually modify sections of it, unpacking the structure, until the internal parts of the original formula are independently controlled.

## Questions for discussion

1    If we assume that UG is not a reasonable hypothesis for the acquisition of language, how should we set about explaining the similar paths and rates of language development in different language communities? (See below.)

2    In what ways do you think the acquisition of different dialects can be compared to the acquisition of different languages? (See below.)

3    I have only touched on the issue of the discourse pragmatic skills of bilinguals. What issues arise when we think about how individuals can function not only with two (or more) grammars (syntax, morphology, semantics, etc.), but also with two (or more) sets of ways of *using* their languages – to be polite, to ask for information, etc.? What happens when an individual is bilingual in two languages/cultures, one of which, for example, views information as something to be guarded and possessed as a source of power (e.g. in Malagasy), and the other views information as something to be freely shared in the forming of social relationships (e.g. many English-speaking communities)? (See below for some suggestions.)

4    An issue that frequently arises in the literature on child bilingualism is that of *language dominance*. Informally, this is the idea that a child might be more competent in one language than in the other. Given the discussion in this chapter, what problems arise with this definition? How might you define it better? How might you test for language dominance? What are the educational implications of identifying (correctly and/or incorrectly) a child's dominant language? (See below, and the further reading section.)

## Some activities

1    Search the literature for descriptions of the acquisition of a language other than English by a child younger than two. (The

volumes by Dan Slobin (see below) are an excellent place to start.) Extract, from whatever sources you can find, as many sentences as you can, together with the ages at which they were said. Order them by age, and then try to observe the distribution of subjects. (If you are looking at a language you do not know, you will need to work with data that has 'glosses', i.e. morpheme by morpheme translations.) Try to decide whether each sentence has a full noun phrase for its subject, a pronoun, or nothing at all. You will find that many of the utterances you thought were sentences turn out to be only fragments, so make sure that in each case you have a full main verb. Then try to compare what you have found with the claims that appear in this chapter about the dropping of subject pronouns (pro-drop) in early child language.

2    How many exposures does it take to learn a word? Are morphologically complex words harder to learn than simple ones? Are long ones harder to learn than short ones? Are words for concrete things easier to learn than words for abstract ones? Design an experiment to test one or more of these questions using made-up words that 'ought' to be English words, but are not. For example, 'a gloop', 'to cafferate' and 'piffy' are all words that could (phonologically and in terms of bound morphology) be part of the English language, but are not (to my knowledge, though some young person may well have already coined them). Find suitable meanings for your own set of made-up words and ways to illustrate them to children, and try to teach a young child (aged between four and seven) your words. Do not, however, assign meanings to your fake words that are the same as meanings the child already possesses because (as noted earlier) children appear not to like exact synonyms. For example, you could suggest that 'a flinder' is a particular kind of car, but it must be special enough not to be rejected because the child already possesses the word 'car'. You can, if you like, use rare existing words that the child you are studying will not have heard, so long as you are sure the child has not already had any exposure to them. How do the results of your experiment square with the rapid growth of vocabulary reported in the literature? (See below for some pointers.)

3    Use the CHILDES database to retrieve one or more of the bilingual transcripts stored there. (See Appendix 1, p. 208.) Work through the transcript pulling out all the code-switching examples you can find. Catalogue them according to their linguistic structural characteristics (e.g. is the switch at a word boundary, phrase boundary, sentence boundary, etc.) and discuss the types of switching you find, the possible communicative reasons for the switch, and whether the language of the

transcript does or does not provide evidence in favour of the proposition that code-switching correlates with higher levels of bilingual skill.

## Solutions to and comments on discussion questions and activities

Discussion question 1

If there is no genetic underpinning to language acquisition, then similarities must be accounted for by similarities of experience and/or similarities of human information processing that are not specifically linguistic. The burden of proof for either of these approaches (or, more likely, a mix of the two) lies with those who espouse them. Piaget's approach, for example, argued for language acquisition being simply an extension of pre-linguistic experience with the world, and some basic processing mechanisms (assimilation, accommodation). In my view, his account does not come even close to explaining the complexities of wh-movement, or even the success children have with basic word order across the world's languages. I still think it is important, however, to pursue the possibility that there is no specifically linguistic genetic component to language acquisition. If nothing else, without the debate that is sparked off by competing approaches, there would be little chance of genuine advance in the field, and every chance of serious stagnation of ideas.

Discussion question 2

This question is particularly interesting to contemplate in light of current discussions about the rights of minority children to have their particular dialects recognised as bona fide languages rather than treated as corruptions (e.g. the 'ebonics' debate in the US about the validity of Black English dialect). There should not be any doubt that all dialects are equally linguistically sophisticated, even if some are negatively valued politically. Therefore, understanding how different dialects of a language are acquired by children as their first dialect is simply what this book is about. Any given dialect of a language poses exactly the same questions about how it is acquired as any other, just as the acquisition of different languages poses the same questions. A description/explanation of the acquisition of one dialect of a language will, however, need to be adjusted to a greater or lesser extent to account for other dialects of the same language. If the UG story is correct, however, it will not need to be adjusted any more than for different languages.

### Discussion question 3

In a modular view of language ability, pragmatic knowledge and skills are viewed as outside, and independent of, the structural aspects of language; they are also often regarded as part of more general cognition, rather than peculiarly linguistic. Bicultural bilinguals may thus not store their pragmatic knowledge along with the linguistic system it goes with, but rather in a central processor independent of language. This central store would then need to contain information about how languages are used, but without locking the user into only certain kinds of behaviours with a certain language. The implication is that bilinguals can choose to use each of their languages appropriately or not, as they see fit. The ability to use language appropriately is acquired by long years of observation, and often as a result of direct negative evidence (negative evidence that seems to be effective, unlike in the acquisition of syntax). Thus, children are taught overtly how to argue, how to be polite, what information not to give away, and they are often punished for getting it wrong. Learning the differences between language use in more than one culture is a burden on the bilingual, and very hard for the second language learner to get right. Many second language learners feel that the pragmatics of their first language seem so natural, so defining of themselves, in fact, that though they may learn the structural characteristics of the new language, they continue to find it a struggle to behave pragmatically as required.

### Discussion question 4

There are multiple ways language dominance might be defined. These include suggesting that the language that provides the syntax in a code-switched utterance is dominant (but then we have to justify the assumption that the syntax is basic), or we could say that the language that is chosen more easily is dominant (but then we have to say where and when, because in one situation, one language might be most natural, and in another, the other one might be), or we could say that the first language learned is dominant (but then we know that very young children may acquire second languages that they come to view as their main/strongest language). So perhaps we should say that the language the bilinguals themselves view as dominant is dominant (but then on what criteria are they judging?). Some might say that the dominant language is the language of dreams, but even my second language learning children dream in both languages (as evidenced by their talking in their sleep in both English and French). No good test of dominance exists, and the sensible thing to do in my opinion is to define it situationally. So, if a child at school finds it easier/more natural to work in one language than in the other, then that is the dominant language *in that situation*, and appropriate steps need to be taken to develop the language that is non-dominant in that situation.

Activity 2
Some issues to bear in mind: Pictures help children learn words, so do actions (kinesthetic learning). Stories that contextualise words are also very effective. To give your child the best possible chance of learning your words, give him or her a variety of exposures to each word, but make sure each word receives exactly the same number and types of exposure. In testing whether the child knows the word, you might give him or her a sentence completion test, or ask the child to identify a picture, or define the word. Whatever you choose, make sure that you are not setting tasks that are too difficult for the child. Read about metalinguistic awareness in Chapter 8 before you plan your experiment. It would be a shame if your word teaching failed because the means used to test it was beyond your child's capabilities.

## Further reading

If you would like to know where to start in modern Chomskyan linguistic theory, I recommend Radford (1997), which, like his earlier introductions to the same area, is a model of clarity and comprehensibility.

Research on cross-linguistic acquisition has been rendered an enduring and important service by the publication of a series of volumes edited by Dan Slobin (1985, 1992, 1996, 1997). There are currently five volumes, and they cover languages as different as French, Hebrew, K'iche', Warlpiri, German, Greenlandic, Japanese, Polish and Samoan. I recommend these volumes extremely highly because they present together, in an easily accessible form, important data that can form the basis for understanding what is acquired and when. They also present information which any approach to language acquisition, whether it is grounded in linguistic theory and UG or not, must account for in some way.

Goodluck (1991) is an excellent summary of the state of our knowledge of the linguistic characteristics of language development both early and late. In particular, for the purposes of this chapter, she gives a very lucid summary of work in the development of syntax within Chomsky's Government and Binding theory, and provides a very good summary of the theoretical ideas needed to understand the research in that paradigm. Levy (1994) is a volume of papers which address many of the issues introduced in this chapter. Similarly, the two-volume set of books edited by Barbara Lust and her colleagues (1994) provides a summary of current thinking in cross-linguistic language acquisition within a UG perspective. Both books are advanced texts.

Hoffmann (1991) is a useful overview of issues in bilingual language development, as is Romaine (1989). I also recommend the rather older, but still useful, book by Grosjean (1982). Another very readable account is Hakuta (1986). I would suggest that you read the psycholinguistically oriented chapters from these in conjunction with my book; but you should also find the sociolinguistic and language planning aspects of bilingualism covered in these books very useful.

Students interested in reading more about second language acquisition and the debate over whether UG is involved or not might like to look at the set of volumes on this issue published by John Benjamins (Amsterdam). Five of these volumes are: White (1989), Eubank (1991), Huebner and Ferguson (1991), Meisel (1994) and Lakshmanan (1994). These are all advanced texts. A general overview of second language acquisition at a lower level is Larsen-Freeman and Long (1991).

## CHAPTER 8

# When does language development stop?

## Chapter summary

This chapter is about language acquisition beyond early childhood. It tries to give a sense of the kinds of things that are still developing even as late as the late teenage years, including later oral language skills, the ability to read and write, and metalinguistic skills. Since metalinguistic skills start early, this section of the chapter also takes us back, full-circle if you like, to some of the youngest ages we saw at the beginning of this book.

## Later oral language development

While the research literature in education has always focused on later language development, it has only been fairly recently that linguists have turned their attention to language development after the age of about five or six. There are a number of reasons for this relative neglect. One is the sense that the hard part is done by the age of five, and that change thereafter is slow, and mostly schooled rather than developing naturally. Another is that older children are generally shyer and more silent around researchers than younger children and thus exhibit less 'data' for capture (Stephens 1988). Moreover, since older children are aware that their language can be deliberately modified for the audience, their performances are often stilted and less natural than those of younger children. And, finally, older children are much more mobile. The most interesting language may be happening at twenty miles an hour on a skateboard. Clearly, these are not ideal recording conditions!

There are, broadly, two types of studies of later language development available in the literature. The first type are studies of syntactic, morphological or other developments which include both younger and older children because the features

being studied are not acquired until late childhood or adoles-
cence. The second type are those carried out by researchers
interested specifically in the linguistic characteristics of children
in school. Often these studies are broader-based surveys designed
to give an overall picture not of one particular linguistic structure, but of the totality of children's linguistic systems. Both
sorts of studies form the basis for this discussion, and for that
provided by Perera (1984), still an excellent summary, and one
which I have made considerable use of in what follows.

## Preferred clause structures

Although children are capable of using a range of clause patterns
by the time they start school, they tend to use just a few most
of the time (simple, active ones without extensive modification).
Older children and adolescents, however, make increasing use
of the full range of clause types that they learned when they
were young. As Perera says, children progressing through school,
'gradually display greater control and fluency in their handling'
of the different basic clausal types (Perera 1984: 97).

Passive constructions are a rare type of clause structure in
English adult speech, and they are rare in children's speech.
O'Donnell *et al.* (1967) found that only one out of every 120
utterances in the narratives of English speakers studied were
passives, even at age 13;0. (Remember that they are much
more common in the speech of users of certain other languages, such as Inuktitut and Sesotho.) Horgan (1978) studied
passives elicited from children aged 2;0 to 13;0 and found
them used from 3;0 up, but they were not used in any significant
numbers until 5;0, when, as already noted, they were still
pretty infrequent and they were not used by a very large
proportion of the children. Horgan also made what Perera
(1984: 126) notes is a 'rather surprising discovery' – that children showed a preference for a certain type of passive. Some
of her subjects used semantically reversible passives (e.g. 'The
dog was chased by the cat', where it is equally plausible that
the dog should chase the cat) and others used non-reversible
passives (e.g. 'The flowers were watered by the girl', where it
is not plausible that the flowers watered the girl). The odd
thing is that children under 11;0 used either one type or the
other, but not both.

Helen Goodluck (Goodluck and Birch 1988; Goodluck and
Behne 1992) suggests that the period from five to ten is also

one in which children move 'away from a reliance on thematic relations (agent, patient, etc.) in interpreting various constructions' (Goodluck 1991: 99). To see what this means, consider the following sentences from Goodluck:

(1)    Fred kissed Jane before leaving.
(2)    Jane was kissed by Fred before leaving.

Who did the leaving? For (1) you probably said 'Fred', and in (2) you probably said 'Jane'. In other words, you chose the subject of the sentence in both cases. Young children, however, often choose Fred in both of these sentences because they interpret the leaving as being done by the one who did the kissing. That is, their interpretation is based on the roles the protagonists play in the utterance, rather than on syntactic position. As they grow through the middle childhood years, however, their interpretations become increasingly adult-like.

Children in middle childhood must also give up other tendencies which affect their responses to linguistic structures. While children aged five appear to have a good grasp of relative clause structures, sentences which include a number of different protagonists and events often lead them to make mistakes in interpretation. So, for example, Amy Sheldon tested children's interpretations of sentences such as (3) and (4).

(3)    The dog that jumps over the pig bumps into the lion.
(4)    The pig bumps into the horse that jumps over the giraffe.

In (3) the dog does both the jumping and the bumping, but in (4) the pig does the bumping and the horse does the jumping. Children, however, have a tendency to assume that the same animal does both actions in both cases and will therefore misinterpret (4) as meaning that the pig both bumps into the horse and jumps over the giraffe (Sheldon 1974). This kind of interpretation should probably not be regarded as evidence of incomplete learning of relative clauses. Rather, as Goodluck (1990) has suggested, it is probably a strategy for coping with an on-line processing problem when the going gets tough. And in school-based comprehension tasks, the going often does get tough.

There are, perhaps, just a few constructions which children may truly learn during their school years. These include the strange and wonderful constructions of literary language and archaic/historical constructions. If you have ever seen a child struggle to understand Shakespeare, for example, you can quite

clearly see that there is a certain recognition that this is indeed
English, but a clear frustration that it is initially very hard to
understand, and takes work to become easily readable. English
teachers are really asking children to learn to comprehend another
dialect in which word order and other grammatical features are
different enough to mean some genuine new learning.

> Friends, Romans, countrymen, lend me your ears.
> I come to bury Caesar, not to praise him.
> *Julius Caesar*, Act 3, scene 2

is easy enough, but what of,

> What is a man,
> If his chief good and market of his time
> Be but to sleep and feed? A beast, no more.
> Sure he that made us with such large discourse,
> Looking before and after, gave us not
> That capability and godlike reason
> To fust in us unused.
> *Hamlet*, Act 4, scene 4

## Noun structures

Older children start using more adjectives and other premodi-
fiers, such as numbers ('Here's a white puppy', 'I have three
cats'). Post-modification of a noun by using a prepositional
phrase ('The man with the umbrella') is usually acquired during pre-school, but is not much used by the 5;0 to 12;0 age
group, except by high ability children, but then increases in
use after age 12. Perera concludes, on the basis of this and
other research, that adult norms for noun modifiers are not
reached until age 15;0 or 16;0. Interestingly, there seems to
be a preference for simpler subjects and more complex objects:
so, 'Whoever gets the most wins' is less likely to occur than 'I
know how to make televisions' (Fawcett and Perkins 1980).

## Verb structures

Although we tend to think of past tense errors such as, 'I
brung it' as being typical of quite young children, they actually
continue well on into the school years. Fawcett and Perkins'
(1980) data show errors such as 'keeped', 'builded', and 'drawed'
produced by eight-year-olds who are otherwise acquiring the
standard dialect forms.

Carol Chomsky's (1969) study of verb exceptions pioneered linguistic studies of later language development. It looked at the problem posed for children by a verb such as 'promise', which does not behave in the same way as the verbs 'expect', 'want' or 'persuade'. Thus, 'John expected/wanted/persuaded Bill to leave' should, or may, result in Bill leaving. But 'John promised Bill to leave' should result in John leaving. Children continue to have problems with this verb until well into late childhood. She also looked at the difference between adjectives such as 'eager' and 'easy', which not only mean different things, but result in a different set of relationships understood from the sentence. 'John is easy to see' implies that it is easy for someone to see John, whereas 'John is eager to see' implies that John is eager to see someone else, but even eight-and-a-half-year-olds give wrong answers to questions based on this difference.

Other, similar kinds, of persistent errors surround negation. The error, so typical of younger children, of not shifting the tense to the auxiliary in a negative (leading to '*I didn't did it' instead of 'I didn't do it') may not be entirely eradicated until after 6;0. Moreover, children well into their school years still do not get polarity items such as 'some' and 'any' right in their negative sentences (e.g. '*I haven't got some pencils', instead of 'I haven't got any pencils'), and the so-called double negative ('I haven't got no pencils') is common not only among children whose local dialect supports it, but also among those who will eventually lose it. A study carried out by Harris (1975) in which children aged 4;0 to 11;0 were presented with sentences such as 'The teacher did not know that Tim was not absent' and were then asked, 'Was Tim absent?', showed that only 60 per cent of the children could answer correctly. Similarly, Reid (1972) found that seven-year-olds, asked to read 'Tom's mother was anything but pleased' and asked, 'Was Tom's mother pleased?', did much worse than children who read 'Tom's mother was not pleased at all' and were asked the same question.

Even more problems are created by the differences between sentences such as the following:

(5)    Mary knew that John was angry.
(6)    Mary didn't know that John was angry.
(7)    Mary pretended that John was angry.
(8)    Mary didn't pretend that John was angry.

In both (5) and (6) John is angry, but in (7) and (8) he's not angry. The different verbs in the main clauses (know versus pretend) lead to different interpretations of what is going on in the subordinate clauses. Studies of children aged 3;6 to 14;0 suggest that children take a long time to get these differences sorted out and often respond erratically for quite a while (Phinney 1981; Scoville and Gordon 1980). Interestingly, the better readers get these kinds of sentence differences sorted out earlier than poorer readers (Phinney 1981).

## Lexical development

There are nearly 500,000 words in Webster's dictionary. Meanwhile, it has been estimated that the average third grader (eight/ nine-year old) has a vocabulary of between 4,000 and 10,000 words, and the reading vocabulary of an average eighteen-year-old who has stayed in full-time education consists of around 40,000 words (plus another 40,000 for names, places and idiomatic expressions) (Nagy and Herman 1987). Initially, young children learn all their words from their spoken environment (see Chapter 5). But when they enter school and begin to read, they add to their vocabulary through the words they read. Adams (1990) estimates that 800 to 1,200 new words are learned from reading each year. The rest of the estimated 3,000 new words learned each year are picked up from the oral language around children, from direct teaching and overt word learning through vocabulary lists, direct explanations of the words, etc. It is sobering to think that 3,000 words a year is an acquisition rate of about eight new words a day, come rain, come shine, day in, day out!

## Pragmatic aspects of later language development

Although there are a number of quite significant changes in the structural system during the school years, researchers such as Karmiloff-Smith (1986) see much greater changes taking place in the functional system during these same years.

## Connecting text

Developing the structure of extended pieces of discourse is a very significant part of later language development, and it is during this period that children become adept at producing (and reproducing upon request) quite extended stories and accounts in both formal and informal situations. In her study of children aged 4;0 to 9;0 producing narratives from picture books with no text, Karmiloff-Smith found that four-year-olds produce rather differently constructed stories compared with those produced by children over five. Here are two examples (Karmiloff-Smith 1986: 470): the first is from a younger child (under five), the second from an older one (over five):

(9)  There's a boy and a girl. He's going fishing and she's going to make sandcastles. So he takes her bucket and . . . she tries to grab it back and he runs off with it, so she sits there crying by the tree. Now he can do his fishing. He got four fish.
(10) There is a boy and a girl. He's going to catch fish so he takes the girl's bucket and he runs off and catches lots of fish.

**Exercise 1**

What are the differences between these two stories? Take a minute to jot them down before continuing reading.

Clearly, the younger child's story is longer than the older one's, and there are more details provided in the former than in the latter. From this point of view (coverage of information), the younger child appears to have done a better job. However, from a linguistic point of view, there are some things which make the younger child's account less sophisticated than the older child's. One is that the subject of every clause is included in the younger child's story. In the older child's story, we find 'he runs off and catches lots of fish', where the subject of 'catches' is understood to be the boy, but is not expressed. This difference is in fact indicative of a general and broad difference between the two versions of the story. The older child is obeying what Karmiloff-Smith calls the 'thematic subject constraint'. All of the subjects in the second story, once the two protagonists (the girl and the boy) have been introduced in the first sentence, are the same person – the boy. The fact that it is the same person allows the older child to omit explicit reference to the boy in the last clause of the story without losing any information, and the result is a smoother flowing text. The younger child's story does not obey the 'thematic subject constraint'.

## Exercise 2

What are the subjects in the first story above? What is the effect of the way the child uses subjects in this story? (The answer is given at the end of the chapter.)

Obviously, adult stories do not rigidly obey the 'thematic subject constraint', so it is only a matter of time and development before children, too, begin to relax it. By about eight or nine, children begin to use a variety of other linguistic devices to ensure that their stories hang together, including varying between noun phrase, pronoun and zero pronoun (as we saw in the second story above). Here's a more sophisticated version of the story:

(11)    There's a girl and a boy. The boy wants to go fishing, so he tries to get the girl's bucket, but the girl won't let him take it, so he grabs it out of her hand and the girl chases after him, but he gets away from the girl and he starts to fish while the girl sits there crying. He goes home smiling with four fish. (*ibid.*: 471)

## Exercise 3

Analyse the story above in terms of the way the subjects of the clauses work throughout the text, just as you did in Exercise 2. Then examine other indicators that this story was produced by an older and more linguistically competent child. Pay particular attention to the words that link clauses together. Then, go back and compare all three stories in as many ways as you can (content, discourse structure, choice of words, choice of constructions, etc.). (You may want to use a measure of complexity known as T-unit calculation. Instructions for doing this are presented in Appendix 1.) (See the end of the chapter for a solution.)

I have already drawn your attention to the words used to link clauses together. Collectively called 'connectives' – words such as 'and', 'so', 'but' and 'then' – they help stories stick together. Peterson and McCabe (1991) have analysed the connectives that children between 3;6 and 9;6 use in their stories, and the functions they serve. They find that 'and' is the most commonly used connective, perhaps not surprisingly since this is one of the most versatile words in the English language. It can be used to link two ideas together in myriad different ways: indicating the combining of two entities or events (Ann and Mary went to the store), ordering of events within time (I

went to the store and bought some candy), a causal relationship (I hit him and he fell down), etc. Peterson and McCabe
did not find nine-year-olds using 'and' any differently from
four-year-olds, and Scott (1984) found children continuing to
use 'and' extensively up to age 12. However, there is a range
of other connectives children use, 'then' being the second
favourite after 'and', and sometimes being combined with it
('and then'). Other common ones are 'because', 'so' and 'but'.
All these connectives serve semantic purposes in linking ideas
together causally, temporally, etc., but some of them are also
used pragmatically, to do things in the discourse – introducing
narratives, marking digressions, signalling the end of narratives,
etc. Here are a few examples from Peterson and McCabe
(1991):

(12)   Adult:   I bet you see the sun come up in the morning.
        Child:   *But* I saw the zoo. (*But* signals the beginning of a
                 narrative.) (1991: 39)
(13)   Child:   And then I fell down *but* you know what? (*But* signals
                 a digression from the time-line of the narrative.) (1991:
                 40)
(14)   Child:   David was there and my uncle Pete, *and then* I said
                 'Pete . . .' (*And then* signals a return to the time-line of
                 the chronological events of the story.) (1991: 40)

In all these examples, connectives are doing more than might
at first appear. They are connecting together ideas as well as
making clear the structure of the narrative as a successful linguistic event.

## Basic steps in learning to read

Learning to read involves different linguistic skills from those
called for up to this point. For example, children must start
paying overt attention to the sub-components of words. This
is a difficult task, as anyone who has watched a pre-reader
struggle can attest. At the age of almost four, my son became
very interested in what letter words began with and would try
to make sensible identifications. It was clear, however, that he
did not have much, if any, idea of how to listen to the beginning of the word, peel off the first sound, and then identify it
with a letter name. In consequence, he would just guess. 'Mama
starts with a "D", right?' By five, however, he was very good at
this identification, and was beginning to 'sound out' whole words,
with the help of the instruction he received in kindergarten.

(At six, these were skills he transferred quickly and easily to learning to read in French.)

Children must not only grasp the division of words into sounds (to be connected with letters), but also the division into syllables. Good readers break unfamiliar words into syllables whose structure they are able to read fluently, rather than sounding out words letter by letter. Luckily, children generally find the division of words into syllables quite easy. My son's earliest attempts to 'spell' words (at around 3;6) were in fact a sounding out of the syllables, ('El-e-phant spells elephant, right?'). Research suggests that children who can pay early attention to the syllable structure of language tend to be better readers later on, and it may be that syllable awareness precedes sound awareness. (In France, it is standard practice to teach by syllable at first rather than by sound, and the structure of French, which has fewer consonant clusters than English, lends itself well to this method.)

While the most successful readers learn quickly how to build up words from smaller components (known as 'bottom-up' learning), there is a certain amount of 'top-down' learning of whole words as gestalt chunks that goes on naturally. The global method of teaching reading exploits this, and the learning of words from the general print environment of signs and packaging, etc. is also top-down. Top-down learning has the advantage that it gives the child the impression of having entered the world of print, and of being able to read. However, there appears to be no substitute for constructing words out of sounds. The research shows, in fact, that while children do not all respond to reading instruction in the same way (some are more tolerant of/more engaged by approaches that emphasise one method over another), they all need *both* phonics (bottom-up) and a more holistic, meaning-driven (top-down) approach to learning to read.

Learning to read also calls for specific effort to understand the conventions of the writing system, deal with upper and lower case, print versus handwriting, and different typefaces. Children must cope with the fact that while the spaces between words are linguistically relevant because they mark word boundaries, the break created by the end of a line is *not* a linguistically relevant boundary. None of this is easy, and it all takes time, even for the most precocious.

Once readers have the skill, however, they can not only use written language to verify the knowledge they already possess, they can also eventually use written language to learn new information. Chall (1983) has proposed six stages in the development of reading comprehension, predicated on little or no exposure to reading instruction prior to going to school. Children whose parents have worked on reading at home at the pre-school stage often have children who show the skills described below much earlier than the ages given. The fact that this is so shows that learning to read does not happen on an automatic genetic schedule, unlike learning to use spoken (or signed) language:

Stage 1:    An initial reading and decoding stage in which children learn to connect arbitrary letters with spoken sounds (6;0–7;0).

Stage 2:    Children use reading to confirm what they already know from other sources (7;0–8;0).

Stage 3a:   Children begin to use reading to gain new knowledge (9;0–11;0)

Stage 3b:   Children begin to analyse and react to what they have read (12;0–14;0).

Stage 4:    Children begin to recognise that what they read represents multiple viewpoints and voices (14;0–18;0).

Stage 5:    Children/adults are able to use strategies of analysis and selection that allow them to make the most intelligent use of written materials (18;0 and up; many adults never reach this stage).

## Basic steps in learning to write

Several of the large-scale studies of later language development mentioned earlier in this chapter were carried out for the express purpose of understanding the writing abilities of school-aged children (Loban 1976; O'Donnell et al. 1967; Hunt 1965). Although these studies provide a fairly sparse database on which to base major conclusions about children's writing, their results do give some indications of major milestones in writing development.

It seems that between the ages of 7;0 and 18;0, the average length of clauses in writing increases. Hunt (1970) suggests that clause length grows from 6.5 words at age 8;0 to 8.6 words at age 18;0, while skilled adult writers are estimated to have an average clause length of 11.5 words. As in spoken language, the number of passive constructions is relatively small, but more passive constructions are used as children develop their writing skills. Coordination as a way of combining clauses decreases as subordination becomes more used in writing. However, all types of subordinate clause do not develop identically. Relative clauses show the greatest increase in number; adverbial and nominal clauses show less obvious increases in frequency, changing most in the variety of different types of each that are used, depending on the task they are used for. The frequency of sentence adverbials such as 'however', 'on the other hand' and 'therefore' increases as children come to understand the importance of these 'signposts' for the reader.

At the phrase level, Perera (1984) reports increases in the complexity of various types of phrases: for example, noun phrases have more adjectives before the head noun ('the little old crooked man'), and more prepositional phrases following the head noun ('the man with an umbrella with tassles on top'). Within the verb phrase, the tense and aspect system becomes more elaborated and this contributes to the complexity of the language used, at least in response to some tasks.

Kroll (1981) has suggested that there are four broad phases in learning to write:

I   *Preparation phase*   In this phase, children learn to form letters, handle a pencil, and copy words for themselves.

II   *Consolidation phase*   Children can write independently of a model to be copied, but they use in their writing only those constructions that they already use in speech, and in the same proportions. Children are probably about 7;0 when they reach this second phase.

III   *Differentiation phase*   Writing and speech become recognisably different, using some different constructions and with more of the more literary constructions appearing in the writing. Children are estimated to be about 9;0 or 10;0 when they move into this phase.

IV   *Integration phase*   The separate control of speaking and writing are complete, so that the writer can deliberately manipulate the differences and even deliberately mix them for effect. Few writers actually achieve this stage of development.

In general, 'Grammatical development in writing does not occur in a smooth, steady progression but proceeds in a series of spurts followed by fairly stable periods during which, presumably, newly acquired constructions are being consolidated. Spurts of growth are reported as occurring at about age 9 . . . and at 13 . . . and then again at 17' (Perera 1986: 497).

The last two sections have focused on linguistic and psycholinguistic milestones in the acquisition of reading and writing.

There are also, of course, many serious sociolinguistic issues surrounding the development of literacy in children. These issues
include the role of literacy in the home as compared with the
school, issues of literacy as empowerment, and cross-cultural
comparisons of literacy practices. There is a substantial literature on these sorts of issues, and, if you are interested, I urge
you to consult authors such as Duranti and Ochs (1988), Ochs
(1988), Bernstein (1971, 1990), Halliday (1978), Heath (1983),
Andersen (1992), Michaels (1991), Miller (1993), Villanueva
(1993) and Rothery (1989).

## Metalinguistic development

Although I have alluded to the need to be aware of the structure
of language in order to read and write, I have not yet focused
on metalinguistic development in general. The remainder of this
chapter does exactly that.

In Chapter 1, we saw how difficult it is to be sure what
children know about language. In that chapter, we were concerned with knowledge in the sense of 'competence'. We
were concerned, that is, with the *implicit* knowledge of their
language that children possess and that we can deduce from
listening to them use that knowledge as they speak. We saw
there that one of the problems in determining what children
know in this sense is that they cannot tell us themselves. Very
young children are not able to reflect on the knowledge they
possess or to respond to direct requests for grammaticality judgements. However, they do show, from a very early age, the first
glimmerings of being able to reflect on the system they are
using.

### Early childhood

One of the earliest metalinguistic behaviours to appear is the
ability to correct one's own speech. Clark (1978), Clark and
Andersen (1979), Iwamura (1980) and McTear (1985), among
others, have observed the repairs that children under five make
to their speech. It seems that as young as 18 months they will
repair their own utterances, either spontaneously because they
realise there is a structural or functional problem, or because
their interlocutor makes it clear they do not understand, or
demands a better attempt. They will, for example, correct the
pronunciation of a word, sometimes working through a variety

of different pronunciations for the same word (Scollon 1979) before either settling on one particular pronunciation, or (apparently) abandoning the attempt. Here are a couple of examples from Brenda, the child studied by Ron Scollon (Scollon 1979: 103,104) at the age of 1;7.

(15)   Brenda is repeating each of the numbers up to ten said by the adult. When she gets to seven, she makes two attempts at it:
A:   Seven
C:   /ʃedɛn . . . sewɛn/
(16)   In this example, the adult demands a better attempt:
A:   No, you can't step on my microphone!
B:   /məikrəʔə/
A:   Microphone! Come on, say it right.
B:   /məikʸu . . . məikʰo/

Slightly older children (aged two and up) will also correct their own syntax and word choices, although not always settling on what an adult would regard as the correct form (see Brenda in example (15) above). Clark and Andersen (1979) suggest that children are likely to correct those aspects of the system they are in the process of actively learning, since at that time they are monitoring those aspects very closely. The sorts of errors that get self-corrected are, therefore, ones which reflect an earlier stage of development, a stage that can now be improved upon. So Brenda's 'sheden' might be how she routinely said 'seven' at an earlier time, but now she realises that it needs improvement.

Older children, by contrast, catch themselves in slips of the tongue, as well as reworking utterances to make them more comprehensible for the person they are talking to. Here are a few examples from McTear (1985: 190–191). (A hyphen indicates the child corrected herself, and three dots indicates a pause.)

(17)   Heather aged 4;0: 'What- who does that say?' (said while pointing to her lunch box which has her name printed on it).
(18)   Siobhan aged 4;3: 'Do you want more some books now . . . some more books?'
(19)   Heather aged 4;10: 'Well I hurt me . . . I hurt myself.'
(20)   Siobhan aged 4;9: 'She . . . my friend Heather knows how to take it off herself.'
(21)   Siobhan aged 4;9: Just put them up . . . up there alright the crayons.'

It is only ever possible to make educated guesses about what exactly such spontaneous corrections actually mean from the

point of view of the child's system, but the following interpretations for these examples are at least plausible. In (17),
Heather replaces the wh-word at the beginning of her question, which was apparently intended to elicit the name of the
owner of the lunch box. She chooses 'who' instead of 'what'
perhaps because she believes people should be routinely referred
to by personal pronouns. The result, however, is not a well-
formed adult question, unless it was intended as part of a much
more complex utterance such as 'Who does that say the lunch
box belongs to'?

In (18), Siobhan appears to be aware that she got the word
order wrong. This is probably a slip of the tongue because
genuine word order errors are rather rare in children's language. Or maybe she originally intended to say, 'Do you want
more?', realised she needed to be explicit for her listener and
say more of what, and then back-tracked to redo the whole
noun phrase.

In (19), Heather replaces an incorrect pronoun with a correct, reflexive, one. In (20), Siobhan replaces the simple pronoun ('she') with a full noun phrase ('my friend Heather')
probably in order to be clearer for the listener. And in (21),
she is providing more information at the end of her utterance
to explicate the rather cryptic 'Just put them up', which specifies
neither what is to be put up, nor where 'up' is exactly. Again
one assumes that this is done for the benefit of the listener,
although they could, in fact, be rewordings for the benefit of
the speaker, trying to clarify her own mind.

The question now is what examples such as these tell us about
children's developing metalinguistic skills. Some researchers,
such as Gombert (1992), would not allow any of these to be
evidence of true metalinguistic skill, because in none of them
are there clear indications that the children are *consciously* aware
of the system they are appealing to when they correct themselves. However, I think it is helpful to see these early self-
corrections as indicative, albeit unconscious, of an emerging
understanding of how the language system works. There is
evidence here, for example, that four-year-olds know that
wh-words come in a variety of flavours, that word order is
important and must be got right, that pronouns are restricted
in the contexts of their use and that a reflexive must be used
when the subject and the object of the clause are the same,
and that the rules of pragmatics involve making one's message
sufficiently clear for the listener.

**Exercise 4**

Here is a short exchange between two little girls (aged 3;9 and 3;6) on their way to pre-school, playing a game where they pretend their names are different. The data were collected by Susan Iwamura and appear in her book on language play (1980). The girls' names are Suzy and Nani (whom Suzy also calls Lani).

1   S:  You say, you say what's my name.
2   N:  Suzy.
3   S:  No. You say what's my *name*.
4   N:  What's your name?
5   S:  Laur-um-Lauren.
6   N:  Say what's *my* name.
7   S:  Your name is Lani.
8   N:  No, no, what's, say 'What's your *name*?' What's *my* name?
9   S:  What's your name?
10  N:  Nan, um, I mean, um, Laurie.
11  S:  Laurie.
12  N:  Laurie.
13  S:  I mean, I mean.
14  N:  What's your *name*?
15  S:  Um, Gwynnie.
16  N:  (laugh)

What are the metalinguistic aspects of this game? What problems arise in the course of the game that the girls must solve in order to make the game work? (See the end of this chapter for a suggested solution.)

While self-repairs are a way of obtaining a natural window on young children's emerging understanding of the linguistic system, another, and much less natural, way is to ask direct or semi-direct questions of children about their linguistic knowledge. A favourite method of getting at adult linguistic knowledge is to ask for grammaticality judgements, and several researchers have attempted to do the same with children (Gleitman, Gleitman and Shipley 1972; de Villiers and de Villiers 1972; Smith and Tager-Flusberg 1982). In one of the earliest studies, Gleitman *et al.* (1972) presented three children aged 2;6 with various kinds of imperatives and asked them to say whether they were 'good' or 'silly'. There were four kinds of imperatives:

1   correct imperatives: 'Bring me the ball!'
2   telegraphic imperatives: 'Bring ball!'
3   inverted imperatives: 'Ball me the bring!'
4   inverted telegraphic imperatives: 'Ball bring!'

Although the results were only suggestive, given the small number of children studied, there did seem to be a preference for seeing the correct and telegraphic imperatives as better than the inverted and inverted telegraphic. Gleitman *et al.* suggest that while it is often hard to know the extent to which children this young have interpreted the request for the identification of silliness as a request about form or about function, there is no doubt that children this young *can* pay close and conscious attention to the formal properties of words and sentences, and thus have 'at least a muddy capacity to be reflective about knowledge' (1972: 160).

Believing that Gleitman *et al.* were probably underselling children's metalinguistic ability, Smith and Tager-Flusberg (1982) replicated Gleitman *et al.*'s 1972 imperatives study, but this time using a version of it developed by de Villiers and de Villiers (1972) in which the children had to 'help' a puppet who 'said things all the wrong way round' to talk properly. The puppet spoke correct or reversed imperatives which the child had to declare were 'right' or 'wrong', and then 'fix up' if they were 'wrong'.

In addition to the imperatives task, Smith and Tager-Flusberg had children aged 2;11 to 5;3 do five other tasks. The children had to determine whether presented sounds were 'talking sounds' or not, tell a puppet named Jed whether words rhymed with his name, and judge which of a list of words and nonsense syllables presented to them were words. They also had to answer questions about an invented language. So, for example, they were taught new words for familiar objects (e.g. a carrot is now called a 'gok') and then asked questions about the objects (e.g. 'Can you eat a gok?'). Finally, they had to help one puppet teach another to talk. They had to recognise and correct faulty morphemes produced by the 'learning' puppet.

While the youngest children behaved pretty randomly, there was some evidence of appropriate responses to these tasks even at around three. The task most likely to be got right was the word referent differentiation task in which a carrot was called a 'gok'. And by age four, there was no doubt that several of these tasks were routinely in the grasp of many of the children. These results fit much better with spontaneous evidence of close attention to language structure by four-year-olds, such as when a four-year-old child said, 'Mommy is it AN A-dult or A NUH-dult?', or another said, when his mother told him to hold on tight, 'Isn't it *tightly*?'

So, before they are five, children have begun to develop quite sophisticated metalinguistic skills. Moreover, although children at this young age tend to have difficulty separating the forms of language from their meanings, in certain tasks (such as the word-referent task), they demonstrate their ability to control the arbitrariness of language surprisingly well. (The issue of the status of words will be taken up again below.)

## Middle to late childhood

While there is considerable discussion over the issue of whether metalinguistic development is a gradual process or one in which significant and qualitative leaps occur, there is little doubt that around the age of seven, children have progressed to the point where they are capable of quite sophisticated performance on metalinguistic tasks. For example, they can judge the grammaticality of sentences by focusing only on structural information (syntax and morphology); they are not misled by the meaning of the utterance as they were at an earlier age. Similarly, when presented with ungrammatical sentences, they can not only correct morphological and minor syntactic aspects of sentences, but can sometimes, if they understand what the sentence means, also engage in major reordering of words and larger constituents (Bialystok 1986b). At seven, they are also beginning to show the effects of being taught to read and are starting to use the grammatical terminology presented in reading classes (noun, verb, etc.), in cases where they are exposed to them (Papandropoulou and Sinclair 1974). Reading teaching methods vary quite widely, and there are plenty of adults who do not know a noun from a verb.

At the pragmatic end of things, they can use sarcastic intonation as well as evidence from the context that what a speaker says cannot have been literally true; however, they do less well when intonational and other cues are not there. Seven-year-olds still have problems with 'dead-pan' sarcasm, in other words (Ackerman 1986). Similarly they now recognise that responsibility for the success of a communication lies largely with the speaker, and are beginning to understand the difference between what is said and what is meant (Bonitatibus 1988). Finally, seven-year-olds can recognise when they have made a faulty inference and can revise those inferences. In other words, where younger children usually get fixated on their first interpretation, seven-year-olds can change their minds if new information shows them that their original assumptions were wrong. If you have ever tried to argue a four-year-old out of a misinterpretation of *anything*, you will be only too aware of how wonderful dealing with a seven-year-old can be!

Two further developments that show milestones around seven are the ability to understand what words are, and the ability to understand and produce linguistic humour. The next two sections are concerned with these developments.

### What is a word to a child?

While children make use of words unconsciously to analyse the language they hear, they do not at first understand the notion of a single word as a separate linguistic entity. By seven, however, this ability has clearly emerged (Papandropoulou and Sinclair 1974). Bialystok (1986a) suggests that children are better able to identify words in some situations than in others. For example, counting words in sentences is harder than counting words in a string of unrelated words because in the former the child is unwittingly processing all the other information carried by a real sentence (the relationships between words, the overall meaning of the sentence, etc.), whereas in the latter, the child can focus on each individual word. And children who have had experience with a foreign language, and thus are used to the idea that the same thing may be called by more than one name, are better able to count words, particularly when they are multiple-syllabled words, than their monolingual counterparts (Bialystok 1986a) However, Rosenblum and Pinker (1983) argue that in fact there is no difference in the two groups' ability to recognise the arbitrariness. There is, however, a difference in how they conceive of the relationship between word and object. When asked to justify or deny a new word for an object, 'monolingual children are more likely to refer to the physical properties of an object . . . whereas bilingual children [are] more likely to refer to the social context of naming or the shared knowledge that results' (358). This is presumably because bilingual children must figure out who understands which language, and where each language is appropriate.

### Exercise 5

Some researchers argue that children are not able to recognise words as separable units of the language until the age of seven. What does the following piece of data from a four-year-old suggest about the course of development of this ability?

Avi:  What does 'Lonesome sushi' mean?
Me:   What do you mean?
Avi:  You know, in the song, 'Lonesome Sue, she's in love with old Sam'.

(See the end of the chapter for a solution.)

Templeton and Spivey (1980) carried out an experiment in which they asked children aged four to almost eight to tell them what they thought words were. They did this by asking the children a series of questions. First, they asked them if a series of words and phrases presented to them were words. For example, 'Is "house" a word?', 'Is "up and down" a word?', 'Is "the" a word?'. For each word, the children were also asked to explain why it was or was not a word. Then the experimenter asked flat out, 'What *is* a word anyway?' Finally, the children were asked, 'Please tell me a long word', 'Please tell me a short word', 'Please tell me an easy word' and 'Please tell me a hard word'. After the response to each question, the children were asked to explain their choice (e.g. 'Why is ____ a hard word?').

The results showed that the children moved through a series of stages in their answers to these questions. At the least developmentally advanced stage, the children thought that words were equivalent to some object or action. Children at this stage would not grant that function words such as 'is' and 'the' were words, for example. Other researchers have noted that young children (under 5;0) begin by thinking that a word is a property of an object like any other property such as its colour or texture (Piaget 1926/1955; Vygotsky 1962), and that they will assume that a long word represents a long or large object. For example, they will assume that the word 'snake' is longer than the word 'button' because a snake is longer than a button (Bialystok 1986a).

At the second stage, children equated words with the saying of them, responding to the question of what a word is, by saying, 'It comes out of your mouth', 'They say something, and they are a piece of things'. At the third stage, there is an effect of exposure to print, so that now words are seen as written as well as spoken entities. Often children did not talk about words being made up of separable units until they had encountered print, and then they would talk in terms of words being made up of letters, rather than sounds.

Finally, children understand that words are sequences of sounds or letters that signify in a systematic way. Children at this stage should be able to separate form and meaning and to succeed in a task such as being asked to select the word ('frog' or 'puppy') which either 'sounds the same' or 'means the same' as 'dog' (Bialystok 1986a). By about seven, children are able to do these kinds of tasks quite well.

Giving word definitions is perhaps the height of sophistic-ated understanding of the nature of words, and the develop-ment of this ability continues into adulthood. McGhee-Bidlack (1991) tested 10-, 14- and 18-year-olds on their ability to give noun definitions. They each had to define eight concrete and eight abstract nouns. She found that it was not until 18 years of age that they began to define abstract nouns in the ways they define concrete ones, that is, mainly by referring to the class of things involved ('A flower is a plant', 'Courage is a state of mind') and to the characteristics of the notion involved ('A flower is beautiful', 'Freedom is being able to do what you want to do'). Up until that age, they tended to use only examples as definitions of abstract items ('Courage is when I stand up to a bully') or to give synonyms ('A bush is a shrub'). The clear conclusion is that giving definitions of abstract nouns is harder than giving definitions of concrete ones, perhaps because it is easier to define words which call for reference to perceptible elements which have size, shape, etc. than those which do not. It is also clear that teenagers become increas-ingly familiar with the metalinguistic form of a definition, and are better able to produce it provided they are given overt opportunities to practise the skill.

Overall, then, this research suggests that the concept of word emerges gradually. Around the age of seven, children seem largely to have grasped the concept, helped in great measure by their exposure to written language in school.

Children's humour

(22)  N:  So? (pause) So?
      S:  So?⎤
      N:  So?⎥
      S:  So?⎥
      N:  So?⎦
      S:  ⎰So, so, so, so, so, so, so, so, so, so, so, ⎰so.
      N:  ⎱So. So. So. So. Now, now, now, now.⎱Now you say yes, and I say no. No, no, no, no.

       S:   Ye-e-es.
       N:   No. ⎡No. No, no, no, no, no, no, no. You say no
                ⎪ and I say yes. ⎧
       S:      ⎪ Ye-e-es.    ⎩No, no.
                ⎣
       N:   Yes, yes, yes, yes. Yes. Your home.
       (from Iwamura 1980)
(23)  Five fat frogs fly past fast
       The fattest frog passes fastest
(24)  Why is a cloud like Santa Claus?
       Because it holds the rain, dear!
(25)  Which is heavier, a half moon or a full moon?
       A half moon, because a full moon is lighter.

Verbal humour includes a range of metalinguistic activities,
including play with familiar word sounds such as (22), tongue
twisters such as (23), puns and riddles, as in (24) and (25),
other 'canned' jokes, rude words, and teasing of various kinds.
The metalinguistic aspects of this humour may centre on the
effects of word choice, as in the humorous use of dirty words,
or punning, like that on 'lighter' in (25). Alternatively, they
may be phonologically/phonetically centred, as with the tongue
twister in (23) or the silly word play in (22). Syntactic jokes
occur when the utterance must be reanalysed in order to produce a different analysis of the string, as in (24) above, where
the joke depends on reanalysing 'rain, dear' as 'reindeer'.

Different sorts of verbal humour appear at different ages, the
earliest being the kind of phonological distortion seen in (22).
For many (e.g. Gombert 1992) this does not count as metalinguistic at all if the child is not consciously aware of the manipulation involved. In (22), we can probably argue that the girls
do indeed know what they are doing, but earlier forms of the
same game, and certainly the kind of babbling type modifications
to sounds done by pre-linguistic children, should not be counted
as metalinguistic.

Phonological humour continues to be popular throughout
childhood, particularly through such forms as humorous verse
which uses the rhythm and rhyme of recognised poetic forms
to produce a predictable, and humorous, effect. Here are a
couple of examples from Keller (1973), cited in Shultz and
Robillard (1980):

(26)  Roses are red,
       Violets are blue,
       I copied your paper
       And I flunked too.

(27) Now I lay me down to rest,
I pray to pass tomorrow's test;
If I should die before I wake,
That's one less test I'll have to take.

The full effect of both of these depends on knowing the amorous verse on which the first is based, and the prayer that is the basis for the second. Another form which is routinely exploited for humorous effect is the limerick:

(28) There was a young farmer of Leeds
Who swallowed six packets of seeds.
It soon came to pass
He was covered with grass,
And he couldn't sit down for the weeds.

The success of children's poets such as Shel Silverstein attests to the enduring lure of silly verse, where the main thrill is created through the *tension* built by the expectations of the rhyme and rhythm and where the *resolution* creates the main humorous effect.

Many argue, in fact, that it is tension and resolution which form the basis for all humour. Shultz and Robillard (1980) argue that at the morphological level, for example, it is the violation of morphological rules which makes play languages such as Pig Latin so funny. A similar violation of rules is involved in the French *verlan*, where the game's name is an example of what it involves. *Verlan* (which is now, incidentally, more than a simple child's game and is used, often aggressively, to flout the authority of adults in economically and socially troubled suburbs of large French cities) involves reversing the order of syllables. 'L'envers' ('backwards') becomes 'verlan', 'mari' ('husband') becomes 'rima', 'copains' ('friends') becomes 'painsco', 'merci' ('thank you') becomes 'cimer', etc. The tension is created by the invented phonological rule, and the humorous resolution occurs when one 'works out' what has actually been said. (Obviously, if such forms are used frequently enough, they lose the humorous effect and become simply additions to the lexicons of their users.)

Most semantically based humour depends on violating rules known as co-occurrence restrictions. These are the rules that make Chomsky's famous sentence, 'Colorless green ideas sleep furiously', meaningless. They are the rules that say, for example, the words 'colorless' and 'green' cannot go together, neither can any colour word and the word 'ideas', and so on. Children's play with these rules results in what is often referred to as 'tangletalk' (Opie and Opie 1959). Here is an example from the Opie volume (1959: 25) quoted in Shultz and Robillard (1980):

(29)   One fine day in the middle of the night,
       Two dead men got up to fight,
       Back to back they faced each other,
       Drew their swords and shot each other.
       A paralysed donkey passing by
       Kicked a blind man in the eye,
       Knocked him through a nine inch wall
       Into a dry ditch and drowned them all.

The penultimate line is not in fact a semantic violation, but a pragmatic one, since there is nothing inherently contradictory about it, just unlikely given our expectations about nine-inch walls. And the line before contains no violation unless one assumes that being blind entails having no eyes.

Besides the kinds of violation of world knowledge mentioned in the previous paragraph, pragmatic humour also involves effects created by such things as failing deliberately to recognise the indirectness of speech in certain contexts. (This is something that the American storybook character Amelia Bedelia is well known for.) For example, if, when someone asks you whether you have the time, you say, 'Yes, I do', and do nothing more, you are either being rude or humorous.

Finally, we might note that there is a kind of (often unintended) pragmatic humour when the rules for humour are themselves broken. I am thinking of those instances where a child only partially understands the script for a joke and yet persists. Here's one I heard recently. The actual joke is: 'I can jump higher than the Eiffel Tower. How come? The Eiffel Tower can't jump.' The version that came out, however, was: Mama, Mama, listen to this one, 'The Eiffel Tower can't jump as high as me!' (laugh).

What makes a joke a joke? While adult definitions depend on notions of carefully crafted tensions and resolution in the content of the joke, children often use the known and expected structure of the joke itself to create the tension and resolution. A knock-knock joke is fun to do just because of its structure. It really doesn't matter what you say.

(30)   Naomi at 5;2:
       N:   Knock knock.

M:  Who's there?
N:  Sandwich.
M:  Sandwich who?
N:  If the bug eats the sandwich, when the kid eats the
    sandwich, the bread'll be all gone. (laughs)

McGhee (1979) has suggested that children's humour develops
in a series of stages. (I summarise them here on the basis of a
discussion in Horgan (1981), whose work on joke telling forms
the basis for one of the activities at the end of this chapter.)

Stage 1:  incongruous actions towards object, such as pretending
          that a leaf is a telephone;
Stage 2:  incongruous labelling of objects and events, such as calling a
          hand a foot;
Stage 3:  conceptual incongruity that leads to word play from around
          the age of three;
Stage 4:  an appreciation of ambiguity begins to emerge around the
          age of seven, and children can now understand riddles.

The ages at which children enter these various stages varies
somewhat, but again we see that the age of seven seems to be
the start of adult-like competence in this aspect of metalinguistic
awareness.

## Explaining metalinguistic development

A number of researchers have tried to pull together all the
various metalinguistic developments we have seen in this chapter
into an overarching framework that aims to explain as well as
describe what happens. As I have hinted at various points,
there is no generally agreed definition of what should be called
'metalinguistic', at least at the younger end of the developmental path. At the more advanced end, all researchers would
agree that when (a) the speaker is talking about explicit knowledge of the language that he or she has *and* (b) the speaker is
consciously accessing the knowledge he or she has in order to
enter the discussion, this is clearly metalinguistic. The difference
between those who credit very young children with metalinguistic awareness and those who do not lies in whether conscious access to the linguistic system is required or not. Those,
such as Gombert (1992), who argue that conscious access is
necessary, do not credit very young children with metalinguistic
awareness.

Annette Karmiloff-Smith (1992) has argued for a model of metalinguistic development which encompasses all these issues and can provide a useful way of thinking about children's abilities. She suggests that at the beginning, knowledge of language is implicit. It guides children's production and comprehension of language, but in terms of the mental representations involved, this knowledge of language is purely procedural and cannot be said to constitute *objective* knowledge. At the following stage, this same implicit knowledge becomes 'redescribed' in a new, more explicit, format. At the next stage, conscious access to the knowledge begins to emerge, and at the final stage the knowledge is not only explicit and consciously accessible, but can also be described verbally. It is at this stage that children can offer definitions and answer direct questions about grammaticality.

Although different parts of the linguistic system pass through these stages at different times, Karmiloff-Smith argues that, in general, children under the age of five are at the first stage, and seven-year-olds are beginning to reach the last stage, although, as we have seen, it is not until well into teenagehood that some metalinguistic skills are perfected.

This review of metalinguistic development concludes this chapter, and, in fact, the whole book. As I hope you are now aware, there is a huge literature on child language acquisition; one which I hope you will explore further, if you haven't already done so. There is much we now know about how children learn their first language or languages, but, as you have seen, there is much still to be understood. Perhaps you will be among those who move our understanding forward. At the very least, I hope you are now among those who can see a little way behind the words that come out of children's mouths to the system that underlies them.

## Discussion of in-text exercises

Exercise 2

You should get: 'there' – 'he' – 'she' – 'he' – 'she' – 'he' – 'she' – 'he' – 'he'. As you can see, there is no consistency. Karmiloff-Smith argues that the younger child's story is not a linguistic unit at all. Rather, it is a collection of sentences that reflects a connection between what the child saw and a linguistic, sentence-bound, way of describing it, but it is not a structured story in the true sense.

Exercise 3

I have italicised the subjects in this story (an 'e' indicates an empty, understood subject):

> *There*'s a girl and a boy. *The boy* wants (e) to go fishing, so *he* tries (e) to get the girl's bucket, but *the girl* won't let him take it, so *he* grabs it out of her hand and *the girl* chases after him, but *he* gets away from the girl and *he* starts (e) to fish while *the girl* sits there crying. *He* goes home smiling with four fish.

(Depending on the particular linguistic theory you espouse, you might also say that the 'him' in 'let him take it' is a subject, even though it is in objective form, since it is understood that it is the boy who can't take the bucket. Also, you might try to count as empty subjects the understood actor of 'crying' (the girl) and 'smiling' (the boy).)

Clearly, this story does not obey the thematic subject constraint, which is indicative of an older child. Other clues that this is more sophisticated come from the use of words that link clauses together, such as 'so', 'but', 'and' and 'while'. The result is longer utterances, and a switching of protagonist in subject position, yielding a more complex, but richer, story. Also, the two forms 'crying' and 'smiling' are quite sophisticated ways of packing information into a story, although the first of these also occurs in the youngest child's story in (9). The last sentence of the story in (11) is particularly sophisticated because the reader must infer that the boy caught four fish from the fact that he goes home smiling with four fish. In both the younger stories, it was spelled out that he caught (or got) the fish.

Compared with the story from the youngest child, the one in (11) selects the information to be presented so as to focus on the tussle between the boy and girl. Unlike the story in (9), it does not mention the intention of the girl to make sandcastles, nor does it mention the tree. The story in (10), between the two other stories in terms of the child's age, seems caught by the thematic subject constraint in a pared-down rendition. Forced by the constraint to keep the boy as the subject, this child is unable to give the listener/reader any feel for the girl's part in what happened. It is all about the boy.

A T-unit calculation (see Appendix 1) would yield a score of 9 T-units for the story in (11). The story in (9) also has 9 T-units, while the one in (10) has 4. There is undoubtedly more that can be said about these three stories, but I'll leave that up to you.

Exercise 4
The main metalinguistic ability shown by this game is the ability to play with the possibility that things can be called other than what they are normally or 'really' called. Also involved, however, is the problem of making a request for a repetition of a question distinct from a request that the question itself be answered. Although the latter, as an embedded question, would, in the adult grammar, have a different word order ('You tell me *what my name is*'), for these girls at these ages it is clear that the direct question order is interpreted as the indirect. Interestingly, the child who invented the game is caught in the same bind as her friend in lines (6) and (7) when it is her turn to be the responder. Finally, there is evidence in line (10) that remembering to maintain the new name is difficult.

Exercise 5
Avi has done a straightforward misanalysis of the word boundary, made possible by his recognition that there is a word 'sushi'. A child without that word in his or her vocabulary is unlikely to be misled. However, even though Avi puts the word boundary in the wrong place, he is clearly able to lift out and query what he thinks is a phrase, which bespeaks an ability to recognise quite clearly the notion of word as separable unit.

## Questions for discussion

1   Some linguistic expressions (such as the ubiquitous 'like' in American English) seem only to emerge as children get older. My son acquired 'like' together with 'ya know' and the requisite 'cool' gestures and intonation when he was 5;6. What other older child/pre-adolescent/adolescent words and phrases are you familiar with? When do you think these emerge? How many of them persist into adulthood? Which ones? Why these and not others?

2   One feature of later language development which I have not discussed is sociolinguistic competence: knowing what to say to whom, and when. What sorts of different ways of speaking do children need to learn? Do these require new grammatical resources from those they learned as younger children? Do they require different ways of using already acquired language? When do children get all the rules of politeness for different situations? (See below.)

3   What position do you take in the debate over what should be counted as metalinguistic and what should not? Evaluate the

different frameworks summarised in this chapter and decide for
yourself what you think constitutes being metalinguistic.

## Some activities

1    Find a picture-book without words and allow children aged 5;0,
     7;0, 9;0 and 11;0 to 'read/tell' the story into a tape recorder
     one at a time. You will need to have each child carry out the
     task alone, and you should do it in a context where it makes
     sense. For example, particularly for the younger children, it will
     not make 'sense' for the child to tell the story if you are there
     in the same room looking at the pictures with the child. The
     child will assume you can see what he or she can see and
     leave out of the story some information that he or she might
     otherwise have put in. However, making a tape for a friend
     who is far away, or who is ill and needs cheering up, might
     just be the kind of 'sense' a young child is looking for. Also,
     you will need to choose a book that is comprehensible to
     the youngest age-group and yet not insulting to the oldest.
     (Raymond Briggs' *The Snowman* would be an excellent choice.)
     After you have tape-recorded the stories, transcribe them
     *exactly* as the children said them (see Appendix 1). Analyse the
     transcripts for the features of narratives discussed in this chapter
     (length, degree and amount of subordination, tracking of
     discourse referents, etc.).
2    If you have access to a group of writers 'in training' (these
     might be from kindergarten to college level), design two
     age-appropriate writing tasks, one of which is close to casual
     conversational language skills (e.g. a personal narrative), and one
     which is more removed (e.g. an analysis of a point of view).
     Ask your group of writers to respond to both prompts and then
     analyse the results in terms of the language used, the success of
     the students at each task, etc.
3    Here are some examples from McTear (1985) of self-repairs.
     For each one, write down what you see as the repair, what
     aspect of the linguistic system it involves, and any other
     analytical observations you can make.
     (a)    Heather (5;1): 'You chopped your head off . . . you got
            your head chopped off.'
     (b)    Siobhan (4;6): 'I could . . . could I cut them out?'
     (c)    Heather (4;0): 'Give me the wee bus. It's going in the car
            wash . . . in the bus wash.'
     (d)    Siobhan (4;9): 'That's why it doesn't stop go-coming.'
     (See below for some feedback.)
4    Here are some examples of the early evolution of joke telling
     from Kelly, the child described by Horgan (1981). Horgan
     organises them in terms of the kind of linguistic manipulations

they employ. Her four categories, in order of appearance, with examples, are as follows (note that these categories are additive; that is, as each appears, it is added to an expanding repertoire, and, at the oldest age, all four types of joke can be found):

(a)  *Violations of semantic categories*    Kelly (1;4) learned the word 'shoe'. 'Several days later, she put her foot through the armhole of a nightgown, saying 'shoe', accompanied by shrieks of laughter.

(b)  *Phonetic pattern games*    At 1;8, Kelly said, 'Cow go moo. Mommy go mamoo. Daddy go dadoo. Ha ha.'

(c)  *Changing established patterns*    At 2;3, Kelly invented the following:
Five socks. Pick up stocks.
Seven ox. Close the gox.
Nine tens. Start agains.

(d)  *Riddle-like questions*    At 2;6:

K:    How do aspirins make?
M:    Huh?
K:    How do aspirins make?
M:    I dunno, how do aspirins make?
K:    They make you feel better.
      At 3;0:
K:    Mommy, do you love me?
M:    Yes.
K:    Do you love me to hit you? Ha, ha!

For each of these data samples, discuss the metalinguistic knowledge involved. (See below.)

5    Construct a reverse Scrabble or crossword puzzle in which the words are already given on the grid (i.e. the puzzle is already filled in); the children win points for a word if they can define it. Make sure that you design the filled-in crossword so that there is a core set of words to which you want children to respond with a definition, as well as additional items as 'distracters'. You will need to make sure that the core set covers the different kinds of words you want defined, and that you have thought through why these particular words are of interest in studying the metalinguistic skill of word-defining. (You could perhaps award higher scores for more difficult words, e.g. those requiring more abstract definitions.) Then play the game by having children receive the score for the word only if they can define it. This will push them to try to define the harder words because they will be 'worth more'. Write up the results of your game.

6    Find a selection of jokes intended for children (from joke books, comics, etc.). For each one, decide:

(a)  what kind of metalinguistic knowledge is required (phonological, lexical, syntactic, pragmatic, etc.);

(b) what kind of real-world (encyclopaedic) knowledge is
necessary;
(c) what aged child is likely to find them funny.
Then, if you are able, try them out on a sample of children by
(a) telling the jokes and seeing if they 'get them', and
(b) asking them to explain why they are funny. Record their
answers if you are able.

## Solutions to and comments on discussion questions and activities

Discussion question 2
There is a large literature on this topic, some of which is
referenced in the chapter. Issues which have been addressed
include how children learn to be polite, how they learn social
routines such as 'trick or treat' for Hallowe'en, and how they
learn to take account of what their hearer knows. These may
or may not require new grammatical resources, depending on
the language involved. Some languages use certain tenses only
for certain purposes, e.g. French has a tense (the *passé simple*)
only for stories and reports, and rarely in spoken form at all.
On the other hard, English and French both use the conditional form for being polite, but that form is also used for
ordinary conditional statements, so it does not call for new
grammatical resources to use the conditional for being polite.

Activity 3
McTear (1985) argues that extracts (a) and (b) represent a
change of sentence type for pragmatic reasons. The first from
active to passive because the child realises that with the active,
the wrong person is affected by the cutting; the second from
declarative to interrogative to make it more tentative and polite. Extracts (c) and (d) are lexical repairs involving a substitu
tion of one lexical item for another within the same lexical set.

Activity 4
Example (a) suggests that Kelly has understood that words are
reliably attached to things, and though there is a resemblance
between what she does with a shoe and what she's doing with
the armhole of her nightgown, it is funny because it is not
'right'.

Example (b) shows Kelly manipulating the structure of words for humorous effect, possibly initially from a modification from 'mommy' to 'mamoo', and then the repeat pattern with 'dadoo'. She wouldn't be able to do this if she were unable to reflect on the structure of what she heard herself saying.

Example (c) depends on Kelly knowing the original rhyme, and producing a new one by modifying the vowels in both portions of each line in the same way. Again, it calls for an ability to hold in memory a set of forms which can then be systematically modified.

Both the examples in (d) call for simultaneous manipulation of the joke format and of the syntax of the utterances on which the joke depends. Interestingly, both jokes call for a division of the crucial utterance into two at a point which is unconventional. In the first case, it produces a question that is ungrammatical, although her mother is clearly able to play along none the less. In the second, it works much better because both the initial question and the punch-line are grammatical. In both cases, however, the metalinguistic ability to stand back from the syntax and to manipulate it is called for.

## Further reading

Two summary chapters of research into language development beyond the age of five are Karmiloff-Smith (1986) and Chapter 3 of Oakhill and Garnham (1988). In addition, Nippold (1988, 1998) is, to my knowledge, the only collection of articles focusing specifically on a broad range of issues in later language development. As mentioned in the text above, Adams (1990) is an excellent survey. It can also be obtained as a short summary of 100 pages or so from the Center for the Study of Reading at the University of Illinois at Urbana-Champaign. Gombert's recently translated book on metalinguistic development (Gombert 1992) is a rich source of information on the main ideas presented in this chapter. It deserves close study. Chapter 2 of Karmiloff-Smith (1992) focuses on her view of metalinguistic development, and is an interesting and challenging approach.

# Tools for studying children's language

In the course of this book, you will find various exercises designed to help you understand, first hand, what it is like to collect and analyse the language of children. Over the years, child language researchers have developed various tools to help them in their research, and a few of the key ones are presented in this appendix so that you can use them too.

## Transcription

You might think that transcribing children's language is just a matter of agreeing on a number of symbols to represent what was said, but it is in fact much more than that. Everything, from the way you lay out the page, to what you decide to write down and what to leave out, to how you choose your symbols, is motivated by assumptions about child language, whether you are aware of it or not. Elinor Ochs discussed many of these issues some years ago (Ochs 1979) and I urge you to read her article. While you may need additional ways of representing specific features you are interested in, the basic conventions you are going to need are:

1   A way of transcribing the linguistic sounds you want to study.
    You could use ordinary spelling conventions, provided you
    don't need to be more precise about a child's pronunciation.
    Be careful, however, that you can justify attributing to children
    the words you think they have said. Don't jump to conclusions.
    Another alternative is to use modified normal spelling to give at
    least some hints as to the child's pronunciation. (So you might
    write 'wabbit' for 'rabbit', for example.) This may also be
    appropriate to certain goals. An even more precise transcription
    would use a broad phonemic transcription. This is a transcription
    that uses a set of symbols such as those shown in Appendix 2.
    These represent the sounds of the language without going into

the details of the precise phonetics. It will represent what in spelling appears as 'sh' as /ʃ/, for example. Likewise, it will represent the vowel in 'cat' as /æ/ but the vowel in 'father' as /a/ because although they are both spelled with an 'a', they are, in fact, different vowels. However, it will not discriminate between the 't' in 'top' and the 't' in 'stop', even though there is a puff of air (aspiration) after the 't' in the first case but not in the second. To do so, you would need to use a narrow phonetic transcription system, and this is only necessary if you are trying to study the phonetics of child speech or to transcribe pre-linguistic vocalisations for which broad transcription is impossible because the child is not using sufficiently adult-like sounds. Pre-linguistic vocalisations will also require you to find symbols for sounds that are not in the adult language. For this you will need to use the full International Phonetic Alphabet (IPA). Any introductory general linguistics or phonetics book should have a copy of the IPA.

2    A means of representing who spoke when. Normally a play script format such as you'll find throughout this book is used (but read Ochs (1979) for the pitfalls). However, you will almost certainly also need to represent other features of the interaction to help the person reading the transcript re-create for themselves what you heard. All the examples below are from McTear (1985).

3    When two or more people speak at the same time, you will need to represent the overlap. One way is to emphasise the portions that overlap, as I have done in Sample 5 in Chapter 4.

4    When speakers interrupts themselves, you can show this by a hyphen:
   H:   do you like his br-her big brother? (156)

5    Sometimes it is helpful to know when people speak one after the other without any pause; not an interruption that causes an overlap, but so rapid a handover from one person to the next that the speech sounds continuous. This can be represented by an equals sign:
   Heather:    Father Christmas is coming today
   Siobhan:    no he's=
   Heather:            =tonight (197)

6    When the speech is so unclear that you can't transcribe it, simply place empty parentheses at the appropriate place in the transcript. However, when you think you know what was said, but you are not sure, put the word(s) you think you heard in the parentheses.

7    When there are pauses long enough to count in seconds, put the number of seconds in parentheses. If you have a stopwatch, use it and record to the tenth of a second. If you don't have a stopwatch, count whole seconds by saying 'ONE-one-thousand-

TWO-one-thousand-THREE-one-thousand-FOUR-one-
thousand, etc.'

Heather:    Siobhan don't forget to bring your bikini round to
my house (3.2) will you will you bring your bikini
round to my house? (118)

8    Use CAPITALS to show a particularly heavily stressed item:

Heather:    I'm only lending it for to play in the Poly playschool

Siobhan:    no I'm lending it for YOU

Heather:    no I'm lending it FROM you (185)

9    You will notice in all these examples that McTear does not use
capital letters at the beginning of utterances or full stops at the
end. He does, however, use '?' to indicate rising intonation, and
'''' to indicate contractions. You will have to decide for yourself
how much standard punctuation you want to use.

The key to a good transcript is consistent use of whatever
conventions you decide on and an explanatory key appended
to your transcript so that someone else will know how to read
it in the way you intend.

## Mean Length of Utterance calculations

There are two kinds of Mean Length of Utterance calculations.
One involves counting and averaging the number of words in
a representative sample of children's utterances, and the other
involves counting and averaging the number of morphemes.
To see the difference, compare the two different counts for a
phrase such as 'living dangerously'. The word count would be
2. The morpheme count would be 5 (liv-ing danger-ous-ly).
MLUm is the abbreviation for the Mean Length of Utterance
counted in morphemes and MLUw is for the calculation in
words.

The following rules were developed by Roger Brown (1973)
(and are presented here from Dale (1976), with some additional comments from me in square brackets). They apply
similarly to MLUm and MLUw calculations except that in the
latter, multi morpheme words are counted as single tokens. It
is usually reckoned that MLU counts are useful only to an
MLU of about 4.0, at which time other measures of complexity, such as T-units (see next section) should be used.

1    Start with the second page of the transcription unless that
page involves a recitation of some kind. In this latter case
start with the first recitation-free stretch. Count the first
100 utterances satisfying the following rules. (A 50-
utterance sample may be used for a preliminary estimate.)

2       Only fully transcribed utterances are used. Portions of
        utterances, entered in parentheses to indicate doubtful
        transcription, are used.

3       Include all exact utterance repetitions . . . Stuttering is
        marked as repeated efforts at a single word; count the
        word once in the most complete form produced. In the
        few instances in which a word is produced for emphasis
        or the like ('no, no, no') count each occurrence.

4       Do not count such fillers as 'um' and 'oh,' but do count
        'no', 'yeah', and 'hi'.

5       All compound words (two or more free morphemes),
        proper names, and ritualised reduplications count as single
        morphemes. Examples: 'birthday', 'rackety-boom', 'choo-
        choo', 'quack-quack', 'night-night', 'pocket-book', 'see-
        saw'.

6       Count as one morpheme all irregular pasts of the verb
        ('got', 'did', 'want', 'saw'). Justification is that there is no
        evidence that the child relates these to the present forms.
        [If you have evidence that they *do* relate them to the
        present forms, then count the irregular past tense forms as
        two morphemes.]

7       Count as one morpheme all diminutives ('doggie',
        'mommy') because these [the ones Brown was studying]
        at least do not seem to use the suffix productively.
        Diminutives are the standard forms used by the child.
        [Some children with an MLU less than 4.0 may show
        evidence of using the diminutive suffix productively. If
        they do, then count such words as two morphemes.]

8       Count as separate morphemes all auxiliaries ('is', 'have',
        'will', 'can', 'must', 'would'). Also all catenatives: 'gonna',
        'wanna', 'hafta'. The latter are counted as single
        morphemes rather than as 'going to' or 'want to' because
        the evidence is that they function so for children. [Same
        caveat applies as above.] Count as separate morphemes all
        inflections, for example, possessive '-'s', plural '-s', third
        person singular '-s', regular past tense '-(e)d', progressive
        '-ing'.

Using these rules will give a rough measure of productive complexity. This procedure can be used with languages other than
English, but adjustments will almost certainly have to be made.

## T-unit calculations

While the complexity of very young children's language can
be measured by calculating the average number of morphemes

per utterance, as above, measuring the number of clauses can be useful with slightly older children. However, when children begin to *combine* clauses in their sentences, a measure closer to the sentence or utterance is needed.

If you have ever looked at a genuine text from either a child or an adult, you will know that finding sentence boundaries is often difficult. In oral text, the intonation clues, etc., frequently leave you with multiple possibilities as to where to put the boundary. In written texts, particularly, children's control of punctuation is so poor that one cannot use full stops and capitals as in any way a reliable indicator of sentence boundary. This is where the T-unit comes into play.

A number of studies looking at older children's language have employed the notion of T-unit (terminable unit) as a sensible measure of spoken or written language. A T-unit is a main clause plus all its dependent clauses, such as relative clauses, complement clauses, adverbial clauses, etc. Crucially, clauses that are joined by 'and' (unless there is deletion of a co-referential subject) are not regarded as part of the same T-unit. Let me give a few examples.

1    Jane went to the store and Bill went to the theatre. (2 T-units)
2    Jane went to the store and bought some Coke. (1 T-unit because the subject of the second conjunct is the same as the first)
3    Jane went to the store and she bought some Coke. (2 T-units)
4    Jane drank the Coke that she bought. (1 T-unit)
5    The girl that drank the Coke has bought another one. (1 T unit)

In general (depending upon the type of text being considered), the complexity of children's language as measured by T-units increases with age.

## Some dos and don'ts of research design

I emphasised in the first chapter of this book the need to combine a theoretically motivated approach to data collection with an openness to alternative hypotheses that might present themselves in light of data collected. Here, I want simply to state some 'dos' and 'don'ts' of research design which might help keep you on the right track.

1    Be honest about the assumptions you are making about children and their language learning/acquiring capacity, even if you have not dignified these assumptions with the title of 'hypothesis'.

2    If you decide simply to record children without a conscious hypothesis in mind, recognise that your choice of methodology does, in fact, reflect certain assumptions, e.g. that children's linguistic systems are accurately reflected in spontaneous interactions.

3    If you go seeking data (whether observational or experimental) on the basis of a hypothesis, make sure that the hypothesis is precise enough to be testable, and that it is properly motivated by reasonable assumptions. Make sure, also, that if your hypothesis is *not* supported, you can give reasons about exactly how and why it is not supported, and that if it *is* supported (hypotheses are never 'proved'), that you are able to articulate exactly why. Your constant aim should be to try to *falsify* your hypothesis, and only when you have genuinely tried to do so, can you be reasonably certain that you are on the right track.

4    Make sure your methods are sufficiently well thought out and sufficiently well described that someone else could reliably replicate what you have done.

5    If you need to do experiments that involve large numbers of children, be sure to work out in advance what kinds of statistical techniques you are likely to need, and to make sure your sample (of children, or of data) is correctly selected to make those statistical techniques appropriately applicable.

## Finding data

Going out and collecting data, as you are asked to do in several of the exercises in this book, is extremely valuable in helping you understand how difficult it can be, and in learning about the kinds of things you can and can't get children to do. However, a lot of people have been collecting a lot of different kinds of data for a long time, and many of them have been kind enough to make it available to the rest of us.

There are quite full data sets available in already published materials, some of which I have (with permission) reproduced for you in this book. Other materials are increasingly being made available electronically through the Internet. If you are a World Wide Web surfer, you can probably find materials in a variety of places, but there is one database that is recognised by all child language researchers, and that is the one developed by Brian MacWhinney and his colleagues at Carnegie Mellon University and known as the CHILDES database. It is extremely rich, and getting richer all the time. It consists of fully transcribed (and in many cases analysed) data, and is where researchers from all over the world have placed their data (in a variety of languages) for other researchers to use. The best way to learn about CHILDES is through the handbooks published by Lawrence Erlbaum Associates (e.g. MacWhinney 1995). Lawrence Erlbaum Associates also publishes a child language bibliography associated with the CHILDES project, available in book or CD-Rom form (Higginson and MacWhinney 1990, 1994).

## Bulletin boards

The CHILDES bulletin board is a forum for sharing ideas and questions, run through Carnegie Mellon University. It disseminates information about child language conferences, and other issues of interest to child language researchers. To join it, ask for information from Brian MacWhinney at brian+@ andrew.cmu.edu.

'Linguistlist' is another electronic bulletin board which keeps linguists of all stripes (including those in child language research) in contact with each other. You should first visit the website at http://linguist.org, where you can find out all about it. Other relevant lists can be found through the linguistlist site. The landscape of the Internet is changing so rapidly that I cannot hope to alert you to all the opportunities out there. Get an account, get 'on', and browse!

## Journals in child language

The following journals are among those in which you can routinely or frequently find research on child language development. Child language research is actually flung wide among linguistics journals, educational journals, clinical journals, etc. Use your library's electronic databases as well as the resources of the Internet in order to search for materials for your particular topic(s).

*Journal of Child Language*
*First Language*
*Language Acquisition*
*Applied Psycholinguistics*
*Behavioral and Brain Sciences*
*Cognition*
*Child Development*
*Language*
*Journal of Psycholinguistic Research*
*Journal of Memory and Language*

## Associations

The only major association specifically for child language is the International Association for the Study of Child Language (IASCL), which publishes a newsletter called the Child Language Bulletin. There is also the Society for Research in Child Development, which has its own journal and conference, including a lot of research in child language, but it is not limited to that aspect of child development.

## Conferences

The two main child language conferences in the USA are the Stanford Child Language Research Forum, held each spring at Stanford University, and the Boston University Conference on Language Development, held each autumn at Boston University. The IASCL has a congress every two years, and it moves around the world. The UK has a yearly conference on language development called the Child Language Seminar. Other countries have their own conferences along the same lines.

## Further reading

If you really get serious about research in child language development, there are a couple of books that you might find useful. A very recent publication that focuses on research in syntax is Dana McDaniel et al. (1996). There is also an earlier book, by Tina Bennett-Kastor (1988).

# Phonetic symbols

Sounds of a language can be divided into natural classes of sounds. For example, whether a consonant is *voiced* or not (i.e. produced with the vocal cords vibrating or not) divides consonants into two groups (e.g. /d/ is voiced and /t/ is voiceless). Similarly, all the consonants that are produced with a sudden release of the airflow form the class of *stops* (e.g. /t/ and /d/). Those that involve the airflow seeping out through a constricted opening that causes friction against the airflow form the class of *fricatives* (e.g. /s/ and /z/). Those that involve resonance in the nasal cavity are *nasals*, and these may be consonants such as /m/ or /n/ or nasal vowels, such as exist in French. Among the vowels, there are natural classes in terms of how high the vowels are (/i/ is high, where /a/ is low), how far forward in the mouth the vowels are produced (/i/ is front and /a/ is back) and how much lip rounding there is (/i/ is unrounded and /u/ is rounded). The consonants, too, can be divided into natural classes depending on where in the mouth they are produced. For example, /b/ and /m/ are both made at the front of the mouth with both lips, /t/, /d/ and /s/ are made with the tongue on the ridge behind the teeth. Consonants /g/ and /k/ are made at the back of the mouth.

There are many more features that can be used to distinguish speech sounds, but when you are trying to decide why a child has produced the particular pronunciation he or she has, it is useful to ask yourself whether what he or she has done draws upon the notion of a natural class. Has the child substituted another sound from within the natural class, or assimilated two sounds so that they become members of a natural class when they were not before.

Listed below are the sounds that appear in this book, with a guide to their pronunciation. I have also provided indications of the features that are argued to characterise them. Some I have referred to above, but others I have only space to name here. I urge you to consult any introductory linguistics or phonetics/phonology text (e.g. Francis Katamba's *Introduction to Phonology* in this series) for further details.

## Consonants

### Stop consonants
/b/ as in the first sound of     'bat' (voiced bilabial)
/p/     'pat' (voiceless bilabial)
/d/     'dot' (voiced alveolar)
/t/     'tot' (voiceless alveolar)
/g/     'got' (voiced velar)
/k/     'cat' (voiceless velar)

### Fricative consonants
/v/ as in the first sound of     'vet' (voiced labio-dental)
/f/     'fetch' (voiceless labio-dental)
/ð/     'they' (voiced inter-dental)
/θ/     'thing' (voiceless inter-dental)
/z/     'zoo' (voiced alveolar)
/s/     'sat' (voiceless alveolar)
/ʒ/ as in the middle sound of     'measure' (voiced palatal)
/ʃ/ as in the first sound of     'shoe' (voiceless palatal)

### Affricate consonants
/d/ as in the first sound of     'judge' (voiced)
/t/     'church' (voiceless)

### Nasal consonants
/m/ as in the first sound of     'mug' (voiced bilabial)
/n/     'nut' (voiced alveolar)
/ŋ/ as in the last sound of     'sing' (voiced velar)

### Glide consonants
/w/ as in the first sound of     'win' (voiced bilabial)
/y/     'you' (voiced palatal)

### Liquid consonants
/l/ as in the first sound of     'love' (voiced alveolar lateral)
/r/     'rat' (voiced alveolar retroflex)
/R/ is a trilled 'r' as in Spanish

### Glottal consonants
/h/ as in the first sound of         'hat' (voiceless fricative)
/ʔ/ is the voiced stop in between the two parts of 'uh-oh'

## Vowels

### Front vowels
/i/ as in the middle sound of     'beat'
/e/                            'bait'
/ɪ/                            'bit'
/ɛ/                            'bet'
/æ/                            'bat'
/ø/ is a front rounded high vowel

### Central vowels
/ə/ the unstressed vowel at the beginning of 'about'

### Back vowels
/u/ as in the middle sound of     'boot'
/ʊ/                            'put'
/o/                            'boat'
/ɔ/                            'cot'
/a/                            'cart'

### Diphthongs (two vowels forming one sound)
/ay/ as in the middle sound of    'hide'
/aw/                          'cow'
/oy/                          'boil'

## Other symbols

1     ː = a vowel is lengthened.
2     A superscript [h] after another symbol means that the sound is aspirated, i.e. that it has a puff of air after it.
3     A superscript [y] after another sound means that there is a little glide after the sound. This produces the same effect as the diphthongs written with a full /y/ as in the list above.
4     ~ = nasalisation of the sound below it.
5     Most of the sounds presented in this book are represented as phonemes and placed between / /. However, a few are represented between [ ], indicating a more detailed, phonetic level, of transcription.

# Bibliography

Ackerman, B. (1986) Children's sensitivity to comprehension failure in interpreting a nonliteral use of an utterance. *Child Development* 57: 485–497.

Adams, M. (1990) *Beginning to Read: Thinking and Learning about Print*. Cambridge, MA: MIT Press. Summary published by the Center for the Study of Reading, The Reading Research and Education Center, University of Illinois at Urbana-Champagne.

Allen, S. (1997) A discourse-pragmatic explanation for the subject-object asymmetry in early null arguments: the principle of informativeness revisited. To appear in R. Shillcock, A. Sorace and C. Heycock (eds.), *Proceedings of the 3rd GALA Conference*. Human Communication Research Centre, University of Edinburgh.

Allen, S. and M. Crago (1992) Active passives in early child Inuktitut. Unpublished manuscript, McGill University.

Andersen, E. (1992) *Speaking with Style: The Sociolinguistic Skills of Children*. London and New York: Routledge.

Astington, J., Harris, P. and Olson, D. (eds.) (1988) *Developing Theories of Mind*. Cambridge: Cambridge University Press.

Atkinson, M. (1982) *Explanations in the Study of Child Language Development*. Cambridge: Cambridge University Press.

Baron, N. (1992) *Growing Up with Language: How Children Learn to Speak*. Reading, MA: Addison Wesley.

Basena, D. (1995) The development of child code-switching: a case study of a four-year-old Lusoga child. Unpublished doctoral dissertation, Northern Arizona University.

Bellugi, U. (1967) The acquisition of negation. Unpublished doctoral thesis, Harvard University.

Bennet-Kastor, T. (1988) *Analyzing Children's Language: Methods and Theories*. Oxford: Blackwell.

Berman, R. (1994) Developmental perspectives on transitivity: a confluence of cues. In Y. Levy (ed.), *Other Children, Other Languages: Issues in the Theory of Language Acquisition.* Hillsdale, NJ: Lawrence Erlbaum Associates, 189–241.

Bernhardt, B. and Johnson, C. (1996) Sentence production models: explaining children's filler syllables. In C. Johnson and J. Gilbert (eds.), *Children's Language, Volume 9.* Mahwah, NJ: Lawrence Erlbaum Associates, 253–281.

Bernstein, B. (1971) *Theoretical Studies Towards a Sociology of Language. Class, Codes and Control: I.* London: Routledge and Kegan Paul.

Bernstein, B. (1990) *The Structure of Pedagogical Discourse. Class, Codes and Control: IV.* London: Routledge.

Bialystok, E. (1986a) Children's concept of word. *Journal of Psycholinguistic Research* 15: 13–32.

Bialystok, E. (1986b) Factors in the growth of linguistic awareness. *Child Development* 57: 498–510.

Bialystok, E. (1991) Metalinguistic dimensions of bilingual language proficiency. In E. Bialystok (ed.), *Language Processing in Bilingual Children.* Cambridge: Cambridge University Press, 113–140.

Bloom, L. (1970) *Language Development: Form and Function in Emerging Grammars.* Cambridge, MA: MIT Press.

Bloom, P. (ed.) (1994) *Language Acquisition: Core Readings.* Cambridge, MA: MIT Press.

Bonitatibus, G. (1988) Comprehension monitoring and the apprehension of literal meaning. *Child Development* 59: 60–70.

Bornstein, M. and Lamb, M. (1992) *Developmental Psychology: An Advanced Textbook.* Hillsdale, NJ: Lawrence Erlbaum Associates.

Brown, R. (1973) *A First Language: The Early Stages.* Cambridge, MA: Harvard University Press.

Brown, R. and Bellugi, U. (1964) Three processes in the child's acquisition of syntax. *Harvard Educational Review* 34: 133–151.

Bruner, J. (1974) The organization of early skilled action. In M. Richards (ed.), *The Integration of a Child into a Social World.* Cambridge: Cambridge University Press, 167–184.

Bullowa, M. (1979) *Before Speech: The Beginning of Interpersonal Communication.* Cambridge: Cambridge University Press.

Carruthers, P. and Smith, P. (eds.) (1996) *Theories of Theories of Mind.* Cambridge: Cambridge University Press.

Carter, A. (1979) Prespeech meaning relations: an outline of one infant's sensori-motor development. In P. Fletcher and M. Garman (eds.), *Language Acquisition* (1st edn). Cambridge: Cambridge University Press, 71–92.

Chall, J. S. (1983) *Stages of Reading Development*. New York: McGraw-Hill.

Chomsky, C. (1969) *The Acquisition of Syntax in Children from 5 to 10*. Cambridge, MA: MIT Press.

Chomsky, N. (1965) *Aspects of the Theory of Syntax*. Cambridge, MA: MIT Press.

Clahsen, H. (1992) Linguistic perspectives on specific language impairment. *Theorie des Lexikons: Arbeiten des Sonderforschungsbereichs*, 282. Seminar für Allgemeine Sprachwissenschaft, Universität Düsseldorf.

Clark, E. (1978) Awareness of language: some evidence from what children say and do. In A. Sinclair, R. Jarvella and W. Levelt (eds.), *The Child's Conception of Language*. New York: Springer.

Clark, E. (1993) *The Lexicon in Acquisition*. Cambridge: Cambridge University Press.

Clark, E. and Andersen, E. (1979) Spontaneous repairs: awareness in the process of acquiring language. *Papers and Reports on Child Language Development*, 16. Stanford, CA: Stanford University.

Curtiss, S. (1977) *Genie: A Psycholinguistic Study of a Modern-Day 'Wild Child'*. New York: Academic Press.

Dale, P. (1976) *Language Development: Structure and Function* (2nd edn). New York: Holt, Rinehart and Winston.

Demuth, K. (1989) Maturation and the acquisition of the Sesotho passive. *Language* 65 (1): 56–80.

de Villiers, J. (1984) Form and force interactions: the development of negatives and questions. In R. Schieffelbusch and J. Pickar (eds.), *The Acquisition of Communicative Competence*. Baltimore, MD: University Park Press, 193–236.

de Villiers, P. and de Villiers, G. (1972) Early judgments of semantic and syntactic acceptability by children. *Journal of Psycholinguistic Research* 1, 299–310.

de Villiers, P. and de Villiers, J. (1979) Form and function in the development of sentence negation. *Papers and Reports on Child Language Development* 17: 56–64, Stanford, CA: Stanford University.

de Villiers, J., de Villiers, P. and Hoban, E. (1994) The central problem of functional categories in the English syntax of oral deaf children. In H. Tager-Flusberg (ed.), *Constraints on Language Acquisition*. Hillsdale, NJ: Lawrence Erlbaum Associates, 9–47.

Dunlea, A. (1989) *Vision and the Emergence of Meaning: Blind and Sighted Children's Early Language*. Cambridge: Cambridge University Press.

Duranti, A. and Ochs, E. (1988) Literacy instruction in a Samoan village. In E. Ochs (ed.), *Culture and Language Development*. Cambridge: Cambridge University Press, 189–209.

Eubank, L. (ed.) (1991) *Point–Counter-Point. Universal Grammar and Second Language Acquisition*. Amsterdam/Philadelphia: John Benjamins.

Fawcett, R. P. and Perkins, M. R. (1980) *Child Language Transcripts 6–12*, Vols. I–IV. Pontypridd: Polytechnic of Wales.

Ferguson, C. A. (1979) Phonology as an individual access system: some data from language acquisition. In C. J. Fillmore, D. Kempler and W. S.-Y. Wang (eds.), *Individual Differences in Language Ability and Language Behavior*. New York: Academic Press, 189–201.

Fillmore, C., Kempler, D. and Wang, W. S.-Y. (eds.) (1979) *Individual Differences in Language Ability and Language Behavior*. New York: Academic Press.

Foster, S. (1990a) *The Communicative Competence of Young Children*. London: Longman.

Foster, S. (1990b) Developmental pragmatics. In H. Winitz (ed.), *Human Communication and Its Disorders: A Review – 1990*. New York: Academic Press, 64–134.

Foster-Cohen, S. (1993) Directions of influence in first and second language acquisition research. *Second Language Research* 9 (2): 140–152.

Foster-Cohen, S. (1995) Modularity and Principles and Parameters: avoiding the 'cognitively ugly'. *First Language* 15: 1–19.

Fowler, A., Gelman, R. and Gleitman, L. (1994) The course of language learning in children with Down syndrome: longitudinal and language level comparisons with young normally developing children. In H. Tager-Flusberg (ed.), *Constraints on Language Acquisition: Studies of Atypical Children*. Hillsdale, NJ: Lawrence Erlbaum Associates, 91–140.

Fraiberg, S. (1977) *Insights from the Blind*. New York: Basic Books.

Galambos, S. and Goldin-Meadow, S. (1990) The effects of learning two languages on levels of metalinguistic awareness. *Cognition* 34: 1–56.

Gardner, H. (1983) *Frames of Mind*. New York: Basic Books.

Gierut, J. (1996) Categorization and feature specification in phonological acquisition. *Journal of Child Language* 23: 397–415.

Gleitman, L., Gleitman, H. and Shipley, E. (1972) The emergence of child as grammarian. *Cognition* 1: 137–164.

Gleitman, L. Newport, E. and Gleitman, H. (1984) The current status of the motherese hypothesis. *Journal of Child Language* 11 (1): 43–80.

Gombert, J. (1992) *Metalinguistic Development*. Chicago: University of Chicago Press.

Goodluck, H. (1990) Knowledge integration in processing and acquisition: comments on Grimshaw and Rosen. In L. Frazier and J. de Villiers (eds.), *Language Acquisition and Language Processing*. Dordrecht: Kluwer, 369–382.

Goodluck, H. (1991) *Language Acquisition: A Linguistic Introduction*. Oxford: Basil Blackwell.

Goodluck, H. and Behne, D. (1992) Development in control and extraction. In J. Weissenborn, H. Goodluck and T. Roeper (eds.), *Theoretical Issues in Language Acquisition*. Lawrence Hillsdale, NJ: Lawrence Erlbaum Associates, 151–171.

Goodluck, H. and Birch, B. (1988) Late-learned rules in first and second language acquisition. In J. Pankhurst, M. Sharwood Smith and P. van Buren (eds.), *Learnability and Second Language Acquisition: A Book of Readings*. Dordrecht: Foris, 94–115.

Goodsitt, J. V., Morse, P. A., Ver Hoeve, J. N. and Cowan, N. (1984) Infant speech recognition in multisyllabic contexts. *Child Development* 55: 903–910.

Gopnik, A. and Meltzoff, A. (1984) Semantic and cognitive development in 15- to 21-month-old children. *Journal of Child Language* 11: 495–513.

Greenfield, P. (1980) Toward an operational and logical analysis of intentionality: the use of discourse in early child language. In D. T. Olson (ed.), *The Social Foundations of Language and Thought*. New York: W. W. Norton, 254–279.

Greenfield, P. and Smith, J. (1976) *The Structure of Communication in Early Language Development*. New York: Academic Press.

Grosjean, F. (1982) *Life With Two Languages*. Cambridge, MA: Harvard University Press.

Hakuta, K. (1986) *Mirror of Language: The Debate on Bilingualism.* New York: Basic Books.

Halliday, M. A. K. (1975) *Learning How to Mean: Explorations in the Development of Language.* London: Edward Arnold.

Halliday, M. A. K. (1978) *Language as Social Semiotic.* London: Edward Arnold.

Harris, R. J. (1975) Children's comprehension of complex sentences. *Journal of Experimental Child Psychology* 19: 420–433.

Heath, S. B. (1983) *Ways with Words: Language, Life and Work in Communities and Classrooms.* Cambridge: Cambridge University Press.

Higginson, R. and MacWhinney, B. (1990) *CHILDES/BIB Database: An Annotated Bibliography of Child Language and Language Disorders* plus the 1994 supplement. Hillsdale, NJ: Lawrence Erlbaum Associates.

Hoffmann, C. (1991) *An Introduction to Bilingualism.* London: Longman.

Horgan, D. (1978) The development of the full passive. *Journal of Child Language* 5: 63–80.

Horgan, D. (1981) Learning to tell jokes: a study of metalinguistic abilities. *Journal of Child Language* 8: 217–224.

Huebner, T. and Ferguson, C. (eds.) (1991) *Cross-currents in Second Language Acquisition and Linguistic Theories.* Amsterdam/Philadelphia: John Benjamins.

Hunt, K. W. (1965) *Grammatical Structures Written at Three Grade Levels.* Urbana, IL: National Council of Teachers of English.

Hunt, K. W. (1970) *Syntactic Maturity in School Children and Adults*, Monographs of the Society for Research in Child Development 35, no. 1.

Hyams, N. (1986) *Language Acquisition and the Theory of Parameters.* Dordrecht: Reidel.

Hyams, N. (1994a) Nondiscreteness and variation in child language: implications for Principle and Parameter Models of language development. In Y. Levy (ed.), *Other Children, Other Languages: Issues in the Theory of Language Acquisition.* Hillsdale, NJ: Lawrence Erlbaum Associates, 11–40.

Hyams, N. (1994b) Commentary: null subjects in child language and the implications of cross-linguistic variation. In B. Lust, G. Hermon, and J. Kornfilt (eds.), *Syntactic Theory and First Language Acquisition: Cross-Linguistic Perspectives. Volume 2: Binding, Dependencies, and Learnability.* Hillsdale, NJ: Lawrence Erlbaum Associates, 287–299.

Hyams, N. (1994c) VP, null arguments and COMP projections. In T. Hoekstra and B. Schwartz (eds.), *Language Acquisition Studies in Generative Grammar*. Amsterdam: John Benjamins, 21–55.

Ingram, D. (1986) Phonological development: production. In P. Fletcher and P. Garman (eds.), *Language Acquisition* (2nd edn). Cambridge: Cambridge University Press, 223–239.

Iwamura, S. (1980) *The Verbal Games of Preschool Children*. London: Croom Helm.

Jackendoff, R. (1994) *Patterns in the Mind: Language and Human Nature*. New York: Basic Books.

Jaeggli, O. and Hyams, N. (1988) Morphological uniformity and the setting of the null subject parameter. *Proceedings of the North Eastern Linguistics Society* 18.

Jakobson, R. (1968) *Child Language, Aphasia, and Phonological Universals*. The Hague: Mouton. (Translated into English by A. R. Keiler; originally published in 1941 as *Kindersprache, Aphasie und allgemeine Lautgesetze*.)

Karmiloff-Smith, A. (1979) *A Functional Approach to Child Language: A Study of Determiners and Reference*. Cambridge: Cambridge University Press.

Karmiloff-Smith, A. (1986) Some fundamental aspects of language development after age 5. In P. Fletcher and M. Garman (eds.), *Language Acquisition* (2nd edn). Cambridge: Cambridge University Press, 455–474.

Karmiloff-Smith, A. (1992) *Beyond Modularity: A Developmental Perspective on Cognitive Science*. Cambridge, MA: MIT Press.

Keller, C. (1973) *Ballpoint Bananas and Other Jokes for Kids*. Englewood Cliffs: Prentice Hall.

Klein, S. M. (1982) Syntactic theory and the developing grammar: reestablishing the relationship between linguistic theory and data from language acquisition. Unpublished doctoral dissertation, University of California, Los Angeles.

Klima, E. and Bellugi, U. (1966) Syntactic regularities in the speech of children. In J. Lyons and R. J. Wales (eds.), *Psycholinguistic Papers*. Edinburgh: Edinburgh University Press, 183–219.

Kroll, B. M. (1981) Developmental relationships between speaking and writing. In B. M. Kroll and R. J. Vann (eds.), *Exploring Speaking–Writing Relationships: Connections and Contrasts*. Urbana, IL: National Council of Teachers of English, 32–54.

Kunsmann, P. (1976) Reduplication as a strategy for language acquisition. Paper presented at the summer meeting of the Linguistic Society of America, Oswego, New York. Cited in Ferguson (1979).

Lakshmanan, U. (1994) *Universal Grammar in Child Second Language Acquisition.* Amsterdam: John Benjamins.

Landau, B. and Gleitman, L. (1985) *Language and Experience: Evidence from the Blind Child.* Cambridge, MA: Harvard University Press.

Lane, H. (1976) *The Wild Boy of Aveyron.* Cambridge, MA: Harvard University Press.

*Language Files* (5th edn) (1991). Ohio: Ohio State University Press.

Larsen-Freeman, D. and Long, M. (1991) *An Introduction to Second Language Acquisition Research.* London: Longman.

Lenneberg, E. (1969) *Biological Foundations of Language.* New York: Wiley.

Levy, Y. (ed.) (1994) *Other Children, Other Languages: Issues in the Theory of Language Acquisition.* Hillsdale, NJ: Lawrence Erlbaum Associates.

Lightfoot, D. (1982) *The Language Lottery.* Cambridge, MA: MIT Press.

Lightfoot, D. (1991) *How to Set Parameters: Arguments from Language Change.* Cambridge, MA: MIT Press.

Lindfors, J. W. (1980) *Children's Language and Learning.* Englewood Cliffs, NJ: Prentice Hall.

Lindfors, J. W. (1987) *Children's Language and Learning* (2nd edn). Englewood Cliffs, NJ: Prentice-Hall.

Lindholm, K. J. and Padilla, A. M. (1978) Child bilingualism: report on language mixing, switching, and translations. *Linguistics* 16: 23–44.

Lléo, C. (1990) Homonymy and reduplication: on the extended availability of two strategies in phonological acquisition. *Journal of Child Language* 17: 267–278.

Loban, W. (1963) *The Language of Elementary School Children,* NCTE Research Report no. 1. Urbana, IL: National Council of Teachers of English.

Loban, W. (1976) *Language Development: Kindergarten through Grade Twelve.* NCTE Research Report no. 18. Urbana, IL: NCTE.

Locke, J. (1993) *The Child's Path to Spoken Language.* Cambridge, MA: Harvard University Press.

Lust, B., Hermon, G. and Kornfilt, J. (eds.) (1994) *Syntactic Theory and First Language Acquisition: Cross-Linguistic Perspectives. Volume 1: Heads, Projections, and Learnability. Volume 2: Binding, Dependencies, and Learnability.* Hillsdale, NJ: Lawrence Erlbaum Associates.

MacWhinney, B. (1995) *The CHILDES Project: Tools for Analyzing Talk* (2nd edn). Hillsdale, NJ: Lawrence Erlbaum Associates.

Malakoff, M. and Hakuta, K. (1991) Translation skill and metalinguistic awareness in bilinguals. In E. Bialystok (ed.), *Language Processing in Bilingual Children.* New York: Cambridge University Press, 141–166.

Marcos, H.(1987) Communicative functions of pitch range and pitch direction in infants. *Journal of Child Language* 14: 255–268.

Markman, E. (1990) Constraints children place on word meanings. *Cognitive Science* 14. Reprinted in P. Bloom (ed.) (1994), *Language Acquisition: Core Readings.* Cambridge, MA: MIT Press, 154–173.

McDaniel, D., McKee, C. and Cairns, H. S. (eds.) (1996) *Methods for Assessing Children's Syntax.* Cambridge, MA: MIT Press.

McGhee, P. (1979) *Humor: Its Origin and Development.* San Francisco: Freeman.

McGhee-Bidlack, B. (1991) The development of noun definitions: a metalinguistic analysis. *Journal of Child Language* 18: 417–434.

McLaughlin, B. (1984) *Second-Language Acquisition in Childhood. Volume 1: Preschool Children. Volume 2: School-Age Children.* Hillsdale, NJ: Lawrence Erlbaum Associates.

McTear, M. (1985) *Children's Conversation.* Oxford: Blackwell.

Meisel, J. (1987) Early differentiation of languages in bilingual children. In K. Hyltenstam and L. Obler (eds.), *Bilingualism Across the Lifespan: In Health and in Pathology.* Cambridge: Cambridge University Press, 13–40.

Meisel, J. (1994) *Bilingual First Language Acquisition: French and German Grammatical Development.* Amsterdam: John Benjamins.

Michaels, S. (1991) The dismantling of narrative. In A. McCabe, and C. Peterson (eds.), *Developing Narrative Structure.* Hillsdale, NJ: Lawrence Erlbaum Associates, 303–351.

Miller, J. (1993) Spoken and written language: language acquisition and literacy. In R. Scholes (ed.), *Literacy and Language.* Hillsdale, NJ: Lawrence Erlbaum Associates, 99–141.

Nadel, J. and Camaioni, L. (1993) *New Perspectives in Early Communicative Development*. London: Routledge.

Nagy, W. E. and Herman, P. A. (1987) Breadth and depth of vocabulary knowledge: implications for acquisition and instruction. In M. McKeown and M. Curtis (eds.), *The Nature of Vocabulary Acquisition*. Hillsdale, NJ: Lawrence Erlbaum Associates, 19–35.

Nelson, K. (1973) *Structure and Strategy in Learning to Talk*, Monographs of the Society for Research in Child Development 38, no. 149.

Nelson, K. (1981) Individual differences in language development: implications for development and language. *Developmental Psychology* 17 (2): 170–187.

Newport, E. (1976) Motherese: the speech of mothers to young children. In N. Castellan, D. Pisoni and G. Potts (eds.), *Cognitive Theory: Volume II*. Hillsdale, NJ: Lawrence Erlbaum Associates.

Newport, E. (1990) Maturational constraints on language learning. *Cognitive Sciences* 14. Reprinted in P. Bloom (ed.), *Language Acquisition: Core Readings*. Cambridge, MA: MIT Press.

Newson, J. (1979) The growth of shared understandings between infant and caregiver. In M. Bullowa (ed.), *Before Speech: The Beginnings of Interpersonal Communication*. Cambridge: Cambridge University Press, 207–222.

Nippold, M. (ed.) (1988) *Later Language Development: Ages Nine through Nineteen*. Austin, TX: Pro-ed (2nd edn, 1998).

Nolan, C. (1987) *Under the Eye of the Clock: The Life Story of Christopher Nolan*. London: Weidenfeld and Nicolson.

Oakhill, J. and Garnham, A. (1988) *Becoming a Skilled Reader*. Oxford: Basil Blackwell.

Ochs, E. (1979) Transcription as theory. In E. Ochs and B. Schieffelin (eds.), *Developmental Pragmatics*. New York: Academic Press, 43–72.

Ochs, E. (1988) *Culture and Language Development: Language Acquisition and Language Socialization in a Samoan Village*. Cambridge: Cambridge University Press.

O'Donnell, R. C., Griffin, W. J. and Norris, R. C. (1967) *Syntax of Kindergarten and Elementary School Children: A Transformational Analysis*. Urbana, IL: National Council of Teachers of English.

Opie, I. and Opie, P. (1959) *The Lore and Language of School Children*. Oxford: Clarendon Press.

Papandropoulou, I. and Sinclair, H. (1974) What is a word? Experimental study of children's ideas on grammar. *Human Development* 17: 240–258.

Perera, K. (1984) *Children's Writing and Reading: Analysing Classroom Language.* Oxford: Basil Blackwell.

Perera, K. (1986) Language acquisition and writing. In P. Fletcher and M. Garman (eds.), *Language Acquisition* (2nd edn). Cambridge: Cambridge University Press, 494–518.

Peters, A. (1977) Language learning strategies. *Language* 53: 560–573.

Peters, A. (1983) *The Units of Language Acquisition.* Cambridge: Cambridge University Press.

Peterson, C. and McCabe, A. (1991) *Developing Narrative Structure.* Hillsdale, NJ: Lawrence Erlbaum Associates.

Pettito, L. (1988) 'Language' in the prelinguistic child. In F. Kessel (ed.), *The Development of Language and Language Researchers: Papers Presented to Roger Brown.* Hillsdale, NJ: Lawrence Erlbaum Associates, 187–221.

Phinney, M. (1981) Children's interpretation of negation in complex sentences. In S. Tavakolian (ed.), *Language Acquisition and Linguistic Theory.* Cambridge, MA: MIT Press, 116–138.

Piaget, J. (1926/1955) *The Language and Thought of the Child.* London: Routledge and Kegan Paul.

Pinker, S. (1994) *The Language Instinct.* New York: W. Morrow and Co. (Also available from Penguin.)

Pizzuto, E. and Caselli, M. C. (1992) The acquisition of Italian morphology: implications for models of language development. *Journal of Child Language* 19: 491–557.

Poplack, S. (1980) Sometimes I'll start a sentence in English y termino en español: toward a typology of code-switching. *Linguistics* 18: 581–616.

Priestly, T. M. S. (1977) One idiosyncratic strategy in the acquisition of phonology. *Journal of Child Language* 4: 45–65.

Pye, C. (1992) The acquisition of K'iche' Maya. In D. Slobin (ed.), *The Crosslinguistic Study of Language Acquisition: Volume 3.* Hillsdale, NJ: Lawrence Erlbaum Associates, 221–308.

Pye, C. (1994) A cross-linguistic approach to the causative alternation. In Y. Levy (ed.), *Other Children, Other Languages: Issues in the Theory of Language Acquisition.* Hillsdale, NJ: Lawrence Erlbaum Associates, 243–263.

Quine, W. (1960) *Word and Object*. Cambridge, MA: MIT Press.
Radford, A. (1990) *Syntactic Theory and the Acquisition of English Syntax*. Oxford: Basil Blackwell.
Radford, A. (1997) *Syntax: A Minimalist Introduction*. Cambridge: Cambridge University Press.
Reid, J. F. (1972) Children's comprehension of syntactic features found in some extension readers. In J. F. Reid (ed.), *Reading: Problems and Practices*. London: Ward Lock International, 394–403.
Reilly, J. (1982) The acquisition of conditionals. Unpublished doctoral dissertation, University of California, Los Angeles.
Rice, M., Wexler, K. and Cleave, P. (1995) Specific language impairment as a period of extended optional infinitive. *Journal of Speech and Hearing Research* 38: 850–863.
Rispoli, M. (1994) Structural dependency and the acquisition of grammatical relations. In Y. Levy (ed.), *Other Children, Other Languages: Issues in the Theory of Language Acquisition*. Hillsdale, NJ: Lawrence Erlbaum Associates, 265–301.
Romaine, S. (1989) *Bilingualism*. Oxford: Basil Blackwell.
Rosenblum, T. and Pinker, S. (1983) Word magic revisited: monolingual and bilingual children's understanding of the word–object relationship. *Child Development* 54: 773–780.
Ross, J. R. (1967) Constraints on variables in syntax. Unpublished doctoral dissertation, MIT.
Rothery, J. (1989) Learning about language. In R. Hasan and J. R. Martin (eds.), *Language Development: Learning Language, Learning Culture*. Hillsdale, NJ: Ablex, 199–256.
Sacks, O. (1984) *A Leg to Stand On*. New York: Simon and Schuster.
Sacks, O. (1985) *The Man Who Mistook his Wife for a Hat and Other Clinical Tales*. New York: Simon and Schuster.
Sacks, O. (1995) *An Anthropologist on Mars*. New York: Alfred A. Knopf.
Schaffer, H. R. (1977) *Studies in Mother–Infant Interaction*. New York: Academic Press.
Scollon, R. (1979) *Conversations with a One Year Old*. Hawaii: University of Hawaii Press.
Scott, C. (1984) Adverbial connectivity in conversations of children 6 to 12. *Journal of Child Language* 11 (2): 423–452.
Scoville, R. P. and Gordon, A. M. (1980) Children's understanding of factive presuppositions: an experiment and a review. *Journal of Child Language* 7: 381–399.

Shattuck, R. (1994) *The Forbidden Experiment: The Story of the Wild Boy of Aveyron.* New York: Kodansha International.

Shatz, M. (1982) On mechanisms of language acquisition: can features of the communicative environment account for development? In E. Wanner and L. Gleitman (eds.), *Language Acquisition: The State of the Art.* Cambridge: Cambridge University Press, 102–127.

Sheldon, A. (1974) The role of parallel function in the acquisition of relative clauses in English. *Journal of Verbal Learning and Verbal Behavior* 13: 274–281.

Shultz, T. and Robillard, J. (1980) The development of linguistic humour in children: incongruity through rule violation. In P. McGhee and A. Chapman (eds.), *Children's Humour.* London: John Wiley, 59–89.

Slobin, D. I. (1973) Cognitive pre-requisites for the development of grammar. In C. A. Ferguson and D. I. Slobin (eds.), *Studies of Child Language Development.* New York: Holt, Reinhart and Winston, 175–208.

Slobin, D. I. (ed.) (1985) *The Crosslinguistic Study of Language Acquisition. Volume 1: The Data. Volume 2: Theoretical Issues.* Hillsdale, NJ: Lawrence Erlbaum Associates.

Slobin, D. I. (ed.) (1992) *The Crosslinguistic Study of Language Acquisition. Volume 3.* Hillsdale, NJ: Lawrence Erlbaum Associates.

Slobin, D. I. (ed.) (1996) *The Crosslinguistic Study of Language Acquisition. Volume 4.* Mahwah, NJ: Lawrence Erlbaum Associates.

Slobin, D. I. (ed.) (1997) *The Crosslinguistic Study of Language Acquisition. Volume 5: Expanding the Contexts.* Mahwah, NJ: Lawrence Erlbaum Associates.

Smith, C. and Tager-Flusberg, H. (1982) Metalinguistic awareness and language development. *Journal of Experimental Child Psychology* 34: 449–468.

Smith, N. V. (1973) *The Acquisition of Phonology: A Case Study.* Cambridge: Cambridge University Press.

Snow, C. and Ferguson, C. (eds.) (1977) *Talking to Children.* Cambridge: Cambridge University Press.

Sperber, D. and Wilson, D. (1995) *Relevance.* Oxford: Oxford University Press.

Stephens, M. I. (1988) Pragmatics. In M. Nippold (ed.), *Language Development: Ages Nine through Nineteen.* Austin, TX: Pro-ed, 247–262.

Stilwell Peccei, J. (1994) *Child Language.* New York: Routledge.

Stoel-Gammon, C. and Cooper, J. A. (1984) Patterns of early lexical and phonological development. *Journal of Child Language* 11: 247–271.

Tager-Flusberg, H. (ed.) (1994) *Constraints on Language Acquisition: Studies of Atypical Children*. Hillsdale, NJ: Lawrence Erlbaum Associates.

Templeton, S. and Spivey, E. (1980) The concept of word in young children as a function of level of cognitive development. *Research in the Teaching of English* 14 (3): 265–278.

Tough, J. (1974) *Focus on Meaning*. London: George Allen and Unwin.

Trevarthen, C. (1979) Communication and cooperation in early infancy: a description of primary intersubjectivity. In M. Bullowa (ed.), *Before Speech: The Beginning of Interpersonal Communication*. Cambridge: Cambridge University Press, 321–347.

Trevarthen, C. and Hubley, P. (1978) Secondary intersubjectivity: confidence, confiding and acts of meaning in the first year. In A. Lock (ed.), *Action, Gesture and Symbol: The Emergence of Language*. London: Academic Press, 183–229.

van der Lely, H. (1996) Language modularity and grammatically specific language impaired children. In M. Aldridge (ed.), *Child Language*. Clevedon, UK: Multilingual Matters, 188–201.

Velten, H. (1943) The growth of phonemic and lexical patterns in infants' language. *Language* 19: 281–292.

Vihman, M. (1996) *Phonological Development: The Origins of Language in the Child*. Oxford: Blackwell.

Villanueva, V. (1993) *Bootstraps: From an American Academic of Color*. Urbana, IL: National Council of Teachers of English.

Volterra, V. and Taeschner, T. (1978) The acquisition and development of language by a bilingual child. *Journal of Child Language* 5: 311–326.

Vygotsky, L. (1962) *Thought and Language*. Cambridge, MA: MIT Press.

Watson, J. S. (1973) Smiling, cooing and 'the game'. *Merrill-Palmer Quarterly* 18: 323–339.

Wells, G. (1981) *Learning through Interaction: The Study of Language Development*. Cambridge: Cambridge University Press.

Wells, G. (1985) *Language Development in the Preschool Years*. Cambridge: Cambridge University Press.

White, L. (1989) *Universal Grammar and Second Language Acquisition*. Amsterdam/Philadelphia: John Benjamins.

Williams, D. (1992) *Nobody Nowhere*. New York: Avon Books.
Williams, D. (1994) *Somebody Somewhere*. London: Doubleday.
Wong Fillmore, L. (1976) The second time around: cognitive and social strategies in second language acquisition. Unpublished PhD thesis, Stanford University, CA.
Wong Fillmore, L. (1979) Individual differences in second language acquisition. In C. J. Fillmore, D. Kempler and W. S.-Y. Wang (eds.), *Individual Differences in Language Ability and Language Behavior*. New York: Academic Press, 203–241.
Wong Fillmore, L. (1983) The language learner as an individual: implications of research on individual differences for the ESL teacher. In J. Handscombe and M. Clarke (eds.), *On TESOL 82: Pacific Perspectives on Language Learning and Teaching*. Washington, DC: TESOL.
Wood, D., Ross, G. and Bruner, J. (1976) The role of tutoring in problem-solving. *Journal of Child Psychology and Psychiatry* 17: 89–100.
Woolford, E. (1983) Bilingual code-switching and syntactic theory. *Linguistic Inquiry* 14: 520–536.
Yamada, J. (1990) *Laura – A Case for the Modularity of Language*. Cambridge, MA: MIT Press.

# Index